ADVANCE PRAISE FOR *JOHN DOS PASSOS'S TRANSATLANTIC CHRONICLING*

"*John Dos Passos's Transatlantic Chronicling* is a wide-ranging and engaging set of essays that extends and enriches the scholarship on Dos Passos. Welcome attention is given to Dos Passos's travel writing, his work with theater, and the Iberian contexts so crucial for his artistic and political development. The collection also does justice to Dos Passos's skills as a capacious chronicler of his time with pieces on how a diverse range of culture informed his writing—from clothes to burial practices to the contemporary cinema. A collection that decisively captures the wide sphere of interest of one of the key writers of left global modernism in the 1920s and 1930s."

—MARK WHALAN, Robert D. and Eve E. Horn Professor of English, University of Oregon

"A trenchant and wide-ranging study of one of America's greatest authors. These essays trace the winding course of Dos Passos's writing and provide timely reflections on the functions of art in interesting times."

—WESLEY BEAL, author of *Networks of Modernism*

"An essential addition to Dos Passos studies, *John Dos Passos's Transatlantic Chronicling* expands one of the field's central debates—the impact of the writer's politics on his representations of history—into the 21st century with new critical perspectives. The multiplicity of voices and approaches in this volume reflects the range of forms—innovative fiction, political and travel essays, experimental drama, memoir—in which Dos Passos expressed the turbulent political, economic, and cultural transformations that propelled the US and the world into modernity."

—LISA NANNEY, author of *John Dos Passos & Cinema* and *John Dos Passos Revisited,* and co-editor of *The Paintings and Drawings of John Dos Passos*

JOHN DOS PASSOS'S
TRANSATLANTIC CHRONICLING

JOHN DOS PASSOS'S TRANSATLANTIC CHRONICLING

CRITICAL ESSAYS ON THE INTERWAR YEARS

Edited by Aaron Shaheen
and Rosa María Bautista-Cordero

The University of Tennessee Press / Knoxville

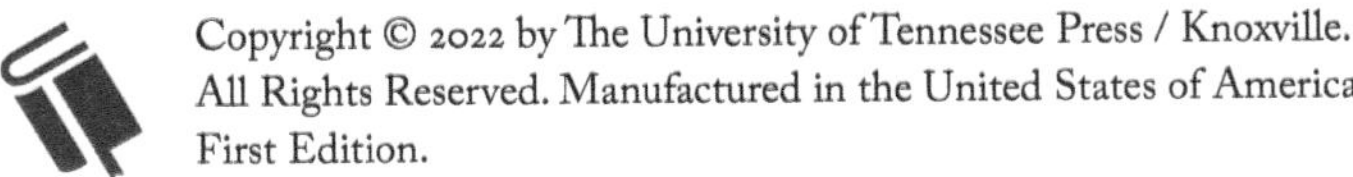

First Edition.

Library of Congress Cataloging-in-Publication Data

Names: Shaheen, Aaron, editor. | Bautista-Cordero, Rosa María, editor.
Title: John Dos Passos's transatlantic chronicling : critical essays on the interwar years / edited by Aaron Shaheen and Rosa María Bautista-Cordero.
Description: First edition. | Knoxville : The University of Tennessee Press, [2022] | Includes bibliographical references and index. | Summary: "This edited collection explores the wartime writings of John Dos Passos. Dos Passos's writings, set against a backdrop of rapidly evolving technology, growing religious skepticism, and political turmoil in the wake of World War I, focus widely on the costs of modern warfare. Contributors in this collection, including scholars from both North America and Dos Passos's native Spain, unpack Dos Passos's novels, essays, and stage plays written during the years between the world wars"—Provided by publisher.
Identifiers: LCCN 2021052506 (print) | LCCN 2021052507 (ebook) | ISBN 9781621907138 (hardcover) | ISBN 9781621907145 (pdf)
Subjects: LCSH: Dos Passos, John, 1896–1970—Criticism and interpretation. | Dos Passos, John, 1896–1970—Political and social views. | LCGFT: Essays. | Literary criticism.
Classification: LCC PS3507.O743 Z65 2022 (print) | LCC PS3507.O743 (ebook) | DDC 813/.52—dc23/eng/20211110
LC record available at https://lccn.loc.gov/2021052506
LC ebook record available at https://lccn.loc.gov/2021052507

Contents

Acknowledgments

The genesis of this edited collection dates back to June 2016 at the Second Biennial John Dos Passos Conference in Madrid, Spain. On a break between panel sessions, the distinguished Dos Passos scholar Lisa Nanney suggested that the strength of the papers presented there, and at the 2014 conference that preceded it, would make for a good edited collection. The present collection is largely the result of those conferences as well as the 2018 conference held in Lisbon, Portugal.

The editors are indebted to a great many people for the completion of this volume of essays, not least of whom are the contributors themselves. These scholars worked, sometimes under hard and rushed deadlines, with great diligence, flexibility, and dedication. Their collegiality is a testament to John Dos Passos himself, who throughout his lifetime fostered a spirit of camaraderie and community wherever he went. Not surprisingly, then, the author passed these traits down to his family. As this collection moved from abstract formulation to concrete reality, Lucy Dos Passos Coggin and John Dos Passos Coggin, in particular, offered the editors and the contributors support in all sorts of ways, from granting permissions for image reproduction to offering insight and anecdotes about the author.

Additionally, the editors would like to thank their colleagues at their home institutions, the Universidad Autónoma de Madrid and the University of Tennessee at Chattanooga. Moreover, they are indebted to the librarians and staffers at the Albert and Shirley Small Special Collections Library at the University of Virginia, where the Dos Passos papers are archived. At the University of Tennessee Press, Thomas Wells and Jon Boggs have shown great competence, patience, and good will as this manuscript has made its way through the various stages of publication. The editors and contributors are also deeply grateful to the two anonymous readers and to the press's editorial board for giving the manuscript a proper and thorough vetting.

Finally, the editors would like to thank their spouses, Jorge Rosenvinge and Amanda Pettit-Shaheen, for their love and support. Being married to a scholar takes a special kind of temperament, one anchored in patience, humor, and an unflagging ability to separate the wheat from the chaff in whatever form the chaff presents itself. To Jorge and Amanda, this volume is dedicated with great love and affection.

JOHN DOS PASSOS'S
TRANSATLANTIC CHRONICLING

Introduction

THE RAW STRUCTURE OF HISTORY

Aaron Shaheen

In the 1932 edition of his 1921 breakout novel *Three Soldiers*, John Dos Passos offers an acute observation about the role of the writer, particularly the fiction writer, in the twentieth century: "We write today for the first generation not brought up on the Bible, and nothing as yet has taken its place as a literary discipline. . . . We must deal with the raw structure of history now, we must deal with it quick, before it stamps us out" (viii). Dos Passos's observation is perhaps too easy for those of us in the early twenty-first century to dismiss. But the writer is putting his finger on perhaps the single biggest rupture in Western reading habits since the invention of the printing press in the mid-fifteenth century. As the most widely read book in the West up to the dawn of the twentieth century, the Bible was generally understood not just as history, but as history with a moral behind it—one that culminated in a telos for the entire world: the Second Coming of Christ and judgment of the quick and the dead. With the Bible setting out a temporal trajectory from the moment of creation to the Apocalypse, various world events—be they from antiquity, the Middle Ages, or at earlier points in the modern era—all had their place and reason.

The great skepticism that accompanied the advancement of science and technology in the late nineteenth century ushered in a generation, despite its gains in literacy, whose knowledge of the Bible was increasingly acquired through hearsay, if it was known at all. With no prevailing metanarrative to grant coherence to temporal flux, the "raw structure of history" was put on display for anyone who cared to notice it. However writers of Dos Passos's generation (and those who would come later) chose to treat history in their works, they had to deal with the clear fact that history would have to be reconceptualized, rewritten, and relearned. These generations would have to ask themselves some fairly pointed questions: If Judeo-Christian metanarratives no longer hold uncontested sway, does the unfolding of history have any coherence? And if so, what guides that coherence? The present volume attempts to address these and other related questions as they arise in John Dos Passos's writings composed between the two World Wars.

The illegitimate son of John Randolph Dos Passos, a prominent New York lawyer, John Roderigo Dos Passos spent much of his youth living with his mother, Lucy Madison, in Europe and going by the name of Jack Madison. While mother and son returned to the States in 1906 so that Jack could enroll at Choate, only with John Randolph's first wife's death in 1910 could the three then live together permanently as a family (Ludington 22–27). Perhaps because he had to live his early life shuttling between the Old and New World, the young Dos Passos was especially sensitive to matters of place and time. As he recalls in his "informal" 1966 memoir *The Best Times*, John Randolph had fairly rigid reading habits, which he passed down to his son: "He abhorred magazines and bestseller novels. No use reading a book you couldn't learn something from. The taste for history he implanted in me as a child surely did take root" (16). For the father, this fascination with history would compel him to publish in 1903 *The Anglo-Saxon Century*, which argues that if the United States forged a deeper relationship with Great Britain (the global powerhouse of the nineteenth century), it was poised at the start of the new century to rise to new levels of international prominence. "It is now manifest," père Dos Passos proclaims, "that to this great [Anglo-Saxon] race is entrusted the civi-

John Randolph Dos Passos (father), date of photo unknown. John Dos Passos Papers, 1865–1999, Accession #5950, etc., Special Collections, University of Virginia Library, Charlottesville, Va.

lization and christianization of the world" (3). Thus, for the son, history—and particularly the very recent history of the twentieth century—would become a lifelong fascination.

As the essays in this volume will show in one form or another, writing in the age of unprecedented technological innovation, religious skepticism, and mechanized warfare posed new challenges for how to understand and render the unfolding of history, whether that unfolding was reflected in fiction, memoirs, or drama. One is even tempted to claim that "History," more than any single character or figure, is the protagonist and subject matter of Dos Passos's various writings. As the author himself wrote in 1928, "The only excuse for a novelist, aside from the entertainment and vicarious living his books give the people who read them, is as a second-class historian of the age he lives in. The reality he misses by writing about imaginary people, he gains by being able to build a reality more nearly out of his own factual experience than a plain historian or biographer can" ("Statements of Belief" 26).

CHRONICLING THE CRITICAL LANDSCAPE

Understanding history's role in Dos Passos's oeuvre has been the project of many critics over the better part of a century. In the past generation and a half, as the twentieth century was either drawing to a close or was indeed over, critics had the increased benefit of historical distance to make their claims about Dos Passos's interwar writings. In criticism spanning from the late 1970s to the late 90s, Barbara Foley, for instance, claims that Dos Passos was "a pioneer in contemporary treatment of fact in fiction" ("From *U.S.A.* to *Ragtime*" 89), and saw in the *U.S.A.* trilogy in particular a melding of the "microcosmic fictional world of the classical historical novel and the documentary immediacy of the contemporary nonfiction novel" ("Treatment of Time" 461). Moreover, for Foley, the four narrative strategies of the trilogy—the Newsreel and Camera Eye sections, as well as the biographical sketches of famous people, and the fictional narratives of twelve main characters—require readers' participation in order to put together the elliptical and "dialectically related" history of the first three decades of the twentieth century: "[T]hrough readerly analysis—aided by authorial coaching—history emerges as a process possessing both determinacy and knowable causality" (*Radical Representations* 431, 432). Michael Denning's *The Cultural Front* (1997) chose the term "modernist history-writing" (170) to describe the *U.S.A.* trilogy, noting that its four different narrative techniques comprise not just "a different history," but "even a different conception of history" (170). In their attempt to chart the "decline and fall of the Lincoln republic" (168–69), however, these techniques are limited in their scope and achievement: the novel's proletarian impulses are time and again overshadowed by white middle-class characters who at best "slum" among ethnic, working-class Others but who cannot fully represent them any more than Dos Passos himself was able to do directly on the page (198).[1]

Among twenty-first-century criticism, Michael North's 2005 *Camera Works* takes a fairly dour view of the trilogy's treatment of history, regarding the elliptical Newsreel sections as consisting of an overabundance of "scandals, ceremonies, sporting events, and human interest stories" (143) that turn "sedentary consumption" in front of a cinema screen (or before a literary text) into a "new kind of doing" (205). Seth Moglen's 2007 *Mourning Modernity* offers a psychoanalytic approach to *U.S.A.*'s rendering of twentieth-century history, showing how the biographical sketches' memorialization of certain leftists who were active during the Red Scare "facilitates an ongoing political commitment and a forward-looking project of radical tradition building" (125). The fictional narratives, however, underscore Dos Passos's melancholic impulse, relying on deterministic naturalism to "represent the destructive social formations produced by monopoly capitalism" (176). More recently, Wesley Beal's 2015 *Networks of Modernism* has argued that the trilogy's four levels of narration create a system of distributed networks that track the course of the early twentieth century. The "unfolding of history" is found "not in any single formal device or even in some combination of the four but in the reader's situation between them" (99); yet what defies articulation in this networked scheme is a "national or social space" that allows for any sense of political or cultural unity, or even any interpersonal connection (31).[2]

The foregoing paragraphs hopefully make clear that most critical examinations of Dos Passos's treatment of time are centered on the *U.S.A.* trilogy, and thus the treatment is therefore largely genre specific, even if the four narrative devices surely expand the boundaries of the novel. Building upon the fine work done by these and other critics, the present collection seeks to expand its vision beyond—though not to the exclusion of—*U.S.A.* To that end, I would like to give due consideration to an interview Dos Passos gave *The Paris Review* in 1962 (finally published in full in 1969), in which he sought a new self-conceptualization to describe his authorial scope:

> Recently, I've been calling my novels contemporary chronicles, which seems to fit them rather better. They have a strong political bent because after all although it isn't the only thing—politics in our time has pushed people around more than anything else. I don't see why

> dealing with politics should harm a writer at all. . . . A lot of very good writing has been more or less involved in politics, although it's always a dangerous territory. It's better for some people to keep out unless they're willing to learn how to observe. It is the occupation of a special kind of writer. His investigation—using blocks of raw experience—must be balanced. . . . A writer in this field should be both engaged and disengaged. He must have passion and concern and anger—but he must keep his emotions at arm's length in his work. If he doesn't, he is simply a propagandist and what he offers is a "preachment." (Sanders 154)

This likely, albeit muted, criticism of leftist writers is perhaps not surprising, for at this point in life (he would die in 1970 at the age of 74), Dos Passos had become an occasional contributor to *The National Review* and a supporter of Barry Goldwater's 1964 presidential campaign. Since the circumstances of the author's disillusion with the Left are well documented in other studies—Lisa Nanney's *John Dos Passos and Cinema* (2019) is among the most recent to do so—this introduction will instead linger on another, but surely interrelated, issue of what does and does not constitute a chronicler.

The chronicle genre has been around since at least the early Middle Ages.[3] Yet as Dos Passos uses it in the *Paris Review* interview with David Sanders, the term is set in opposition to a "preachment" that attempts to instruct or persuade a reader according to a specific set of sociopolitical tenets and a certain view of historical development. If a political writer preaches, a chronicler portrays political situations and politically informed characters and figures but does not lead the reader to any predetermined ideological conclusions. If chroniclers do not ultimately leave the "raw structure of history" unclad, they at least expose the temporary and superficial nature of its vestments. This unwillingness to determine a novel's moral center through which the author can espouse a certain political agenda is fairly consistent throughout Dos Passos's interwar fiction. For instance, even though we are inclined to sympathize with the affable Jimmy Herf in *Manhattan Transfer*, we are rightly hesitant to question if his abandonment of New York—and of his own child—is the right moral choice. The *U.S.A.* trilogy's innovative narrative techniques and its overwhelming cast of characters—all of whom possess the weaknesses and failings found throughout humanity—make preachment from a moral center even less likely.

To be sure, throughout the time under investigation in this collection, Dos Passos's understanding of history *was* politically inflected, as he was heavily engaged in leftist movements and wrote for a number of leftist periodicals, *The New Masses* chief among them. He even voted for the Communist Party candidate, William Z. Foster, in the 1932 presidential election (Nanney 3). But Dos Passos scholars are likely to ensnare themselves in contradictions and dead-ends if they align his interwar career too cleanly with a rigidly defined leftist agenda. The author himself never completely bought into the Marxist view of history. Yet, as Barbara Foley explains, "While Dos Passos was certainly not . . . a Marxist in his overall outlook, he was a radical and a materialist in many of his analyses of—and judgements upon—separate facets of capitalist society" ("The Treatment of Time" 449). Foley is correct to assert that to the extent that readers can detect a political bent in Dos Passos's works, they often do so through the writings' leftist *diagnoses* of the many political and socioeconomic challenges the West faced in these years. These diagnoses are often achieved through an instance of what Roger Griffin terms "epiphanic" modernism—that is, a moment in a modernist text, often rendered through unconventional or experimental techniques, that gives characters and readers alike a "'total' insight beyond the atomized perceptions and spiritually desiccated values that constitute the experiential stuff of modern life" (11). But rarely, if ever, do Dos Passos's interwar writings slip into what Griffin also calls "programmatic" modernism, which offers a clear and rigid set of guidelines for how to achieve "*new ways of living*," which are sometimes illuminated in these epiphanic moments (15; emphasis in original). No wonder, then, that *The New Masses* editor-in-chief Michael Gold regarded *Manhattan Transfer* as flawed: the novel astutely details how industrial capitalism causes Jimmy Herf's "bewilderment," which is rendered epiphanically through "new and experimental" techniques. Yet the novel, Gold further contends, "does not know how to help [Jimmy]," largely because its author did not "ally himself definitely with the radical army" in order to outline an ideological program that could lead his character and the readers themselves out of their modern malaise (25). As John Trombold astutely cautions, left-leaning readers of both yesterday and today were and are bound to be disappointed if looking for an uncomplicated hero either in the pages of Dos Passos's novels or in the author himself (252).

THE TWENTIETH CENTURY RENDERED ABSTRACTLY AND CONCRETELY

In an older but still deeply astute assessment of Dos Passos's view of history, John P. Diggins relies on the distinction made by Italian philosopher Benedetto Croce between the historian and the chronicler. The former, asserts Diggins, offers patterns and meaning to temporal progression, while the latter "treats his materials as inert, empty of determinate content and thus devoid of self-actualizing potential" (334). If the Marxist historian regards material production as the process by which societies evolve over time and eventually culminate in a stateless world where all workers share in the means of production, then the chronicler stands too close to the individual events of that time—as if pressed up against the canvas of a large painting—to be able to gauge whether such events have any deeply rooted antecedents or any far-reaching implications.

Diggins's assessment of time and history, like so many others', is largely focused on the *U.S.A.* trilogy, which surely depicts a number of characters who are caught up, sometimes rather violently and cataclysmically, in the sweep of American and European history from the late 1890s to the 1929 crash of the New York Stock Exchange. In some cases, the characters—labor activist Ben Compton and radical investigative reporter Mary French immediately come to mind—are driven by leftist politics. But if the historian, according to Diggins, is the one who can determine temporal patterns according to a certain political program, be it Marxist or fascist, the program could prove equally spurious, elusive, or tangled, as both Ben and Mary learn over the course of the trilogy. Michael Denning even goes so far as to suggest that Mary's real counterpart in *The Big Money* is not her fellow radical Ben, with whom she has a spurious relationship, but rather the advertising mogul J. Ward Moorehouse, whose living is also made by the use, and the inevitable manipulation, of words. To that end, Denning quotes a rather remarkable statement Dos Passos made in a 1926 issue of *The New Masses*: "Whether [a writer's] aims are KKK or Communist he takes on the mind and functional deformities of his trade. The word-slinging organism is substantially the same whether it sucks its blood from Park Avenue or from [the Brooklyn neighborhood] Flatbush" (20).

Perhaps the best way to articulate the difficulty Ben, Mary, and so many of Dos Passos's characters encounter—a difficulty that is central to the present volume—is that which arises in attempting to reconcile abstraction and concreteness. Indeed, throughout his entire life, Dos Passos maintained a deep distrust of unchecked political and economic abstractions and the echo chambers that would allow those abstractions to take on monstrous aims. To the extent that he sympathized with radical causes throughout the interwar years, he did so because he agreed with Marxism's own leeriness of capitalist abstraction. According to the *Communist Manifesto*, in the age of industrialism, "all that is solid melts into air"—an acknowledgment of capitalism's penchant for abstracting items of "use value" into "exchange value," whereby a cow no longer holds the practical equivalent of twenty chickens, as it may have in a traditional barter economy, but rather a certain number of dollars, francs, or pounds, whose abstract value could fluctuate over the course of a single day (Marx and Engels 16, 15). Marx and Engels's famous revision of Hegelian idealism sought to ground dialectics in material production, thus giving abstraction the weight of history, which could be measured rather viscerally in laborers' blood and sweat.

But Dos Passos's unwillingness to offer his readers a "program" (to use Roger Griffin's terminology) during the interwar years can be read through a chronicling lens, wherein he maintains a healthy amount of suspicion that the reconciliation of abstract and concrete was yet to be proven, if it could be proven at all. When recalling his time working for *The New Masses* in 1926, he explains, "Never much of a hand to work with organizations, I justified my connection with *The New Masses* to myself as a means of getting firsthand knowledge of the labor movement. The hardcore dogmatists were already leery of my attitude. Though I hadn't yet read Roger Williams I was already the Seeker in matters political as he was the Seeker in matters religious" (*Best Times* 162). There are two points worth unpacking here, the first of which is that, in his participation with the Left's major periodical, he privileged the tangible over the ideological: he could take on assignments that would allow him to meet actual laborers, whose flesh-and-blood reality he sets up, even mutedly, in opposition to the Left's "hardcore dogmatists," who were inclined to place abstraction above people. Second, he finds spiritual kinship, even in retrospect, with Roger Williams, the Separatist colonist-preacher, whose protestations against the inseparability of church and state in the Massachusetts Bay Colony, as well as his insistence on freedom of conscience in theological matters, made him an exile and the subsequent founder of Rhode Island. Williams therefore labeled himself a seeker, realizing that the more that theological precepts were hardened into institutions, the more both the precepts and the institutions became corrupted and dangerous.

As Dos Passos puts it in his 1959 essay "Looking Back on *U.S.A.*" with regard to institutional corruption, "[T]he basic tragedy my work tries to express seems to remain monotonously the same: man's struggle for life against the strangling institutions he himself creates" (237). By this point, the author had experienced his own institutional disaffiliation. His abandonment of leftist politics cost him a number of friends, including Ernest Hemingway and John Howard Lawson. Why did the break occur? Lisa Nanney recalls an awkward encounter she once had at the Prado Museum in Madrid with the storied critic Alfred Kazin, who told her that Dos Passos's irreversible rightward lurch began with José Robles (160), a longtime friend of the author who left his teaching post at Johns Hopkins in 1936 to return to his native Spain and serve as a translator on behalf of the Republican forces during the Spanish Civil War. Likely fearing that Robles had learned too much confidential information in his role as translator, and suspecting him (falsely) of betrayal, the Soviets secretly executed him, a move that Hemingway eventually justified to Dos Passos as the unavoidable collateral damage of warfare. This dark story has already been the subject of many studies, including more recently the 2006 book *The Breaking Point* by Stephen Koch and the 2015 documentary *Robles, Duelo al Sol* by Sonia Tercero Ramiro. There is little I can add to these excellent investigations here, but what is clear is that, in learning of Robles's execution at the hands of the Soviets, Dos Passos came to realize that the Left was no better equipped than Franco's fascists to reconcile abstract political principles with flesh-and-blood humanity. "Understanding the personal histories of a few of the men, women and children really involved [in the Spanish Civil War] would," he remarked in a 1939 editorial titled "The Death of José Robles, "free our minds somewhat from the black-is-black and white-is-white obsessions of partisanship" (309).

This leeriness toward the rigidities of abstraction arose, if not before, then at least during his years as an undergraduate at Harvard, from 1912–1916. There in Cambridge theories of all sorts abounded, Marxism and Marxist derivations chief among them. Dos Passos followed the career of the radical John Reed during these days, but the undergraduate's enthusiasm was tempered by the knowledge that so much of what he liked about his own life was shaped by the genteel tastes of men like his father, whose "professional successes," explains biographer Virginia Spencer Carr, "depended upon the growth of industrialism" (66). Moreover, apparently what most interested the young Dos Passos about Reed's writings was not the social, political, and economic issues they brought up, but rather Reed's stylistics, his ability to blend personal impressions with objective reporting (Carr 67). Dos Passos, always at least a little bit of an outsider since his childhood days in exile, seemed to keep at arm's length the socialist abstractions that swept up so many of his fellow undergraduates.

The later years of Dos Passos's time at Harvard played out against the backdrop of World War I. In the aforementioned 1969 *Paris Review* interview, the author admitted, "I got quite a little out of being at Harvard, although I was kicking all of the time I was there, complaining about the 'ethercone' atmosphere I described in [the] Camera Eye [sections of the *U.S.A.* trilogy]"

John Dos Passos (*seated, second from right*) on the editorial board of the *Harvard Monthly*, 1916. Robert Hillyer, also pictured (*seated at right*), joined the author as an ambulance driver in the Verdun sector of the Western Front in 1917. John Dos Passos Papers, 1865–1999, Accession #5950, etc., Special Collections, University of Virginia Library, Charlottesville, Va.

(Sanders 150–51). Apparently the anti-German sentiment at Harvard that was catalyzed by the Great War became so fevered that dialogue with skeptics was futile: "You couldn't talk about it" (151). When he set off for France in 1917 to see the war firsthand as a member of the Norton-Harjes Ambulance Corps, he found what he had been looking for in futility at Harvard. "I suppose that World War I then became my university," he recalled (151). The experience offered him what he found most striking in the writings of John Reed: not political abstractions that help to explain how certain events play into a larger historical trajectory, but a dynamic tension between personal experience and objectivity: "You *saw* the war. I don't know if it was on the more or less seamier side of combat, but in the ambulance service you did have a more objective point of view towards the war. After all, the infantryman must be carried away by the spirit of combat, which is quite different from sitting around and dragging off the wreckage" (151). And yet for all the relative objectivity that ambulance service afforded him, it also gave him the ability to experience the bloodshed and to see in a very visceral way the war's effects on the human body, the human mind, and the natural landscape.

Make no mistake, "dragging off the wreckage"—usually in the form of mangled, amputated, or decomposing young men—*did* offer valuable experience and insight that history books' academic objectivity could not provide. And if there is anything that Diggins's excellent article overlooks in his understanding of Dos Passos's view of chronicling is that it seeks to offer a deeper level of humanity to history, even if that humanity is doomed to immolation in the face of modernity or is unaware of the larger historical forces that ensure such doom. To that end, I would like to return to one particular episode from Dos Passos's wartime experience as it is recalled in *The Best Times* and as it is also verified in his first novel, the 1920 *One Man's Initiation: 1917*. In the span of less than a page (four relatively short paragraphs, in fact), *The Best Times* reveals a fascinating mental migration. The author recalls the time he spent with fellow American ambulance driver Robert Hillyer during the off-hours musing about poetry and other artistic and philosophical matters. Dos Passos recalls dividing humanity into two camps: the useful "producers" who are concerned with "building up mankind," and the destructive

John Dos Passos in the American Red Cross Ambulance Corps, Milan, Italy, 1917. John Dos Passos Papers, 1865–1999, Accession #5950, etc., Special Collections, University of Virginia Library, Charlottesville, Va.

"exploiters," "who spread illusions and caused wars and destroyed civilization as fast as the producers built it up" (44–45). The recollection then moves to the time when the author first encountered Henri Barbusse's recently published wartime memoir *Le Feu*. "[It] moved me to frenzy, but already I'd seen enough of wartime France to discover other sides to the story. War was the theme of the time. I was in a passion to put down everything, immediately [as] it happened, exactly as I saw it" (45). Finally, in the very next paragraph, the narration turns very visceral: "The chance of death sharpened the senses. The sweetness of the white roses, the shape and striping of a snail shell, the taste of an omelet, the most casual sight or sound appeared desperately intense against the background of the great massacres" (45).

The trajectory I want to chart here in this passage of only four paragraphs is one that moves from the abstract to the concrete. Dos Passos initially divides the world into two groups whose boundary is solid and easy to discern: "Black was black and white was white" (45). Not surprisingly, he lists himself among the morally superior "exploited." But in his subsequent mention of *Le Feu*, he reads about war from a different perspective, and even though Barbusse's leftist views about war and politics were generally in keeping with Dos Passos's at the time, readers are reminded that world-shaking events are multiperspectival; and with that multiplicity, he concludes that the way to bring that experience to readers is to move away from abstraction to concrete sensory detail. Evaluating the "great massacre" in vaguely Marxist terms of the exploiters who presumably started the war and the producers who fought it collapses into overwhelming sensory immediacy of white roses, snail shells, and the taste of omelets.

Lest we might dismiss *The Best Times* as a form of historical correction or revision on the part of a man who sought to distance himself from his earlier leftist leanings, we can look to the first novel Dos Passos wrote, *One Man's Initiation*, whose main character, Martin Howe, flees the crass commercialism of his American homeland and joins an ambulance corps, just as his creator did. In a scene that takes place in a trench dugout, Martin plays cards with a trio of French soldiers, each of whom represents a distinct view of historical progression. As an anarchist and a socialist respectively, Lully and Merrier look to the future: "Ours is now the duty of rebuilding, reorganizing," remarks Merrier. Lully then claims, "Abolish property, and the disease of the desire for it, the desire to grasp and have, and you'll need no government to protect you. The vividness and resiliency of the life of man is being fast crushed under organization, tabulation" (112). These perspectives are offset by the Norman, who instead proposes a return to the medieval Church: "There remains only religion. In the organization of religion lies the natural and suitable arrangement for the happiness of man. The Church will govern not through physical force but through spiritual force. . . . The freedom the Church offers is the only true freedom. It denies the world, and the slaveries and rewards of it. It gives the love of God as the only aim of life" (109). Notably, Martin does not side with any one person in this debate, even though the Norman's medieval Catholicism is worlds and centuries apart from the radicalism of Merrier and Lully; the very idealism of the three men's diverse perspectives is enough to reinvigorate Martin. "With people like that we needn't despair of civilization," he tells his fellow ambulance driver Tom Randolph as they walk back to their beds in a nearby barn (116). As he drowsed, he imagined his French idealists as "men with eager brown faces and eyes gleaming with hope, and [he] saw their full red lips moving as they talked" (116). As this scene unfolds, it begins with a discussion of politico-historical abstractions; but in keeping with what Mikhail Bakhtin calls novelistic "polyphony," those abstractions come from different perspectives, and as Martin recalls the men who voiced them, he does so in very tangible, corporeal ways, a reminder to himself and to the reader that these three men's concrete humanity must not be overlooked amid their philosophizing.

The Best Times offers a more condensed version of abstraction's collapse into concreteness after the war, when Dos Passos returns to Europe on assignment as a reporter: "As the correspondent for a labor paper I wasn't much of a success. Though I was thoroughly interested in syndicalism and socialism and trade union matters, I was continually distracted by scenery and painting and architecture and the *canto hondo* and the grave rhythms of flamenco dancing. And the people, the people, the infinitely tragical, comical, pathetic and laughable varieties of people" (80–81). The more the young Dos Passos interacts with the people on a tangible basis, they do not appear to him in abstract terms as "workers" or "producers" but as individuals who possess the expected contradictory natures that can be seen only when they are engaged directly and personally.

These passages suggest that *The Best Times* itself is not just a chronicle of Dos Passos's interwar years told from the perspective of a man then already over seventy who had become disillusioned with the leftist historical narratives that once intrigued him. Just as importantly, the memoir is a veritable meta-chronicle, freighted with a self-consciousness about its own construction and its own tensions, which are not unlike the tensions of a younger Dos Passos being chronicled in its pages: in each case, the contest between abstraction and concreteness takes center stage before a certain historical backdrop.

Upon recalling his ship passage home from the Great War in a first class cabin, in which he socialized cozily with a general, an Episcopal chaplain, and a Y.M.C.A. man, he remarks, "I never could keep the world properly divided into gods and demons for very long" (71). If, from a distance, these individuals were among the "exploiters" who caused, perpetuated, or propagandized the war, up close they were a reminder to the author that perhaps the abstract labels he might slap on them are a softer form of dehumanization than what he experienced in the war—but dehumanization nevertheless. His willingness to apply abstractions too readily reveals his own "demonic" side.

These passages from *The Best Times* help us to understand a more refined definition of chronicling, which Dos Passos used in a speech he delivered in November 1960 to the students of Carleton College:

> A chronicler has to use the stories people tell him about themselves, all the little dramas in other people's lives he gets glimpses of without knowing just what went before or just what will come after, the fragments of talk he overhears in the subway or on a streetcar, the letter he picks up on the street addressed by one unknown character to another, the words on a scrap of paper found in a trash-basket, the occasional vistas of reality he can pick out of the mechanical diction of a newspaper report. ("Contemporary Chronicles" 27)

For Diggins, the ephemeral nature of many of these elements—scraps of paper, overheard talk on the subway, and so forth—show not only the chaos of a "society that was spiritually dying," but also "the lawless nature of historical events" (334, 335). In the four-part narrative sequences of the *U.S.A.* novels, these crises are most apparent; but they also appear earlier in Dos Passos's career, though in more muted ways, in the tripartite narrative focus of *Three Soldiers*, the impressionism of *One Man's Initiation*, the musings on myth and history in *Rosinante to the Road Again*, or the montages of *Manhattan Transfer*. Moreover, though I cannot take issue with Diggins's belief that Dos Passos regards the West as nearing a point of spiritual and moral collapse, I also find chronicling the most effective means by which people may be humanized, even if their humanization does not count for much in the age of mechanized warfare, instant gratification, and sensationalized media. They offer a concreteness that compels readers to see themselves as participants, even if unwitting ones, in the vast sweep of historical circumstance.

In the essays that follow this introduction, we will return to those interwar years, which saw not only the United States's involvement in World War I, but also the country's subsequent industrial and economic ascendancy, which eventually came to an end by the early 1930s and left millions of Americans destitute and hopeless. In that time, fascist and communist regimes took hold of much of Europe. The effects of the Great Depression persisted until the heightened economic productivity brought about by a second world war, which proved even more horrific than the first. Over the course of these turbulent decades, the political, social, racial, gender, and religious landscapes changed dramatically. This collection attempts to give adequate treatment to Dos Passos's early and mid-career writings—be they in the form of memoir, fiction, or drama—which themselves sought to chronicle some of the most consequential and violent events of the interwar period. In one way or another, these eleven essays examine Dos Passos's attempt to understand, to *chronicle*, how the "raw structure of history" would be clothed and reclothed by the many political, social, and economic abstractions that emerged out the first four decades of the twentieth century.

For greater coherence, we have chosen to group the essays in this collection in four sections, each one detailing the different, albeit overlapping, ways Dos Passos chronicled interwar life. The first of these consists of essays that deal in one form or another with the author's chronicling of war and its aftermath. As a volunteer ambulance driver in France during World War I, Dos Passos saw the concrete gruesomeness of combat on bodies, buildings, and landscapes. From that war came the author's chronicling impulse, which would carry over to his literary treatments of the Spanish Civil War in the mid-1930s. In chapter one, Victoria Bryan focuses on burial practices as they appear in Dos Passos's first novel, *One Man's Initiation*, and later in *1919*, the second novel of the *U.S.A.* trilogy. In the former text, volunteer ambulance driver Martin Howe, accustomed to the American system of burial whereby fallen soldiers are returned home for final interment, is deeply troubled by the hasty and impersonal manner in which the corpses of the Great War are placed into the ground near where they fell. The efficiency of these burials matches the swiftness with which young men are conscripted, trained, and killed. Then, turning to the coda of *1919*, titled "The Body of an American," Bryan explains how even solemn and sacred landmarks like the Tomb of the Unknown Soldier become justifications for the efficiency of slaughter that was ushered in by the Great War's reliance on industrialized weaponry.

In chapter two, Keiko Misugi analyzes how American post–World War I imperialistic policies across Europe affected the lives of a generation of American youth, particularly those like the so-called Lost Generation, who were reluctant to return to the United States, which they regarded as provincial, closed-minded, and prudish. At the same time, as Misugi's assessment of *1919* reveals, those such as Dick Savage who stayed in Europe after the war proved complicit in promoting and solidifying American imperialist attitudes.

The third chapter of the volume offers a new perspective on Dos Passos's 1939 *Adventures of a Young Man*, which was inspired by the aforementioned execution of his friend José Robles, and which has therefore been regarded as the author's personal renunciation of the political Left. Rather, Rosa María Bautista-Cordero analyzes Glenn Spotswood as a representative of those desperate and disillusioned Americans who left their homeland during the depths of the Great Depression and joined the International Brigades on behalf of the Republican Army during the Spanish Civil War. In drawing to a close with Glenn's death, the novel, argues Bautista-Cordero, places heavy blame on the abstracting tendencies, shared by both communism and fascism, that render the Brigaders as little more than "human cannon fodder."

Devoted entirely to the groundbreaking 1925 novel *Manhattan Transfer*, Part II of the collection offers analyses of Dos Passos's efforts at chronicling American commercial culture during the 1920s. In the first essay, William Brevda discusses how the novel depicts fashion as a tool of personal identity and cultural conformity. In the "roaring" decade of the 1920s, which sought a "return to normalcy" after the tumultuous years of the Great War, the straw "boater" hat and the Arrow collar were two such items of fashion that had reached all new levels of visibility. As the novel reveals, however, their prominence in consumer culture could give rise not just to a sense of sartorial conformity, but even mobocracy and violence.

In chapter five, Alberto Lena analyzes how *Manhattan Transfer* managed to build dramatic tension through the use of cinematic methods of fragmentation and montage. While most studies of the novel's filmic techniques are based on the innovations developed by D. W. Griffith, Sergei Eisenstein, and Dziga Vertov, Lena places his focus on the legendary director and producer King Vidor, whose 1928 film *The Crowd* offers on the screen the same sense of panic, visual claustrophobia, violence, and urban frenzy found in the pages of Dos Passos's 1925 novel.

In chapter six, Lauro Iglesias Quadrado situates his analysis of *Manhattan Transfer* in a larger historical framework by surveying the role of the chronicler, which dates at least as far back as the Middle Ages. Second, the essay traces the evolution of that role and pits it against the modern notion of a novelist. These distinctions are brought to bear on Dos Passos's novel as Quadrado identifies a number of scenes in which historical forces—ranging from bootlegging and speakeasies to the growing popularity of jazz and vaudeville—thrust themselves visually and audibly into the lives of the various characters.

The third section of the collection focuses on Dos Passos as a chronicler of political ambivalence and uncertainty in the age of totalitarianism. In chapter seven, Jessica E. Teague explores the author's attempt to catalyze a national theatre movement founded on revolutionary principles. His 1928 trip to Russia, which put him in contact with filmmakers Sergei Eisenstein and Dziga Vertov, helped him develop new strategies to revolutionize theatre back in the United States, where glitzy Broadway spectacles made serious experimental drama harder to come by. As a cofounder and director of the short-lived New Playwrights Theatre, Dos Passos attempted, albeit with little success, to strike the right balance between modernist dramatic innovation on the one hand and mass appeal on the other.

In chapter 8, David Murad explores the collection of essays titled "The Republic of Honest Men," which Dos Passos wrote during his trip to Spain in 1933, and which was later collected in *Journeys Between Wars* (1933). Despite the lack of attention it has received from critics, "The Republic of Honest Men" is, according to Murad, a "prescient chronicling of the emotions, attitudes, and defeats of 1930s Spanish life and politics." Displaying an acute understanding of the complexity of the situation in which Spain was immersed during the fragile Second Republic, Dos Passos emerges once more as a critical, yet impartial, chronicler of many of the events that led to the Spanish Civil War in 1936.

In chapter 9, the final chapter of the third section, Addison Palacios focuses on the *U.S.A.* trilogy to show how Dos Passos chronicled the shifting class allegiances of the American intelligentsia throughout the New Deal era. Taking Walter Benjamin's formulation of the role of artists and authors in social causes as a starting point, Palacios suggests that Dos Passos's views of mental labor attempt to envision authors as bona fide producers. As such, "word slinging" intellectuals attempt to align their efforts, albeit with varying levels of success, with the larger labor movement in order to achieve revolutionary results that resonate far beyond the literary page.

Section IV comprises the final two chapters in the volume. In them, their authors assess how Dos Passos chronicles the growing cultural and political divisions between the United States and Europe in the interwar period. Eulalia Piñero Gil first assesses *Rosinante to the Road Again* (1922), a collection of essays that Dos Passos wrote based on his experiences traveling throughout Spain in the late 1910s and early 1920s. Piñero Gil argues that while Dos Passos attempts to use Spain's long history as a foil to highlight Americans' sense of rootlessness, *Rosinante* ultimately recognizes in both countries, but especially in Spain, a struggle to reconcile tradition with modernization in their different and sometimes conflicting regions.

In the final chapter, Fredrik Tydal assesses the relationship between Europe and the United States as it is depicted in a number of Dos Passos's interwar works, both fiction and non-fiction. Tydal discusses how the image of Europe develops from one of fascination—and even envy—in the author's early writings, to one of disillusionment after 1937, when he returned home from witnessing the Spanish Civil War. This shift in attitude, Tydal contends, began during the Sacco and Vanzetti trial, which saw Dos Passos drawing heavily on the founding mythology of the United States in order to explain what had led the two defendants to emigrate from Italy to the New World. The totalitarian regimes that took hold of much of Europe during the interwar years further compelled Dos Passos to regard the United States in a more favorable light than he ever had in his earlier works.

The essays found in this volume attest not only to the time- and situation-specific nature of John Dos Passos's chronicling, but also to his chronicling's timelessness. As much as we try to clothe the "raw structure of history" with different and finely adorned ideological vestments, we find that after a long enough while they start to wear thin and show their ruptured seams. New ones come to replace the old ones, and they too become threadbare in their time. In his role as chronicler, Dos Passos understood this lesson better than many of his contemporaries, which is why, perhaps for more than any other reason, he was unwilling to commit himself unequivocally to any of the "-isms" that sprang out of the twentieth century. His impulse to chronicle—his desire to document and measure an abstraction's worth by the ways it affects actual human beings—proves instructive to those of us in the present century, who cannot tell what the next five years hold for humanity, much less the next hundred years.

ACKNOWLEDGMENTS

I would like to extend a heartfelt expression of gratitude to this volume's co-editor, Rosa María Bautista-Cordero, who has added critical insight to this introduction throughout every step of its composition. Her friendship, hard work, professional acumen, and continual good humor have made collaboration on this volume a true pleasure.

NOTES

1. Barbara Foley's *Radical Representations* concurs: "[T]hroughout Dos Passos's *U.S.A.*, which purports to represent the totality of American society through its spectrum of typical fictional characters, not a single black (or other non-white) character is featured as a protagonist. Moreover, Dos Passos's few black and Latin characters are portrayed through a mutually reinforcing racist and homophobic discourse that presupposes the reader's assent" (193–94).
2. Among other notable works that explore either directly or indirectly Dos Passos's treatment of history, see Cecelia Tichi's *Shifting Gears: Technology, Literature, Culture in Modernist America* (1987), Donald Pizer's *Dos Passos' U.S.A.: A Critical Study* (1988), Janet Galligani Casey's *John Dos Passos and the Ideology of the Feminine* (1998), and more recently Tom McEnaney's *Acoustic Properties: Radio, Narrative, and the New Neighborhood of the Americas* (2017), Mark Whalan's *World War One, American Literature, and the Federal State* (2018), Lisa Nanney's *John Dos Passos and Cinema* (2019), and Aaron Shaheen's *Great War Prostheses in American Literature and Culture* (2020).
3. One is reminded, for instance, of the *Anglo Saxon Chronicle*, initiated (and at times authored) by King Alfred the Great in the late ninth century. And in her preface to the Oxford edition of Thomas Malory's late-medieval *Le Morte Darthur*, Helen Cooper describes the chronicle genre as one that "presents speeches and actions, not thoughts and motives, and the inner life of [Malory's] characters has to be deduced from those. . . . Yet the effect of the narrative is extraordinarily powerful. The sparseness of Malory's style constantly invites the reader to fill in the gaps, to supply the motives that produce the recorded reaction of aggression, or tears, or passion, or an answer at cross-purposes, or on rare occasions a smile" (xvii). When considering the *U.S.A.* trilogy's narrative portions, which trace from a certain distance the goings-on of twelve main characters, we can see a similar strategy. Like Arthur, Guenivere, and Lancelot, J. Ward Morehouse, Eleanor Stoddard, Charlie Anderson, and Margo Dowling are all rendered on the page more by their actions and dialogue than by revelations of interior complexities. When narrative introspection enters into the trilogy, it does so through the "Camera Eye" sections, which depict the life and psyche of the author in such detail that a reader likely feels the onset of claustrophobia.

WORKS CITED

Bakhtin, Mikhail. *Problems of Dostoevsky's Poetics.* Translated by Caryl Emerson, U of Minnesota P, 1984.

Beal, Wesley. *Networks of Modernism: Reorganizing American Narrative*. U of Iowa P, 2015.

Carr, Virginia Spencer. *Dos Passos: A Life*. Doubleday, 1984.

Casey, Janet Galligani. *John Dos Passos and the Ideology of the Feminine*. Cambridge UP, 1998.

Cooper, Helen. Introduction. *Le Morte Darthur*, by Thomas Malory, Oxford UP, 2008, pp. vii–xxii.

Denning, Michael. *The Cultural Front: The Laboring of American Culture in the Twentieth Century*. Verso, 1998.

Diggins, John P. "Visions of Chaos and Visions of Order: Dos Passos as Historian." *American Literature*, vol. 46, no. 3, 1974, pp. 329–46.

Dos Passos, John. *The Best Times: An Informal Memoir*, 1966. Open Road, 2015.

———. Introduction. *Three Soldiers*, by Dos Passos, 1921. Modern Library, 1932, pp. v–ix.

———. "Looking Back on *U. S. A.*" *John Dos Passos: The Major Nonfictional Prose*, edited by Donald Pizer, Wayne State UP, 1988, pp. 235–37.

———. "The New Masses I'd Like." *The New Masses*, June 1926, p. 20.

———. *One Man's Initiation: 1917*, Allen and Unwin, 1920.

———. "Statement of Belief." *The Bookman*, Sept. 1928, p. 26.

Dos Passos, John R[andolph]. *The Anglo-Saxon Century and the Unification of the English-Speaking People*. G.P. Putnam's Sons, 1903.

Foley, Barbara. "From *U.S.A.* to *Ragtime*: Notes on the Forms of Historical Consciousness in Modern Fiction." *American Literature*, vol. 50, no. 1, 1978, pp. 85–105.

———. "The Treatment of Time in *The Big Money*: An Examination of Ideology and Literary Form." *Modern Fiction Studies*, vol. 26, no. 3, 1980, pp. 447–67.

Gold, Michael. "A Barbaric Poem of New York." *The New Masses*, Aug. 1926, pp. 25–26.

Griffin, Roger. "Modernity, Modernism, and Fascism: A 'Mazeway Resynthesis.'" *Modernism/modernity*, vol. 15, no. 1, 2008, pp. 9–24.

Koch, Stephen. *The Breaking Point: Hemingway, Dos Passos, and the Murder of José Robles*. Counterpoint, 2005.

Ludington, Townsend. *John Dos Passos: A Twentieth-Century Odyssey*. Carol and Graf, 1998.

Marx, Karl, and Frederick Engels. *The Communist Manifesto*. 1848. Translated by Frederick Engels, Charles Kerr and Co., 1912.

McEnaney, Tom. *Acoustic Properties: Radio, Narrative, and the New Neighborhood of the Americas*. New York UP, 2017.

Moglen, Seth. *Mourning Modernity: Literary Modernism and the Injuries of American Capitalism*. Stanford UP, 2007.

Nanney, Lisa. *John Dos Passos and Cinema*. Clemson UP, 2019.
North, Michael. *Camera Works: Photography and the Twentieth-Century World*. Oxford UP, 2005.
Pizer, Donald. *Dos Passos' U.S.A.: A Critical Study*. UP of Virginia, 1988.
Sanders, David. "The Art of Fiction XLIV: John Dos Passos." *Paris Review*, Spring 1969, pp. 147–72.
Shaheen, Aaron. *Great War Prostheses in American Literature and Culture*. Oxford UP, 2020.
Tercero Ramiro, Sonia, director. *Robles, Duelo al Sol.* Time Zone Producciones, 2015.
Tichi, Cecelia. *Shifting Gears: Technology, Literature, Culture in Modernist America*. U of North Carolina P, 1987.
Trombold, John. "From the Future to the Past: The Disillusionment of John Dos Passos." *Studies in American Fiction*, vol. 26, no. 2, 1998, pp. 237-56.
Whalan, Mark. *World War One, American Literature, and the Federal State*. Cambridge UP, 2018.

PART 1

CHRONICLING WAR AND ITS AFTERMATH

1

WARRING BODIES

World War I Burial Practices in John Dos Passos's *One Man's Initiation: 1917* and *1919*

Victoria M. Bryan

As Stephen Prothero suggests in *Purified by Fire*, the corpse serves as "a threat to social order" (1), and the corpses produced as a result of World War I are no exception. The United States's decision to join the war effort in 1917 marked an increase in international interaction and cooperation. Such military effort indicated an intention to get involved in international politics on an unprecedented scale, and as a result, the US became privy to the impact on the human body of a technologically advanced war effort. World War I produced corpses that reminded civilians that the "quiet afterglow of the nineteenth century"—as John Dos Passos has referred to the period between the US Civil War and World War I—had been shattered by highly mechanized, widely broadcast, large-scale death (Preface 7). Though the fighting did not take place on US soil, the effects of warfare were reported widely in the United States. Citizens consumed news of the bloodshed overseas in greater quantities than had been available during previous conflicts, leading to increased exposure to the effects of war despite the distance between US citizens and the battlefields of Europe.

Just as war dead can challenge social order, with the right kind of planning and the right kind of memorialization, they can be exploited as artifacts for the justification of war. As combatant nations struggled under the weight of high casualty rates, ideas for large-scale memorials and monuments, like the Tomb of the Unknown Soldier and international military cemeteries came to fruition. Even though the United States resisted the influence of some international burial practices—like leaving buried soldiers in the land on which they fell and opting instead to identify entombed bodies and return them to the States for "proper" burial—it followed the examples of other combatant nations in the creation of memorial monuments. The burial imagery in John Dos Passos's *One Man's Initiation: 1917* and *1919* illustrates modern forces at work as a result of the cultural, technological, and political changes brought about by World War I and the resulting need to bury and commemorate high numbers of war casualties. If the corpse, as Prothero points out, represents "a threat to social order" in peacetime, the war dead came to serve as tools for nationalism and justification of warfare.[1]

As the war progressed, and as authors attempted to make sense of the world's first modern war effort, the indefinable nature of mass death and modernized killing became undeniably clear. Modris Eksteins writes memorably in *Rites of Spring* that "[f]rom its start . . . the war exerted a singular fascination by its very monumentality and, as it progressed, its staggering ineffability" (208–09). While that monumentality was felt heartily in Europe and has inspired volumes of research on the impact of the war on European consciousness, researchers often overlook the impact of World War I on the American consciousness. Pearl James's *The New Death: American Modernism and World War I* focuses on the shortsightedness of arguing that the United States was not impacted by World War I as heavily as were other combatant nations. The highly mechanized nature of the war and the intensely shifting nature of dealing with the dead that the war forced upon Americans should not be understated: "[T]he war disrupted people's ability to prepare for, witness, and ritualize death according to customs of deathbed attendance, funerals, and burials" (7) that were established in the decades leading up to the conflict, but these rituals were already disrupted by shifting modernizing forces. Wartime impacted such disruptions considerably further.

In *One Man's Initiation: 1917*, Martin Howe illustrates such interruptions through his focus on the problematic nature of American idealism and the distinctly American gaze he brings to his interactions overseas. Howe volunteers as an ambulance driver in World War I, and sees his time in France not as an opportunity to help further US power in the world or to glorify his home country, but as a time to witness a world-altering event. Frustration with his life at home and his time at war generate a respect for France's culture and an admiration for leftist political ideas. Howe comes to believe that the capitalist nature of warfare and the greed of American politicians—not the need to keep US citizens safe from foreign threats—constitute the basis for war. As such, he turns a skeptical eye toward commodification and very pointed displays of national grief in the face of what he comes to recognize as systematized murder.

In light of their cynicism about the usefulness of war, Howe and his fellow soldiers reference throughout the novel the prevalence and seemingly abhorrent nature of leaving soldiers buried in impersonal and hastily built military cemeteries. Though burying soldiers on the land on which they died was common in European wars, this practice stood in direct opposition to the US's (albeit short) history of returning soldiers to US soil for burial after they had fallen in battle overseas. Though he criticizes American idealism about warfare and what it accomplishes, Martin does not fully eschew an idealistic worldview—particularly when it comes to burial and how it plays out in times of war.

In having the viewer experience these European burial scenes through Martin's American eyes, Dos Passos comments on the troublesome (though necessary) practice of hurried wartime burial in the eyes of his contemporary US culture. By the early twentieth century, Americans placed a great deal of emphasis and spent exorbitant amounts of money on elaborate burial practices meant to serve the living. Seeing fallen European soldiers buried in hastily dug graves, sometimes with coffins and sometimes without, eventually stripped of their worldly possessions before internment, Howe struggles with what his American eyes understand to be a mistreatment of the body and a lack of respect for the loved ones who have lost soldiers in war. Those who survived the fallen would not get to visit these graves often (if at all) to mourn or remember; they would not get to use the funeral as a time to grieve and gain closure.

For Howe and his comrades, then, military cemeteries are not only lonely, sad places. They are places that cheapen the process of burial and rob the living of the very purposes behind burial practices. As James's study points out, the idea of leaving bodies buried in international soil was deeply problematic for the families of fallen soldiers waiting back home. Upon being told of their loved ones' deaths, "[f]amilies wrote to the war department asking 'Are the bodies of the soldiers who died now embalmed?' 'What kind of casket has been used for burial?' 'Will it be possible to allow relatives to have caskets, containing bodies returned to this country, open for inspection?' 'Can a tentative date for starting removal of bodies to this country be given?'" (22). An overwhelming number of families of fallen soldiers wanted the bodies of their loved ones returned for burial; but, as James points out, those families often waited for years for their loved ones' arrivals, and in some cases, these periods of interrupted and prolonged mourning lasted well into the 1920s as families awaited the delivery of the bodies (22–23). It stands to reason, then, that modernist American writers like John Dos Passos would portray "the 'work of death' as unfinished, unsatisfactory business" (James 22).

Interestingly, this description of wartime burial as an "unfinished, unsatisfactory business" extends to the "Body of an American" section that closes

Dos Passos's *1919*. Perhaps the best-known addition to burial trends to come out of World War I was the Tomb of the Unknown Soldier. This tomb and memorial structure—now one of the US's most revered war memorials—was a French, Italian, and British invention that was later incorporated into commemorative and mourning practices in the United States when American congressmen and politicians were emotionally moved by the European interment ceremonies for their unknown soldiers. The final section of Dos Passos's *1919* addresses the implementation of this memorial in the United States. While the Tomb of the Unknown Soldier valorizes the US soldiers who died during the conflict, Dos Passos's account of this interment ceremony illustrates international cooperation in shifting memorial practices even as it insists on exploring governmental exploitation of corpses created by international military efforts. In the name of honoring the dead, government entities around the world built these memorial structures to reinforce the necessary nature of warfare and the honorable sacrifice made by the soldiers who chose to go into battle.

ONE MAN'S INITIATION: 1917, INTERNATIONAL MILITARY CEMETERIES, AND SOLDIERS FIGURED AS DEAD BODIES

For Martin Howe and many of his companions in *One Man's Initiation,* disappointment with American idealism is inseparable from disillusionment with the war. While they do not *idealize* France, they do enjoy its novelty in light of all of their disappointment with the United States's international military involvement. From the beginning of the novel, Dos Passos figures Howe as the voice of reason in relation to overzealous enthusiasm for war and bloodshed.[2] In this first chapter, Howe "has never been so happy in his life" (45), as he is making his way to France to join the war efforts; but this happiness does not come from his dedication to the war. Throughout the novel, he speaks often about the idiocy of the war, the hopelessness of it, and the notion that "it isn't natural for people to hate that way [the way he believes it is necessary to hate in order to kill]" (72). As early as the first chapter, shortly after being figured as the happiest he has ever been in his life while he is in transit to France, Howe alludes to his skepticism of the war and its motivating factors, saying "I wonder if it's all true . . . " (47), alluding to the widely broadcast reports about German atrocities. By the end of the novel, his anti-war sentiments have only strengthened, and he proclaims to the French soldiers Lully, Dubois, Merrier, and Chenier, that the United States does not fully understand the war, that

Americans "are like children" who believe everything they are told without question, and that he has come to consider the United States's involvement in the war to be "a tragedy" (157). His friend Tom Randolph adds that their entrance into the war eliminates the US's "only excuse for existing" (157)—the separation from corrupt European politics that came with the States's victory in the American Revolution. Howe carries Randolph's declaration further by arguing, "all the quiet and the civilisation and the beauty of ordered lives that Europeans gave up in going to the new world . . . gave them opportunity to earn luxury, and, infinitely more important, freedom from the past, that gangrened ghost of the past that is killing Europe today with its infection of hate and greed and murder" (157). For Howe, a nation's past marked by hatred and greed and systematic murder of young men causes a country to rot spiritually under the demands of a more modern age.

Howe may be fed up with American idealism, but that is because he recognizes the United States's squandered opportunity to actually lead the world to a new kind of freedom. He does not dislike the US so much as he dislikes the fact that the US used nationalistic ideals and false slogans to pull people into supporting its entrance into the war. He has enjoyed his travel to France (as much as one could while running an ambulance to and from attack zones) because it has exposed him to a new and adventurous environment, but he does not think that France is free from the kind of problematic nationalism and problematic government that he sees in the United States. He and his companions do not admire France because of the valor that supposedly comes from war or because they find European nations somehow more admirable than their own country. In fact, he laments that the US's entrance into the war has made them into a "military nation, an organised pirate like France and England and Germany" (157–58). Instead, they admire France as an exoticized land full of history, tradition, and art.

This quest for "othered" and exotic places positions Howe and his traveling companions for overseas burial and for leaving close friends interred in international American cemeteries—a standard and necessary European practice for centuries before World War I. Military forces could not leave bodies unburied as doing so could result in health or morale crises. Since worldwide warfare has not played out on American soil, leaving American soldiers buried in overseas cemeteries was a custom that the United States had not yet encountered and was not inclined to accept as an overarching practice. War within the United States necessitated the formation of cemeteries and burial performances in places that made geographic and economic sense and that did not create the need for extensive transportation of bodies (the most notable example being the cemeteries formed during and immediately following the Civil War). Such practicality did not, however, extend beyond the boundaries of American soil.

Yet, as Dean W. Holt argues, "The Spanish-American War in 1898 and the Philippine Insurrection in 1900–1901 marked a new era in the history of American burial policy. It was probably the first time in history that a country at war with a foreign power had disinterred its soldiers who died on foreign soil and brought them home to family and friends" (2). A group of civilian morticians called the Quartermaster Burial Corps disinterred American soldiers buried in mass or poorly marked graves, identified the bodies, and then gave the fallen soldiers' next of kin the option of having the soldier buried in an international American cemetery or having the soldier's body shipped home for burial. If the next of kin chose the latter option, the body was embalmed in preparation for shipment home. Upon return of the body to American soil, the next of kin had the option to reinter the soldier in a private or national cemetery (Holt 2–3). The United States thus became the only country to offer this practice as an option to the families of soldiers, a practice that remains to this day.[3] In fact, after World War I, many national cemeteries in the United States faced the reality that fallen soldiers were coming home in such high numbers that national (and several private) cemeteries had to be expanded, reorganized, and, in some cases, relocated in order to accommodate the masses of war dead returning to American soil.[4]

American novelists responding to World War I often reference this necessary practice of burying soldiers in the soil on which they fought instead of sending their bodies home for internment, but do so with a sense of discomfort at having to leave the body so far from his homeland. Indeed, Lisa M. Budreau suggests that the United States's "unrestrained erection of monuments and the unquestioned return of the war dead, were abruptly threatened by radical revision" (2) because of its involvement in WWI. As this was the United States's first large-scale international conflict—significantly larger than the military conflicts of the very late nineteenth century and very early twentieth century—Budreau argues that "graves scattered across Europe and the United States, and remains that lay unidentified or simply no longer existed, complicated efforts to collectively mourn the dead just as distant battlefields and government restrictions prevented cooperative efforts to mark the war in a personal and meaningful way" (2). Similarly, Steven Trout's work illustrates that this era was memorialized extensively "through some of the most grandiose remembrance projects in American history" (1), including efforts to take up meaning-making in literature and cinema, resulting in a diverse cultural narrative about what it means to engage in international military conflict and the loss of life that results.

Disruptions to established methods of mourning gave way to a subset of American literature intent on offering representations of inherently modern processes for memorialization. Some of these representations—specifically in *One Man's Initiation*—focus on this practice and the funeral rites practiced on European soil. At several points in the text, Dos Passos depicts burial grounds and makeshift cemeteries, both from a distance and in a tangible manner. In one short and powerful scene, the narrator describes from a distance the "close-packed wooden crosses" that mark the soldiers' burial ground, from which comes "the sound of spaded earth" (113). He includes imagery of "wheeled carts piled with shapeless things in sacks [that] kept being brought up and unloaded and dragged away again" (113). This particular burial scene is distant and depicts bodies that are so impersonalized and stripped of individuality that the narrator does not even describe them as bodies, but instead as "shapeless things in sacks." The suggestion here is that these burial grounds are quickly established as collections of impermanent and conveniently located makeshift graves, the temporary nature of which negates the most important tenets of war burial.

Dos Passos's major concerns with war burial in this novel consist of maintaining the autonomy of a soldier's body, focusing on the sacrifices he made during his service, and allowing a soldier's death to illustrate the economic basis of warfare. Despite the prevalence of burial imagery in this novel, one of the few scenes that features an *actual* burial makes up the entirety of a short section inserted in chapter seven. Several men charged with burying the war dead in one of the shoddy war cemeteries find themselves with a conundrum. The section starts with the sergeant of the stretcher-bearers saying, "It's a shame to bury those boots" (140) as the stretcher-bearers are about to lower the body of a dead soldier named Lieutenant Dupont into his grave. Dupont is the only character actually named in this scene, as if his burial has returned the individuality that warfare otherwise strips from living soldiers. The sergeant has identified one of the burning questions of warfare: how does one maintain the autonomy of a soldier's body during burial when the boots, on one hand, are very precious and expensive commodities during wartime, but on the other hand, belong to the dead soldier? To remove them would violate the autonomy of the body and would feel comparable to stealing. Several of the sergeant's men respond, saying "Shall we take them off? It's a shame to bury a pair of boots like that," and "So many poor devils need boots," and "Boots cost so dear" (140). The men in this scene present valid concerns; quality boots were necessities during trench warfare to avoid the danger and pain of trench foot, but they became exponentially expensive as the war wore on. Obviously, burying a soldier with his boots does not change the fact that he is dead, nor does it change the way he died. Taking his boots would, however, violate the body's sovereignty and deny the body the simple respect it deserves. The stretcher-bearers choose to recognize the fact that he died because of his duty in the military; he died a soldier, so harvesting his gear from his body carries an air of disrespect. They only hesitate once more while lowering Lieutenant Dupont into the ground when another stretcher-bearer asks them to wait because he has found an available coffin for the dead soldier. The stretcher-bearers bury Dupont with his boots still on, and though the sergeant clearly feels a bit uncomfortable burying something "so dear nowadays" (141), the burial scene carries an air of respect and pride as a result of their decision to forego harvesting his supplies and show respect to his body.

Any comfort the reader takes in the stretcher-bearers' respect for Dupont's body, though, is dashed by chapter ten when Howe visits a cobbler who has taken up shop in soldiers' quarters. Howe is looking to buy shoelaces, and this man has made a business out of carving the discarded boots of dead soldiers into shoelaces to sell to soldiers who are still alive. Dos Passos describes the cobbler surrounded by "piles of old boots, rotten with wear and mud, holding fantastically the imprints of the toes and ankle-bones of the feet that had worn them" (171). The anxiety with which Dos Passos imbues this scene is comparable to the anxiety expressed by the stretcher-bearers earlier in the novel; but Howe does not seem to feel that anxiety. He notes the way the candle light makes the boots appear to "move back and forth faintly, as do the feet of wounded men laid out on the floor of the dressing-station" (171). Howe laughs nervously as he tries to make conversation with the cobbler, but the moral conundrum faced by the stretcher-bearers over what to do with a soldier's boots after he has died does not arise between Howe and the cobbler. The cobbler talks openly about procuring the boots from the nearby hut where the burial crews "pile up the stiffs before they bury them . . . leav[ing] lots of their boots around" (172). He goes on to point out that "some day another fellow will be making laces out of mine" (172), indicating that the boots are tied more to a representation of a wartime life cycle rather than a symbol of bodily autonomy.

By the end of the novel, the boots have come to symbolize something separate from a dead soldier's body. They are no longer kept on soldiers as they are carried off for burial. Instead, the soldiers and the boots are discarded in two separate piles, indicating a separation of body from commodity. The pile of boots shows the need for material goods to keep the war going. Moreover, when coupled with Lully's declaration in the previous chapter that "[t]he rich must be extinguished; with them wars will die" (163), the separation suggests that the economic motivation for warfare is not simply a connection Dos Passos hints at in this novel, but one of which the soldiers are acutely aware. By the end of the novel, despite his naivety in the face of war tactics, Howe has come to realize that as far as modern warfare goes, men are replaceable, but boots are not. The governments that run the war can draft more men, but the production of boots is too slow to keep up with the wear and tear of warfare. In other words, the sovereignty of the body and the respect for individual lives disappears in the face of the need to fuel war.

Dead and dying soldiers become more prevalent as the novel progresses, and this death imagery colors the novel as thoroughly as burial imagery. Both make a distinct imprint upon Howe as he becomes notably familiar with the difference between a living person and a dead body, and with the power of warfare to perform burial of its own accord. One of Howe's first encounters with the bodily effects of war comes when he sees the body of a man who had a grenade explode in his pocket, and the description of his mangled body is colored by Howe's attempts to make sense of what the body looked like intact before being blown up. Howe cannot easily take in the sight; he has to absorb it slowly, comparing the abdomen and legs that are now just "a depression, a hollow pool of blood" (71–72) to the space "[w]here the middle of the man had been, where had been the curved belly and the genitals, where the thighs had joined with a strong swerving of muscles to the trunk" (71). Howe thinks of this man often, and of all of the other "huddled, pulpy messes of blue uniform half-buried in the mud of ditches" (108). Warfare, in other words, performs acts of burial without the help of the burial corps. Dust, dirt, and mud all serve similar purposes in this novel. When these elements are present, they generally point to soldiers being buried by warfare. The dirt that falls on Howe's face in chapter four as he tries to sleep in barn with a bombing nearby suggests burial imagery to come. Dust accompanies the soldiers who pass Howe and Randolph as the camions take them off to battle. Dust chokes and confuses and gets kicked up as soldiers get carted off to war. Mud, however, serves as a substance that a body can sink into. When Howe and Randolph visit the theatre while they are on leave, one of their Australian companions makes a toast to mud, saying, "The war'll end when everybody is drowned in mud" (94), suggesting an awareness of the ability for warfare to kill and bury soldiers without the actual agency of a person to perform the burial. This declaration is similar in nature to the declarations of the soldier who goes mad toward the beginning of the novel and tries to stab his sergeant-major because he believes the only way to end the war is to "kill everybody, kill everybody" (79).

In various scenes in the novel, mud becomes thicker and more stifling as soldiers move closer to battle. The camions return from battle covered in mud. The novel's very first graveyard scene features men covered in mud digging graves, as if they are burying themselves. When battles end, soldiers and mules are depicted "huddled . . . half buried in the mud of the ditches" (122) near camions that have been blown up and overturned. The mud that marks miserable battles in this novel also seems to suck soldiers into it, burying them—living or dead—in the land on which they fought. Even though the US government will eventually continue its practice of returning bodies to their families for burial after the war is over, Martin Howe (and Dos Passos's American readership) must come to terms with the reality that initial internment overseas is a necessary practice, as much a modernization of warfare as any of the weaponry Howe encounters in this novel.

This consistent juxtaposition of the soldier's body with imagery of death and burial positions these soldiers as dead bodies even while they are still very much alive. Howe's first recognition of the effects of war comes as he sits at a cafe on a quiet afternoon shortly after arriving in Paris. In a scene that Aaron Shaheen calls the "most consequential" in the novel (127), a woman "swathed in black crepe veils" and a bandaged soldier take their seats at a table near him. Howe finds himself staring into the latter's young-looking face with a "triangular black patch" where the soldier's nose should have been "that ended in some mechanical contrivance with shiny little black metal rods that took the place of the jaw" (54). The soldier's eyes look frightened, as if he either experiences shell-shock or perhaps finds himself unsure of how to navigate the world with his newly disfigured face. Howe describes the soldier's eyes as being like "those of a hurt animal, full of meek dismay" (54), and finds that he cannot look away from them. The impact of modern warfare on a soldier's body is horrifying in this passage, but of particular interest is the woman's mourning attire. She interacts with this soldier as if she were his mother. Obviously, he has not died, but she still dresses in mourning. Perhaps she has lost another son or loved one, but the juxtaposition of this disfigured soldier and this mother-figure suggests that the impact of the war on this soldier's body has caused his figurative death within his family. He will never exist as he did before the deforming effects of modern warfare, so this mother-figure mourns. After seeing the soldier, when Martin looks in the faces of his fellow soldiers or the eyes of beckoning women, he sees the injured soldier. These injuries are so pervasive that Martin sees them on people who are healthy, suggesting that men going to war, who are as yet untouched by the physical effects of modern weaponry, are already imagined as dead bodies.

References to the smell of a soldier's body, blood, and sweat permeate descriptions of the barracks, hospital tents, and the French landscape. One particular encounter with the odor of death and bodily decay occurs when Howe and Tom Randolph enter a hospital tent and are caught by "[a] stench of sweat and filth and formaldehyde" that gives "them a sense of feverish bodies of men stretched all about them, stirring in pain" (76). The soldiers are further described as being "cadaverous" (111); they have a "dirty smell" (79), and they give off the stench of "chloride" and "filthy miserable flesh" (148). Not only are these soldiers injured and dying, but they are also being targeted by enemy fire. Howe listens to one account of an enemy plane "chas[ing] an ambulance ten miles along a straight road . . . trying to get it with a machinegun" (58). Warfare does not just perform burial on its own; it also targets the sick and injured, ensuring high death counts and the absolute necessity of overseas burial. Furthermore, with the prevalence of chemical warfare during this military conflict, gassed soldiers abound, and they are treated as if they are already dead. The soldiers reflect on the fact that the gas "corrodes the lungs as if they were rotten in a dead body" (47), and the soldier that Howe and Randolph rush to the medical tent after a battle is regarded as "pretty near dead now" (125) and thus not offered much medical attention. Soldiers who are injured, soldiers who are gassed—essentially, soldiers who go to war—are destined for death.

Because modern warfare disfigures a body so thoroughly, Howe begins to see death, in the words of Prothero, as "a kind of alchemy" (1). For Howe, war does not simply change a person from an individual into a cog in the war machine. Warfare destroys the body, changing it from an autonomous person into an inhuman mass of grotesque remains. Merrier, one of Howe's companions at war, says he has expected to die every time he has gone to battle, but that he does not expect it this time for some reason, so he thinks this might be the battle that kills him. Howe has a hard time seeing the connection between this lively person and "those huddled, pulpy masses of blue uniform half buried in the mud of ditches" (108), saying "Dead he [Merrier] would be different" (108). Shortly after this exchange—and for the duration of the novel—Howe starts envisioning his own death. He imagines what his body will feel like when he has been shot and killed. His reflections on his supposedly imminent death are indignant and skeptical. He thinks that it is "silly that he might be dead any minute," asking, "What right had a nasty little piece of tinware to go tearing through his rich, feeling flesh, extinguishing it?" (149). The bullet would not simply extinguish Howe's life; it would extinguish his physical flesh, changing his form completely as he moves from life to death.

As Howe encounters more seasoned soldiers and as he witnesses more death, his frustration with warfare and governmental greed that necessitates systematized large-scale slaughter grows stronger. Such encounters take place in "tobacco-stinking, sweat-stinking rooms" (85) and are often accompanied by soldiers gambling against death with the "death-dance of the guns" in the background (86). He juxtaposes the soldiers gambling with money and warring nations gambling with soldiers' lives. The stark comparison, taken with Howe's assertion that the kind of hate that seems to propagate warfare cannot be a natural human emotion, suggests that something besides hatred serves as the impetus for war. The overt socialism found in the conversation at the poker game attended by Howe, Randolph, Merrier, Lully, Dubois, and Chenier draws attention to both the capitalistic motivations for warfare and the reality that war's perpetuation of the violence done is politically motivated by greed. Each soldier reflects on what he believes is the impetus for war, the solution to such a destructive manmade invention, and the way to rid the world of such violence—much of which centers on socialist or anarchist worldviews (with which Dos Passos may have sympathized). This lengthy chapter illustrates the idea that when soldiers become pawns for political and capitalistic gain, avarice, not hate, becomes the driving force behind the killing.

Dos Passos figures these soldiers as fodder for war, fighting for a nation that is gambling their lives away by positioning them as dead bodies that can be disposed of easily. The soldiers are often shown gambling against the backdrop of whistling shrapnel and exploding bombs. In chapter four, for example, Howe sits in a dugout watching his bunkmates play cards. They invite him to play, but amid the sounds of battle outside the dugout he decides he does not want to join because "it would be so silly to be killed in the middle of one of those grand gestures one makes in slamming the card down" (85) on the gaming table. He then makes a direct connection between gambling and dying at war by immediately reflecting on "all the lives that must, in these last three years, have ended in that grand gesture" (85). Howe not only zeroes in on the commodified nature of warfare; he also expounds on the fact that the practice of war risks the lives of young men, some of whom seek valor while others are reluctantly conscripted. He asks at the end of the chapter, "Is it death [the soldiers] are playing, that they are so merry when they take a trick?" (86), indicating recognition that all participation in warfare is a gamble and that what is at stake is not simply money (though for the men in office who make the decision to go to war, money is a very real motivator), but actual human lives. Howe and many of his companions become acutely aware by the end of the novel that the monetary motivations of warfare are sought and enjoyed by men who do not go to war themselves, leaving those who do participate at the mercy of men they will never meet. The decisions are depersonalized and dehumanized, leaving the soldiers figured not just as dead bodies, but as commodities to be gambled away. Toward the end of the novel, Howe begins to see the battlefields, woods, dugouts, and other areas upon which the violence of warfare is enacted "as a gambling table on which, throw after throw, [are] scattered the random dice of death" (149). The dice are thrown by people who never experience warfare, while the men who fight are figured as little more than corpses that serve in international wagers and are eventually discarded.

With such clear figurations of soldiers as dead bodies, the declaration by one of the Australian soldiers that "[t]he war'll end when everybody is drowned in mud" (94) becomes all the more significant. This sentiment is mirrored in the last chapter of the novel during Chenier's last living moments after an enemy attack. Attempting to make conversation with and care for the dying soldier, Howe asks if Merrier, Lully, and Dubois survived the attack. Chenier replies, "Why ask?. . . Everybody's dead. You're dead aren't you?" (173). Despite Howe's hopeful response—"No, I'm alive, and you. A little courage. . . .We must be cheerful" (174, ellipsis in original)—the novel's final exchange solidifies the likeness of living soldiers to dead bodies, a point Aaron Shaheen makes in comparing the scene to the undead figures in Abel Gance's 1919 film *J'Accuse* (which used actual French soldiers as extras while they were on leave from the front) and T. S. Eliot's 1922 *Waste Land* (143). Chenier's stance on the unimportance of each soldier's life is indicative of the mentality that permeates the war as these characters have experienced it.

1919 AND THE TOMB OF THE UNKNOWN SOLDIER

On top of the overwhelming evocation of soldiers as either the living dead or as fodder for warfare in post–World War I literature, Dos Passos's wartime writing examines the steps taken by many countries toward commemorating the fallen soldiers throughout the conflict. The hastily built cemeteries served in this capacity on a small scale, but the largest international movement toward commemorating the fallen was the creation of unknown soldier memorials in major countries involved in World War I. Laura Wittman calls this memorial trend "a quintessentially modern confrontation with death" (7). Such memorials were inventions of the Italians, the French, and the British, who began a trend that quickly spread to countries like the United States and Germany.

The interment of the Unknown Soldier at Arlington National Cemetery on November 11, 1921. Library of Congress.

The anonymity of the Unknown Soldier, the "communicable meaning" of his interment, and the arguable dehumanization that results from his burial color the final section of Dos Passos's *1919*, the second novel in the *U.S.A.* trilogy. This section, titled "The Body of an American," centers around and seeks to explain the establishment of the Tomb of the Unknown Soldier as well as his transportation and reinternment. This section begins with a rendition of President Warren Harding's proclamation that America should observe two minutes of silence and fly the American flag at half-mast on Armistice Day in 1921 to honor the dead of World War I and to commemorate the Unknown Soldier who would be interred that day. Dos Passos's choice to open this section with this proclamation sets the tone of the nation after World War I for his readers. In doing so, he illustrates that the president found it necessary to offer some kind of nationwide mourning ceremony for those who lost loved ones during the war. Dos Passos opens this section with stream of consciousness–style language depicting Harding's address: "Whereasthe Congressoftheunitedstates byaconcurrentresolutionadoptedon the4thdayofmarch" (375). His decision to present the proclamation in such rushed grammar and syntax—taken alongside information about America's reaction to British and French interment ceremonies for their unknown soldiers—signals the haste to follow the example set by other government-sanctioned mourning.

Dos Passos utilizes other official documents to reflect the environment of mourning that permeated America immediately following the war. He also utilizes the address given by President Harding at the interment ceremony for the Unknown Soldier, but this language is presented in standard American English with proper punctuation, spacing, spelling, mechanics, and so forth, though he only includes certain excerpts from President Harding's address. He includes the first few lines of the address—"We are met today to pay the impersonal tribute; the name of him whose body lies before us took flight with his imperishable soul" (377)—and then skips to a moment much further into the speech, recounting Harding's assertion that "as a typical soldier of this representative democracy [the Unknown Soldier] fought and died believing in the indisputable justice of his country's cause" (377). The idea that this soldier *necessarily* died "believing in the indisputable justice of his country's cause" is a stance that *One Man's Initiation* does not support. This soldier's anonymity makes it impossible for us to know if he actually believed in America's cause or if he was (like Martin Howe) fighting with any number of other allegiances or motivations at the heart of his service.

The anonymity of the Unknown Soldier that Dos Passos frames in this section mirrors the anonymity that President Harding illustrated in his address at the interment. Early in his address, he acknowledges that we cannot "know his station in life, because from every station came the five millions" ("President"). Before this acknowledgement, he describes the Unknown Soldier in anonymous terms, saying, "He might have come from any one of millions of American homes. . . . He may have been a native or an adopted son; that matters little because they glorified the same loyalty, they sacrificed alike" ("President"). Harding figured this soldier as an anonymous sacrifice to the cause for which America fought, using this anonymity to bolster his passing as a sacrifice made in the name of nationality. Laura Wittman argues that important characteristics of Unknown Soldier memorials in all combatant nations include anonymity and sacrificial language. As mentioned, Wittman claims that the Unknown Soldier's anonymity was precisely what allowed for his symbolism, but also "a shocking acknowledgement of modern warfare's unprecedented reduction of the individual to an expendable cog in the machine" (9). Harding certainly did not intend for the Unknown Soldier to be viewed as "an expendable cog in the machine," but as war strips individuality and identity from a soldier in the name of national security, that soldier's reduction to something cog-like is impossible to avoid.

That cog-like nature of fallen soldiers is central to Dos Passos's account of the returning of the Unknown Soldier. Veteran burial generally intends to return individuality to the soldier by focusing on his life before the war, saluting him for his service and sacrifice during battle, draping the casket in the American flag, and marking the gravesite with his name and service details. The inability to name this soldier—the very fact that he stays unnamed and unidentified—solidifies his anonymity. Dos Passos's fictionalized retelling of the returning of the body, however, shows soldiers selecting the body that will be sent home and named the Unknown Soldier. He shows them in the "tarpaper morgue at Chalons-sur-Marne in the reek of chloride of lime and the dead" selecting "the pine box that held all that was left of" (375). The sentence is left intentionally unfinished, and Dos Passos breaks for a new paragraph there, leaving a lengthy blank space that should hold the soldier's name, but cannot. He imagines the GIs playing "enie menie minie moe" (375) while selecting the remains that will be sent home for memorialization, saying "Make sure he aint a dinge, boys, make sure he aint a guinea or a kike, how can you tell a guy's a hundredpercent when all you've got's a gunnysack full of bones, bronze buttons stamped with the screaming eagle and a pair of roll puttees" (375). This statement calls up a racist cultural anxiety about the Americanness of the soldier, but also elicits an anxiety about how one can tell if a whole person is in that coffin when modernized warfare did not simply kill soldiers, but demolished their bodies. In doing so, modern warfare worked against the practice of returning individuality to the soldier after he fell on the battlefield. Despite all of President Harding's rhetoric, despite the valorization of the Unknown Soldier's sacrifice, Dos Passos focuses on the fact that his continued anonymity is the very quality that allows him to serve a cog-like function in the machine of war and make an argument in favor of American involvement in massively deadly war efforts throughout the world.

The purpose behind this practice, of course, is to memorialize all of the soldiers who lost their lives during the war by housing one unidentified soldier in an elaborate tomb. Neil Hanson argues that the creation of this type of memorial was a significant move not only because it helped to define the implementation of tombs for unknown soldiers from various nations, but also because "rank and file soldiers had always been seen as the lowest of the low, the sweepings of the gutters. They were mere cannon-fodder and their names and exploits were rarely recorded or memorialized" (330). The war was not, however, the only force at work in the shifting of burial and commemorative practices during this time period. Wittman argues that "The Unknown Soldier was at once a representation of the body of the nation and of the human body, both felt to be ruptured, perhaps permanently, by the war and by modernity" (3). The modern world necessitated a change in the process of meaning-making in relation to death and mourning because of "the rise of nationalism, scientific and technological innovation, secularization and religious pluralism, the development of psychoanalysis and anthropology, and multiculturalism"; all of these factors, Wittman argued, "contribute[d] to a crisis in mourning" that coalesced into the need to commemorate the masses of war dead and make sense of the widespread loss the war inflicted on the involved nations (6). "In short," Wittman explains further, "by the end of the First World War, death was something that Western culture could no longer interpret adequately, and this is what the Unknown Soldier Memorial sought to expose and explore" (6). Inadequate interpretative abilities aside, the commemorative impulse and the memorial structures it inspired (and continues to inspire in the twenty-first century) motivates fictive reflection driven by a desire for meaning-making, even if that meaning is not fully understandable (as Wittman would argue) in an age of mechanized warfare.

Dos Passos utilizes this same kind of anonymity and inadequacy of interpretation, but not solely to make the Unknown Soldier stand as an indecipherable symbol for all of the American war dead. Dos Passos describes a conglomerate anonymity who came together under the title of the Unknown Soldier. He calls the Unknown Soldier "John Doe" and conspicuously conceptualizes this figure as a single being. However, instead of attributing the *possibility* of several backgrounds to this soldier (as President Harding does in his address), he writes several histories into his background as if all of these possibilities come together to create this soldier's multi-faceted background. For example, he writes that the Unknown Soldier was "born and raised in Brooklyn, in Memphis, near the lakefront in Cleveland, Ohio, in the stench of the stockyards in Chi, on Beacon Hill, in an old brick house in Alexandria Virginia, on Telegraph Hill . . . " and speaks to his socioeconomic status by claiming that he was raised "across the railroad tracks, out near the country club, in a shack cabin tenement apartmenthouse exclusive residential suburb" (376). Further, he writes of his career, saying that he "worked for an exterminating company in Union City, filled pipes in an opium joint in Trenton, N.J. Y.M.C.A secretary, express agent, truckdriver, fordmechanic, sold books in Denver Colorado" (377). The anonymously interred soldier is not physically made up of the body parts of several different soldiers; he is, instead, a nameless representation of all of the soldiers from diversified backgrounds who will never be identified and buried in American soil. Despite burial's intention of returning individuality to a soldier, this unidentified soldier is meant to offer closure to a diverse and widely spread population of homes now missing the men sent off to war *specifically because* of his anonymity.

Dos Passos carries this anonymity into his discussion of "John Doe" going into the army, but does so in terms of the anonymity that the army imposes on its soldiers. Of "John Doe," he writes, "Naked *he* went into the army" (377, emphasis mine), but shifts to the second person to describe his pre-enlistment physical, saying "they weighed you, measured you, looked for flat feet, squeezed your penis to see if you had clap, looked up your anus to see if you had piles, counted your teeth, made you cough, listened to your heart and lungs, made you read the letters on the card, charted your urine and your intelligence . . ." (377). This highly mechanized and impersonal description betrays the disposable nature of soldiers in World War I, which Laura Wittman notes when discussing "modern warfare's unprecedented reduction of the individual to an expendable cog in the machine" (9). "John Doe" forfeits his individuality upon joining the army, but Dos Passos extends this discussion of his anonymity, engaging in speculation as to how the soldier became unidentifiable. In one of the few instances when Dos Passos gives this soldier a voice, the doughboy says, "I lost my identification tag swimmin in the Marne" (378), a statement that provides a concrete explanation for his complete lack of identity after death, but one that also signifies *immersion* in World War I and the massive death toll accrued at the Battle of the Marne. Dos Passos positions "John Doe" as a man stripped of his identity as soon as he became immersed in the Marne River—the site of the battle that takes his life.

At the end of this section, Dos Passos recounts the transportation of the Unknown Soldier from France to the United States and the progression of his burial ceremony in fairly accurate, although exceptionally brief, detail. Just as he utilizes the imagery from Harding's address when he describes the personal history of the Unknown Soldier, he accurately represents the burial ceremony and the military funeral honors bestowed upon his body as they actually played out on Armistice Day in 1921. He includes the selection of the Unknown Soldier, his being laid to rest in the pine coffin, his trip home on a battleship, and his interment in the sarcophagus in the Memorial Amphitheater in Arlington National Cemetery. He includes the imagery of draping the American flag over the coffin, the bugler playing Taps, President Harding leading the crowd in the recitation of the Lord's Prayer, and the act of awarding the Unknown Soldier various awards of bravery and valor, including American, French, Belgian, Italian, Romanian, Polish, and Native American awards and commemorative tokens (379–80).

The motivation behind a memorial like the Memorial Amphitheater is very different from that of the Tomb of the Unknown Soldier, however. The Memorial Amphitheater was originally meant solely for memorialization of the war dead rather than interment of an unknown soldier. The sarcophagus for the Unknown Soldier was not built until later when the similar tombs in Europe became so popular that America decided to follow suit. Neil Hanson argues that the implementation of the Tomb of the Unknown Soldier in combatant nations was necessary from a commemorative standpoint because

> [t]he grieving families of [fallen soldiers] were robbed even of the consolation of a funeral and a grave-site, and for them the grave of the Unknown Warrior. . . became the tomb and tombstone of their lost loved ones. In almost every other combatant nation an unknown soldier was also buried at some national shrine and, just as in Britain, each at once became the focus of a pilgrimage that continues to this day. (xv–xvi)

Hanson illustrates here that the practice of actually interring an unidentified body serves a different purpose—a grave to visit, a site at which to mourn the dead—than that of the amphitheater, which is primarily honor-based rather than commemoration-based, and focuses on service and deeds rather than on a body destroyed by war.[5] The US's motivation for adding the tomb to the amphitheater aligned with Britain's motivation: politicians "hoped that by creating monuments and rituals commemorating the military victory, they might help to heal, or at least 'camouflage,' the social divisions caused by the war. . . . The Unknown Soldier, it was hoped, would both validate the war and provide just such a unifying symbol" (412). Laura Wittman argues, though, that the monument's celebration of anonymity was the more significant element of its symbolism and that the tombs act as a reminder of the expendability of soldiers. She does not argue, however, that the Unknown Soldier memorials are pacifist sites, but that they "sought to commemorate the psychological and social conflict of veterans, and of a culture that rejected mass death as incomprehensible and dehumanizing yet needed desperately to feel that so many had not died in vain, that suffering and death could still have a common, communicable meaning" (9). A memorial structure can speak to this kind of meaning, but a tomb containing the body of an unidentified soldier carries with it something more substantial. Such a structure holds a tangible sacrifice within it, and the tangibility adds weight to a fallen soldier's commemoration that a memorial structure does not.

The last two sentences of this excerpt—which read, "All the Washingtonians brought flowers. Woodrow Wilson brought a bouquet of poppies"

(380)—not only close this section (and the novel as a whole) with images of mourning and commemoration; these two sentences also juxtapose imagery of American burial practices with European symbols of mourning. Dos Passos utilizes language and mechanics in the last few paragraphs of this section, which is hurried and somewhat disjointed. He creates long, rambling lists; he breaks for new "paragraphs" that are less than a full sentence long; and he begins these "paragraphs" with the word "and" (note the lower case "a"). A good sampling of this rushed language comes when he describes the mourners at the ceremony who "thought how beautiful sad Old Glory God's Country it was to have the bugler play taps and the three volleys made their ears ring" (379). This rushed and hectic tone subsides in the penultimate sentence, when he writes, "All the Washingtonians brought flowers" (380). The succinct, direct nature of this sentence contrasts the language Dos Passos utilizes immediately preceding it while also representing a standard American mourning practice—that of bringing flowers to a funeral. In the final sentence of the novel, Dos Passos writes "Woodrow Wilson brought a bouquet of poppies" (380). Bringing flowers is a distinctly modern quality of the American funerary tradition,[6] and bringing poppies specifically ties the US to European tradition, as the poppy—a flower that grows well in disturbed earth—was widely associated with the war dead in British literature responding to World War I. Dos Passos utilizes the poppy's association with burial and remembrance practices here, but he utilizes this association as a distinctly *European* practice that solidifies the United States's entrance into international politics.

Though the Tomb of the Unknown Soldier was not a patently American invention, it stands as an important symbol of shifting American burial and mourning practices in the wake of World War I. The memorial was created to commemorate each lost or fallen soldier who went unfound or unidentified, but in doing so, it combines these lost or fallen soldiers into one amalgamated being stripped of individuality and devoid of distinctive motivations for enlisting, going to war, and fighting in Europe. As Dos Passos points out in this final section of *1919*, the Tomb of the Unknown soldier does not return individuality, as some wartime burial practices aimed to do. Instead, the monument combines all unidentified soldiers into one composite being with many possible backgrounds, many possible motivations, and many possible relationships to government and warfare; but in all cases they are used as tools for political posturing and justifications for a bloody and devastating war effort.

Studies of the Great War often marginalize the American dead since the American death toll of around 120,000 was so much lower than that of other combatant nations. Furthermore, though World War I is often heralded as a major catalyst for the modernist period in literature, studies of burial practices often marginalize the importance of World War I compared to the importance of the Civil War, Reconstruction, and World War II. John Dos Passos's *One Man's Initiation* and*1919* illustrate the distinct, oft-noted impact World War I had on American literature—the loss of faith in American ideals and the crisis of understanding that resulted from a highly mechanized, highly bureaucratized war effort. American writers often reflect upon the idea that this generation turned reverently to Europe for leadership, ideas, and guidance. The impact this impulse had on American burial and commemorative practices and policies—including the maintenance of international American military cemeteries, the practice of returning bodies to the United States for burial, and the implementation of the Tomb of the Unknown Soldier—was likewise vast. More importantly, however, the impact that this cultural shift had on American fiction writers during the interwar period affected their literary responses to this moment, as they attempted to respond to this crisis in mourning related to commemorative and memorial practices.

Despite such a crisis, World War I also marked a formative moment in American burial and mourning practices precisely because it brought the general population into contact with death in ways unprecedented since the mid-nineteenth century. Dos Passos's novels illuminate the falsities of the motivation for warfare. *One Man's Initiation: 1917* and *1919* demonstrate the economic drive and political posturing required to send soldiers to death and shows soldiers engaging with these realities on and off the battlefield. The increased death toll and the highly mechanized nature of dying introduced by this modern war created a crisis in the face of which many modern novels scrambled to reflect a changing system of burial practices.

NOTES

1. Worth noting here is that the memorialization of the war dead was never a homogenous project. As Steven Trout argues throughout *On the Battlefield of Memory*, World War I memorials often served different purposes for different groups of people, and the memory of the United States's first international conflict was visited and revisited in various media throughout the decades that followed. Notably, Trout's *Memorial Fictions* examines how the Great War "brought millions of American soldiers into a shared vision of their homeland" and catalyzed "the emergence of a truly national culture" (9). This chapter does not intend to argue that war dead were *only* used to promote nationalism and justify warfare. Trout's work is a testament to the fact that remembrance projects from this time period

took up multiple arguments surrounding warfare and the sacrifices that come with it. Dos Passos's writing, however, seems concerned with the manufacturing of nationalism out of the bodies of fallen soldiers used as pawns in a war propagated by men far more powerful and rich than they would ever be.

2. Kenneth Holditch presents a thorough discussion of Howe's position on this foolish approach to war in "*One Man's Initiation*: The Origin of Technique in the Novels of John Dos Passos." It should be noted, however, that Howe's understanding of the nature of war and the United States's childish and uninformed support of it exist despite his naivety throughout the novel that any one concept (be it a certain kind of politics or a certain kind of warfare, etc.) could serve as an answer to all of humanity's troubles. In "Dos Passos's World War: Narrative Technique and History," Lois Hughson discusses how Howe's disconnection from the war and his naivety in relation to Dos Passos's first attempt to convey the impact of World War I resulted in his "realization of the failure of his traditional technique to embody what the war meant to him" (49).
3. The United States does not, however, perform the same services to foreign soldiers who die on American soil. Many German and French POWs who died in American POW camps are interred in American national cemeteries.
4. This was coupled with the rapid urbanization of American cities and already decreasing burial space and resulted in an extension (of sorts) of the Rural Cemetery Movement (or Garden Cemetery Movement) experienced in the mid-1800s. As Holt reports, "[w]ith nearly 5 million veterans of World War I eligible for future interment in a national cemetery, it was evident that existing national cemeteries in the vicinity of large cities would not be able to provide sufficient gravesites" (185). Established cemeteries in urban areas were running out of space (though they were not necessarily becoming as run down as the churchyard burial grounds in New England did) and, as a result, more burial ground had to be acquired somehow. Highly urbanized areas, then, began acquiring space in suburban areas for the purpose of expanding the existing national cemetery space. This dilemma resulted in congressional approval to buy private land and develop it for the expansion of national cemetery facilities.
5. On March 5, 1921, President Woodrow Wilson signed into law Congress's resolution authorizing "the exhumation and return of one unidentified American soldier, for reburial in the new Memorial Amphitheater of Arlington National Cemetery on Armistice Day (now known in the US as Veterans' Day), 11 November 1921" (Hanson 412).
6. Jessica Mitford writes in *The American Way of Death* that "[f]uneral flowers, today the major mourning symbol and a huge item of national expenditure, did not make their appearance in . . . America until after the middle of the nineteenth

century" (147). They eventually became a staple of the modern American burial tradition and a symbol of the rural countryside to which cemeteries were moved during the nineteenth century. The Rural Cemetery Movement, which consisted of moving burial plots from the center of towns to their outskirts, began shortly before the Civil War and continues the work that, Jonathan Sterne argues, preservative technologies began by physically separating the world of the dead from the world of the living (292). Traditionally, people buried their dead in churchyard burial grounds in the center of their town or city. Bodies were not embalmed and coffins were designed to break down with the body once they were both in the earth. As populations rose across the Western world, so did the number of corpses in need of burial space. Churchyard burial grounds in the centers of towns became putrid sites of exposed decay. Stanley French writes that "[b]cause of the rapidly increasing population the old graveyards became so crowded that they were frequently little more than stinking quagmires—chronically offensive and occasionally serious public health hazards" (74). In response, burial grounds moved from city centers to garden-like burial plots in areas comparable to present-day suburbs (French 70–81).

WORKS CITED

Budreau, Lisa M. *Bodies of War: World War I and the Politics of Commemoration in America, 1919–1933*. New York UP, 2010.

Dos Passos, John. *1919*. 1932. Houghton Mifflin, 2000.

———. *One Man's Initiation: 1917*. 1920. Cornell UP, 1969.

———. Preface. *One Man's Initiation: 1917*, by John Dos Passos, 1920, Cornell UP, 1969, pp. 7-10.

Ekstein, Modris. *Rites of Spring: The Great War and the Birth of the Modern Age*. Mariner, 1989.

French, Stanley. "The Cemetery as Cultural Institution: The Establishment of Mount Auburn and the 'Rural Cemetery' Movement." *Death in America*, edited by David E. Stannard, U of Pennsylvania P, 1974, pp. 69–91.

Hanson, Neil. *The Unknown Soldier: The Story of the Missing of the Great War*. Doubleday, 2005.

"Harding Asks for Two Minutes of Silent Prayer for the Unknown Dead on Armistice Day." *The New York Times*. 21 Oct. 1921, p. 12.

Holditch, Kenneth. "One Man's Initiation: The Origin of Technique in the Novels of John Dos Passos." *Explorations of Literature*, edited by Rima D. Reck, Louisiana State UP, 1966, pp. 115–123.

Holt, Dean W. *American Military Cemeteries*, 2nd ed., McFarland, 2010.

Hughson, Lois. "Dos Passos's World War: Narrative Technique and History." *Studies in the Novel* vol. 12, no. 1, 1980, pp. 46–61.

James, Pearl. *The New Death: American Modernism and World War I.* U of Virginia P, 2013.

Mitford, Jessica. *The American Way of Death.* Simon and Schuster, 1963.

"President Harding's Address at the Burial of the Unknown American Soldier." *The New York Times.* 12 Nov. 1921, p. 4.

Prothero, Stephen. *Purified by Fire: A History of Cremation in America.* U of California P, 2002.

Shaheen, Aaron. *Great War Prostheses in American Literature and Culture.* Oxford UP, 2020.

Sterne, Jonathan. *The Audible Past: Cultural Origins of Sound Reproduction.* Duke UP, 2003.

Trout, Steven. *Memorial Fictions: Willa Cather and the First World War.* U Nebraska P, 2002.

———. *On the Battlefield of Memory: The First World War and American Remembrance, 1919–1941.* U Alabama P, 2010.

Wittman, Laura. *The Tomb of the Unknown Soldier, Modern Mourning, and the Reinvention of the Mystical Body.* U Toronto P, 2011.

2

THE LOST GENERATION AND US TRANSATLANTIC IMPERIALISM IN *1919*

Keiko Misugi

John Dos Passos's *1919* (1932), the second volume of the *U.S.A.* trilogy, paints a tableau of American society and its people during World War I (1914–1918). As Dos Passos's title refers to the post-armistice year of the Paris Peace Conference, a significant dimension of *1919* is the author's treatment of how American imperialistic policies across Europe affect the lives of a generation of American youth. *1919*, in short, portrays Western European nations—with the possible exception of Spain—as a virtual frontier where US trans-Atlantic imperialism cultivated a new base. Indeed, in spite of its late entry into the war in April 1917, the United States presented itself as a crucial power that settled the European conflict, thus successfully securing its eminence over Western Europe's economic, military, political, and cultural domains. European manifestations of American expansionism surface, in particular, in *1919*'s biographical sketch of Woodrow Wilson. The impact of US hegemonic impulses in Europe on members of the "lost generation" that unfold in the novel's narrative sections—and are seen most extensively in the figure of Richard Ellsworth Savage—further spotlight this tension. In the narrow sense of its usage with capitalization, "the Lost Generation" refers to a group of young American writers including Dos Passos, Ernest Hemingway, F. Scott Fitzgerald, and e. e. cummings, who all showed remarkable creative force in dealing with the complexities of the modern world. Many of these writers became expatriates in Europe, especially Paris, where Gertrude Stein, the godmother of the generation, held her famous cosmopolitan salons for these and other avant-garde artists. The experiences and perceptions of these writers, however, reached further to youth who came of age in the turmoil of World War I. Moreover, the brutality that modern technology wrought on the psyche of this generation overshadowed them. They could find no alternative to traditional values, and instead often resorted to aimless hedonism.

The character Richard Ellsworth Savage in *1919* stands as a quintessential figure of this generation. Richard, or Dick, is a literary-minded youth who heads to the European warfront as a volunteer ambulance driver. Though having experienced the battlefront in France and Italy, he can find no meaning in the war and imagines an escape to seemingly neutral Spain, the country Dos Passos fondly represents as an antithesis to sweeping modernity in his fictive travelogue and essays, *Rosinante to the Road Again* (1922). Spain, indeed, occupies a distinct place in Dick's mind as a romantic utopia, uncontaminated by the American display of imperialistic interests across Europe. Dick ultimately succumbs, however, to the currents of US imperialism and becomes one of its agents in postwar Paris. It is these inner workings of US hegemony over greater Europe—where Dick Savage serves as the epitomic agent—that I investigate.

Previous scholarship on Dos Passos's trilogy has often been concerned with its relevance to radical politics, especially its opposition to American capitalism.[1] Yet the trilogy—and *1919* in particular—also reveals both overt and covert ways that US imperialism permeated Europe. To this end, Mark Whalan recently analyzed the impact of the oil industry and emergent petromodernity in the *U.S.A.* trilogy. He conveys how Dos Passos accentuates the workings of the "petrostate," which exemplify a dimension of twentieth-century US imperialism upon which I elaborate in this article. Whalan reveals how the economic and cultural dimensions of oil position the limited resource to become the fuel of the future as well as US efforts and struggles to secure its control over other nations, especially Great Britain, France, and the Netherlands. Fictional characters revolve around the oil industry throughout the trilogy as they chance upon one another and develop relationships not only in the United States, but also in Mexico, Italy, France, and Egypt. Moreover, the critic speaks to Dos Passos's trepidation about the close relationships between the government and the oil industry in *1919*, which "dwells most explicitly on the geopolitical dimensions of this emergent petromodern state" (168). Through his inquiry into various layers of petromodernity in the trilogy, Whalan clarifies how Dos Passos treats state involvement in the infiltration of the US oil industry to gain advantage over European nations and the subsequent influence on people's lives through global consumption of oil.

This article further develops Whalan's assessment by exploring the trans-Atlantic expression of US imperialism through the representation of Woodrow Wilson and perceptions of the lost generation as exemplified in the figure of Richard Savage. By examining the impact of the American empire on the members of the lost generation, I elucidate how *1919* critiques the reign of US trans-Atlantic imperialism in the distinct context of World War I. Moreover, this discussion of *1919* surveys the depths of trans-Atlantic US expansionism in the guise of American democracy as a liberating and redemptive force across Europe during World War I and its aftermath. In a broader context, the argument posed here aims to accentuate the relevance of Dos Passos's perspective today, when twenty-first century imperialism has moved into the corporate sphere of the global economy and information technology.

US IMPERIALISM

The growth of US imperialism is as long as the history of the nation itself. Ever since the founding of the United States, the national government has demonstrated a proclivity for expanding power and exercising its dominion beyond its boundaries.[2] Starting with the thirteen colonies along the eastern shore of the Atlantic in the late eighteenth century, the US expanded westward in the nineteenth century under the aegis of "Manifest Destiny." Once the 1890 US Census declared there was no longer open frontier to claim on the continent, the US turned overseas to spread its wings. The Spanish-American War of 1898 became a pivotal moment when the US emerged as a rising imperialist power on the world stage. Spain itself was once considered the greatest empire on earth; its explorer ship carrying the Italian Christopher Columbus reached the North American continent in 1492, changing the course of world history. Five centuries later, the American victory over Spain marked the beginning of a new era for US imperialism.[3] Establishing Cuba and Puerto Rico as its protectorates, the US extended its power to encompass Central America and the Philippines in the Pacific; it also annexed Hawaii as an official territory in 1898. This was the era of Theodore Roosevelt, whom Dos Passos dubbed the "Happy Warrior" (485)[4] in another biographical section of *1919* and who became a glorious symbol of US expansionism. The twentieth century increasingly saw the nation's dominance extend into political, economic, and cultural spheres overseas.

When the war in Europe broke out in 1914, America's isolationist policy known as the Monroe Doctrine continually curbed interference in European affairs. The US, however, occupied a prime position to exert its financial influence over Allied Europe along with the aid of American military power. President Woodrow Wilson exercised every effort to maintain the nation's neutrality to serve his ambition of proving American preeminence as a peacemaker in the European conflict. Nevertheless, the financial interdependence of the US and its Allies forced US entry into the war by April 1917. With its ample monetary and human resources, the US embarked on a mission to secure victory in order to ensure its place as world leader. At the post-war Paris Peace Conference to settle the Treaty of Versailles in 1919, the US president pursued the creation of a new world order, edified by American moral supremacy and backed by its economic and military might. Historian N. Gordon Levin argues that President Wilson aimed to achieve "a peaceful liberal capitalist world order under international law, safe both from traditional imperialism and revolutionary socialism, within whose stable liberal confines a missionary America could find moral and economic pre-eminence" (vii). Wilson was not so much a disinterested idealist as an aggressor, utterly self-righteous if not hubristic in favor of US hegemony.[5] His internationalism worked in synchrony with nationalism.

Furthermore, the refashioning of the mode of dominion took place in the early twentieth century, especially through Wilson. Theodore Roosevelt unabashedly used his "Big Stick" in Latin America and the Caribbean, while William Taft extended "Dollar Diplomacy," especially in the Caribbean. Both presidents wielded financial power and exerted political pressure in imperialistic pursuit. Wilson, however, went further to combine wide-range operations across economic, political, military, and cultural—including moral—spheres in order to enhance US influence overseas and determine the course of US imperialism thereafter.[6] Subsequently, the approach to imperialism shifted from territorial acquisition to assertion of pervasive power in various domains of life beyond US borders. European powers, however, were not ready to concede to such a proposition. Wilson's own nation, moreover, failed to support his aims, preferring instead to retreat to unilateralism by shunning membership to the League of Nations, the brainchild of Wilsonianism.

Among common citizens of the Allied nations, however, the penetration of American-style democracy and materialism became so apparent that it attested to the triumph of a nonterritorial mode of US imperialism over European nations.[7] "[A] form of domination exists in the modern world," John Tomlinson posits, "not just in the political and economic spheres but also over those practices by which collectives make sense of their lives" (7). Wilson's presidency, then, "accelerated the growth of America's power in the world, increased its moralistic zeal, and enlarged government's role in spreading economic and cultural influence" (Rosenberg 63).[8] Even as Wilson failed in his campaign for his own country, the US succeeded to some extent in achieving his vision of a "brave new world . . . with the collective humbling of all the European powers at the feet of the United States," so that "the exceptional position of America at the head of world civilization would be inscribed on the gravestone of European power" (Tooze 54). In these ways, Wilson emerged as a conveyor of US economic, political, and cultural imperialism—the new mode of domination in postwar Europe.

"MEESTER VEELSON"

Dos Passos titles the biographical sketch of President Wilson in *1919* "Meester Veelson," mimicking a French accent to emphasize his inflated reception by the populace at the time of the Paris Peace Conference. The sketch represents how Wilson steered expansion of the American empire across Europe through financial, military, political, and cultural control over these nations.

When Wilson became President in 1913, his diplomacy effectively adhered to the Monroe Doctrine—that is, he was not necessarily indifferent to strengthening US influence over Central America. In "Meester Veelson," Dos Passos cites a line from the president's 1914 speech: "*I wish to take this occasion to say that the United States will never again seek one additional foot of territory by conquest,*" after which the author punctuates, "And he landed the marines at Vera Cruz" (567). Even when he was attempting to mediate the European conflict, Wilson pushed sending US troops to the Dominican Republic, Haiti, Mexico, and in Cuba. As Adam Tooze writes of Wilson's exploitation of "hard power," "[h]is naval expansion programme and his assertion of America's grip on the Caribbean approaches was more aggressive than that of any predecessor" (44).[9] Wilson's unrelenting interventions prove his strong will for dominion over other countries. For European powers, on the other hand, Wilson's ambition reveals a different dimension. His insistence on neutrality was precisely driven by his towering aspiration to prove the righteousness of the US counterpoise in opposition to the obsolescence of imperialist powers involved in fruitless massacres, as N. Gordon Levin points out. Even so, despite his earlier promises, he was forced to bring the country to war with growing German antagonism and financial entanglements in the Allied countries.[10]

Dos Passos complains of President Wilson's betrayal by accentuating his compliance with warmongering capitalists. As "the danger to the Morgan loans and the stories of the British and French propagandists set all the financial centers in the East bawling for war," Wilson finally declared war and proclaimed, "*Force without stint or limit, force to the utmost*" (567).[11] In fact, as Tooze points out, "[b]y the end of 1916, American investors had wagered two billion dollars on an Entente victory. The vehicle for this transatlantic operation . . . was a single private bank, the dominant Wall Street house of J.P.

Morgan" (38). The nation thus garnered control over Europe initially through financial agency, and then through its military. Once Wilson proposed the Fourteen Points in January 1918 to initiate international negotiations, furthermore, the pursuit of political hegemony across Europe became apparent.[12] Wilson aimed to preside over not only the antagonistic Central Powers but also the Allied nations through his proposal to claim global leadership. Although his demands had to be curbed by shrewd Old World statesmen, his proposal would lay the foundation for the League of Nations and affect the course of world history thereafter. It was certainly ironic that Wilson was unable to persuade US Congress to endorse his European success, only to exhaust himself to the point of incapacitation in futile efforts.

In contrast to the congressional unpopularity of his postwar foreign policy, the president's grip on the popular imagination of Europe was phenomenal and stands as some measure of the triumph of US cultural imperialism. In his biographical sketch, Dos Passos emphasizes the majestic reception Wilson enjoyed in Europe. He landed there for the Paris Peace Conference as "the most powerful man in the world" (568).[13] The Wilsons were the honored guests of the European sovereigns: "[T]he day after Christmas they were entertained at Buckingham Palace; at Newyears they called on the pope and on the microscopic Italian king at the Quirinal" (569).[14] The sketch compares Wilson, along with French and British prime ministers Georges Clemenceau and Lloyd George, to poker players who deal with the postwar order like a deck of cards (570).

Dos Passos represents Europeans' enthusiasm for Wilson as liberator and cultural conqueror. War-ravaged Europe welcomed American-assisted liberation from bombings, massacres, and destitution: "In Europe . . . they read in the papers that Meester Veelson was for peace and freedom and canned goods and butter and sugar" (568). The US represented a life of liberty, democracy, and material fulfillment. Such a statement reminds us of the discourse of "empire of liberty" that Thomas Jefferson famously endorsed. Anthony Bogues argues that "[w]hile conventional imperial rule usually meant violence that originated in founding violence, for Jefferson an empire of liberty was possible because a state could 'conquer without war'" (13). If, Bogues continues, "[a]n empire of liberty as imperial power . . . recognized the natural unfolding of human destiny as embodied in ways of life that were founded on conceptions of American liberty" (14), the dominion of such an empire enforces American exceptionalism with the gospel of the nation's democracy and moral supremacy. In that case, Wilson becomes conqueror and evangelist. Dos Passos illustrates how the European populace awaited their imperial missionary:

"(Did Meester Veelson know that in the peasants' wargrimed houses along the Brenta and the Piave they were burning candles in front of his picture cut out of the illustrated papers?)" (569). He even compares Wilson's proposals to Martin Luther's *Theses*, which sparked the Protestant Reformation: "(Did Meester Veelson know that the people of Europe spelled a challenge to oppression out of the Fourteen Points as centuries before they had spelled a challenge to oppression out of the ninetyfive articles Martin Luther nailed to the churchdoor in Wittenberg?)" (569). The gospel Wilson carries, however, is not merely sacred but is equally loaded with material blessings, supported by the American Relief Administration and thus kindling desire for the freedom of consumption that the US represented.

Western Europe had borne great empires of the past and established the world order in the earlier centuries. Nevertheless, with the end of World War I, the US became recognized as the world leader with its own brand of freedom and democracy. Restoration of such values in Europe by way of financial reinforcement, military intervention, and political ascendancy ensured the wholesale success of US cultural imperialism. Dos Passos illustrates his disappointment with Wilson for the gulf between his promises and reality by rendering an ironic picture of the president and his empire.

THE LOST GENERATION AND EUROPE

While Dos Passos delineates Wilson as an agent of US imperialism in his biographical sketch, the narrative of Dick Savage complements this theme by showing how the empire penetrates the expatriate life of the lost generation. Here we must note that during and after World War I, understanding Europe as an arena in which US imperialism extended itself would characterize the experience of the lost generation in Europe as a solely American affair. Europe then came under substantial influence of the American empire from across the Atlantic. As the war enabled a generation of American youth to experience Europe firsthand, an experience once available only to privileged classes, many sailed across the ocean as enlisted personnel or as volunteers for humanitarian relief organizations. Like bourgeois tourists who visited great cities to admire historical architecture and masterpieces of art, they sought experiences—not necessarily education in refinement and sophistication—but the picturesque, romantic, and adventurous in morally and sexually more liberated Europe.

By the Armistice in 1918, a substantial portion of the lost generation was transported to Europe; "almost four million men were to be in uniform, half of them in France" (Kennedy 169). There were also volunteer ambulance driver organizations, which gave those with misgivings about army enrollment a chance to support the Allied forces or to obtain a close look at the warfront without going to battle. The American Red Cross, the American Ambulance Field Service, and the Norton-Harjes Ambulance Corps were the most notable. One of the literary minded among them, Malcolm Cowley, once observed, "the ambulance corps and the French military transport were college-extension courses for a generation of writers" (*Exile's* 38).[15] And a critic would describe the Norton-Harjes, for which Dos Passos served in France, as "the most distinguished of all the lost generation's finishing schools" (Kazin 345). Such opportunities in foreign lands were eagerly sought after. Instead of experiencing something entirely alien, however, there was a certain continuity in their European experiences with intra-continental US imperialism as they landed in a Europe much affected by American empire.

Unlike most of his contemporaries, Dos Passos was well acquainted with Europe from an early age. Born in Chicago in 1896, he spent much of his childhood in Europe.[16] He travelled extensively throughout Europe, having learned French as his first language. From 1911 to 1912, he visited France, Italy, and other Mediterranean countries before entering college. Upon graduating from Harvard in 1916, he was eager to become a volunteer worker in the European war. He made a compromise to study architecture in Spain the following fall, however, due to his father's reluctance to his plan. He thoroughly enjoyed his sojourn, as he wrote to a friend, "I am so fascinated by Spain" (Dos Passos, *Fourteenth* 66), until January 1917 when his father's sudden death summoned him home.[17] Returning to Paris in the summer of 1917 as a volunteer ambulance driver, he was already fairly conversant with European civilizations. In August 1918, due to anti-war and anti-government sentiments detectable in his demeanor and in his intercepted letters, he was discharged from the Red Cross and sent home. Impatient to return to the scene, however, he immediately enlisted in the army. On the day after Armistice Day he sailed to Europe again and stayed mostly in Paris until his discharge in the summer of 1919.

Like many other Lost Generation writers after World War I, Dos Passos spent much time in Europe. Spain retained a special place in his heart.[18] He returned there to work on his writing from August 1919 to April 1920. In the 1920s and early 1930s, when he was writing *1919*, he would take occasional trips to Spain among other destinations. The Spanish Civil War (1936–1939), however, overshadowed his love affair. His disapproval of the Soviet Communist Party that largely oversaw the Spanish Republican forces made him take his leave of the country and bid a final "Farewell to Europe," as the title of his 1937 essay conveys.[19]

Spain, nonetheless, seems to have played a decisive role in forming Dos Passos's view of the world in his youth. In contrast to the mainstream of his generation, he had a better command of European languages and a deeper understanding of their cultures. His youthful passion for Spain especially seems to have contributed to distancing himself from US imperialism, even when it seemed most compelling on the European continent.[20] Townsend Ludington justly argues for the writer's representation of Spain in *Rosinante to the Road Again* as a foil to America: "Against the qualities he admired [in Spain] he set the raw power and materialism of a rapidly industrializing United States, and the contrasts he noted became part of the basis for his interpretation of modern life in his major work, the trilogy *USA*" ("'I am so fascinated'" 318). The writer's observations of Spain, its people and the land, in short, provided him with insight as to how to avoid being absorbed by the modern world, and rather, remain steadfast to his own position vis-à-vis overwhelming US imperialism.

To be sure, the fictive portrait of Dick Savage resembles Dos Passos to some extent.[21] But the crucial difference lies in Dick's inability to distance himself from US imperialism. He holds literary ambitions, while coming from a troubled household where his father, an ex-convict, lives apart from him and eventually dies in Cuba. Originally from Oak Park, Illinois, he grows up in Trenton, New Jersey, to be befriended by Mr. Cooper, a lawyer and politician, who sees him through Harvard, where he cultivates his literary talent and leftist ideology. He then becomes a contributor to the *Harvard Monthly*, the *Harvard Advocate*, and a few other magazines where his poems are published.

Dick makes his debut in Europe in 1917. Even as a pacifist, he decides to join an ambulance service, which at least ensured him a college degree as compensation. He signs up for the Norton-Harjes to sail for France and later joins the American Red Cross in Italy. There he befriends similarly minded youth. As one of them says, they take a "Cook's tour" of Europe (522), as if they were consumer tourists. Experiencing crushing air raids, visits with prostitutes, and periods of pensive gloom, one of them says: "'[T]his ain't a war, it's a goddam madhouse'" (518) or a "'whorehouse'" (443). Nevertheless, as sensitive, intellectual youth, they abhor the devastation and absurdity of warfare. One professes the misery of humankind: "'I'm ashamed of being a man . . . it will take some huge wave of hope like a revolution to make me feel any selfrespect ever again'" [ellipsis in original] (520). They see no purpose or justice in the face of human atrocities and idiocy. Dick shares much of this frustration and disillusionment. Chafed by political manipulation and human depredation, he compares war to a "cockeyed lunatic asylum," and in his letters to his friends back home he eludes to how gruesome the realities of war can be (529). Censors spot the scornful content of his "asylum" letter, and with that, Dick is discharged from the Red Cross on account of his insurgent ideology. Given no chance to explain himself, Dick is left demoralized by the whole situation.

SPAIN AS A FOIL

Spain thus emerges as one corner of Europe where Dick lays his last hope. Upon his dismissal, Dick purchases a pocket compass, which symbolizes his desperate need for a guiding principle. He considers taking refuge in Spain, dodging enforced repatriation, and crossing the border from Bordeaux, "then, once in a country free from nightmare, [he would] decide what to do" (538). Spain would be his utopia where he could pursue his career as a revolutionary poet. Combining his literary and radical idealism, he is excited by his self-appointed mission that "he must write some verse: what people needed was stirring poems to nerve them for revolt against their cannibal governments" (538). Eugenio Suárez-Galbán defines Spain as "the last good land" (367) and María de Guzmán as "a last frontier" (xxix) for American literary expatriates. Dick assumes that Spain would provide him with an ideal environment as well as the resources for his artistic and ideological passions. He thus imagines himself "living in a sunscorched Spanish town, sending out flaming poems and manifestoes calling young men to revolt against their butchers, poems that would be published by secret presses all over the world" (538). He would justly accuse governments of cruel oppression and quicken people to rise up against such abuse; his messages were intended to be no mere propaganda, but poetry that conveys beauty and truth. Accordingly, he thinks of verses from "A Song in Time of Order, 1850" by Algernon Charles Swinburne, which eulogizes the rebels of the Italian Revolution of 1848: "*While three men hold together / The kingdoms are less by three*" (538). Their resilient opposition to the repressive states would be his paradigm, and he would be a Swinburne of the modern world of suffering, a revolutionary poet in Spain.

The daydream, however, is short-lived. Encountering his college friend Ned Wigglesworth on his way to Bordeaux, Dick abandons the Spanish plot. His friend is no one to hold up to a serious cause, and he cannot fully detach himself from the imperialist war. He drinks away his journey home with Ned and throws the compass overboard. As soon as he arrives home, he becomes a second lieutenant, through the intervention of Mr. Cooper and family connections; he confirms his acquiescence to the imperialist US by enlistment. Back to Europe as an army officer, he becomes a complicit supporter of the imperialist war, exorcising his independent thinking and revolutionary passion.

Dick's infatuation with Spain, though it evaporates with ease, deserves close examination. To his eyes, the country is situated as a foil, or an antidote, to what he sees in imperialist war-torn Europe. Dick thus romanticizes Spain in a quixotic manner, which falls short of reality. The essence of idealized Spain in Dick's mind is crystalized in the phrase a "country free from nightmare." It reminds us of the words of Stephen Dedalus in James Joyce's *Ulysses*: "History . . . is a nightmare from which I'm trying to awake" (Joyce 28). Dedalus, an apprentice writer, is set to refute a view that "[a]ll human history moves towards one great goal, the manifestation of God" (Joyce 28). Given the intricate, violent history of Ireland, Dedalus cannot believe that humankind is evolving toward glorious triumph. Likewise, what Dick has witnessed in World War I is not in accordance with progressive views of history. Even his last service with the Red Cross in Paris engraves the wretchedness of human fate on his mind. When finished carrying buckets of amputated limbs about the hospital, he cannot help thinking of "the faces and the eyes and the sweatdrenched hair and the clenched fingers clotted with blood and dirt and the fellows kidding and pleading for cigarettes and the bubbling groans of the lung cases" (538). What he observes is nothing but human ruin borne of modern warfare. World War I, originally called the Great War, was the first struggle of modern technology—air raids, machine guns, and mustard gas in trenches—that resulted in millions of casualties on either side. The war is shorthand for modernity. But Dick cannot make any sense out of it.

In contrast to these war-torn countries full of nightmares, for Dick, Spain appears to be the "last good frontier." Spain in actuality, however, was far from such assumptions of innocence. It had sustained its own horrors and torments in the course of history, and the arrival of modernity only complicated matters. Medieval Spain was both a locus of struggle and the eventual coexistence of Muslims, Christians, and Jews after invasions by Muslims through 1492 when the Reconquista was completed. The reign of Christian Spain, however, was less benign as the infamous Spanish Inquisition to repel heresy testified to with its brutal torture regime and executions by burning (Pierson 50–51). From the sixteenth to seventeenth centuries, the Spanish Empire enjoyed its Golden Age. But in the process of modernization, the country suffered a protracted decline, which met its final blow with the loss of Cuba and the

Philippines in the Spanish-American War. When World War I began in 1914, Spain was obliged to remain neutral for its accumulation of both domestic and international conflicts. While the war in Europe ignited controversies between Spanish supporters of the Allies and Central Powers, domestic divisions among ideologies, classes, and regions raged. More fundamentally, Spain was utterly unprepared to fight the war because of its scarcity of financial and military resources. It also had to attend to the ongoing, often violent unrest in Morocco, the last remnant of its imperial glory.[22] Even the brief prosperity it enjoyed by supplying the belligerent powers aggravated cleavages within the country. As Francisco Romero writes, some politicians tried to "keep Spain out of the war but it was beyond their power to prevent the war from entering Spain" (Romero 32). The Spain that Dick dreamed of as "free of nightmare" was, on the ground, virtually nonexistent.

Yet, Dick yearns for an Arcadian refuge from the tumult of modernization that endangers his individuality. As the war imposes national unity upon its people, Dick has to suffer offenses to his individual freedoms, particularly in the form of thought-control. His dismissal by the Red Cross on account of his insurgent ideas makes clear that he is not allowed to exercise freedom of speech. A man at the army intelligence service tells Dick that he has no right to speak his own mind: "'I think it's perfectly criminal to allow yourself the luxury of private opinions, perfectly criminal. It's war time and we've all got to do our duty'" (537). The slightest hint of defiance endangers his citizenship in the empire. Moreover, one of the American Red Cross officers informs Dick how insignificant an individual is in the machinery of the imperialist war:

> "The American people is out to get the kaiser. We are bending every nerve and every energy towards that end; anybody who gets in the way of the great machine the energy and devotion of a hundred million patriots is building towards the stainless purpose of saving civilization from the Huns will be mashed like a fly. I'm surprised that a collegebred man like you hasn't more sense. Don't monkey with the buzzsaw." (536–37)

Such discourse is perfectly in tune with the propaganda disseminated by the Committee on Public Information (CPI) to invoke "national unity and mobilization" for the war (Iriye 49). One historian went so far as to claim "[e]xaggeration, fear-mongering, distortion, half-truth . . . were the stuff of the CPI's 'mind mobilization'" (Paterson 666). Individual human existence is denigrated in the grand system called "war," where mindless masses are maneuvered and self-righteously driven to hate and kill their enemies. Dick is not only deprived of the freedom to speak his mind, but also reduced to a subhuman existence through the machinery of war—which is altogether indifferent to individual will or unique ideas.[23]

While Dick's narrative reveals the pressure upon individuality during the war, representation of Spain in Dos Passos's *Rosinante* upholds the distinctive sense of self among its people. By comparing Dick's narrative and *Rosinante,* we should be able to discern the nature of US imperialism as delineated in *1919* more clearly. The first-person narrator of *Rosinante*, presumably the writer himself, recognizes a strong sense of individuality in Spain. He summarizes that "'[l]ife is a dream'" to Spanish people, and that "[o]nly the individual, or that part of life which is in the firm grasp of the individual, is real" (*Travel Books* 25).[24] This notion is best expressed by the protagonists of the nation's great classic: "Don Quixote, the individualist who believed in the power of man's soul over all things, whose desire included the whole world in himself; Sancho, the individualist to whom all the world was food for his belly" (*TB* 25). Whether idealistic or sensual, the spirit of Spain is rooted in a tradition that espouses unfaltering independence of the human soul. A faith in individuality that has endured over centuries is what appears to distinguish Spain from the rest of Europe.

The narrator locates the source of individuality in Spanish pluralism, as he finds "many Spains" (*TB* 25). He observes that "Spain as a modern centralized nation is an illusion" (*TB* 25–26). Calling attention to the variety of languages spoken in the country, he enumerates Castillian, Gallego-Portuguese, Basque, Catalan, and Valencian to illustrate the inherent heterogeneity of its regional cultures and peoples (*TB* 26). He further demonstrates how various topographies have fostered singular communities where individual minds have been traditionally rooted:

> A bleak upland country mostly, with a climate giving all varieties of temperature, from moist African heat to dry Siberian cold, where people have lived until very recently, —and do still, —in villages hidden away among the bare ribs of the mountains, or in the indented coast plains, where every region is cut off from every other by high passes and defiles of the mountains, flaming hot in summer and freezing cold in winter, where the Iberian race has grown up centerless. The pueblo, the village community, is the only form of social cohesion that really has roots in the past. (*TB* 44)

Separated by mountains and diverse coastlines, each pueblo stands as an independent community in which inhabitants lead their lives with values rooted in the land. Such local stability forms a matrix for decentralization and autonomy. The narrator thus maintains that "[t]his intense individualism, born of a history whose fundamentals lie in isolated village communities—*pueblos* . . . is the basic fact of Spanish life" (*TB* 24–25). Unlike that of Dedalus or his opponent, history here seems to be based on the inevitable dynamics in small communities. Each region and each village bears distinct features that undermine any effort to bring them under coercive control, as the narrator defines the country "essentially centrifugal" (*TB* 26). Dos Passos observes the multiple Spains shaped by independent minds as a natural response to the topography of the land.

While Dick fails to recognize Spain's realities, the narrator of *Rosinante* is aware of the problems of modernization descending upon Spain. At times, the narrator seems to assume rural Spaniards' absolute immunity to modernization that was sweeping European countries. He observes that, elsewhere, "things changed, cities were founded, hard roads built, armies marched and fought and passed away; but in Almorox the foundations of life remained unchanged up to the present" (*TB* 24). However, he cannot help recognizing imminent change threatening Spain. A lecturer in Madrid censures Spain's so-called "progress" as the "Europeanization of Spain," and denounces it as "an aping of the stupid commercialism of modern Europe" (*TB* 30). He even claims with raw sarcasm: "Better no education for the masses than education that would turn healthy peasants into crafty putty-skinned merchants; better a Spain swooning in her age-old apathy than a Spain awakened to the brutal soulless trade-war of modern life" (*TB* 30–31). To this fellow, Spain's vanishing status in modern Europe is less undesirable than it is obsolete and impoverished. Unlike Dick, *Rosinante*'s narrator is aware of the dilemmas the country must confront and questions its longevity in the current European climate:

> The problem of our day is whether Spaniards evolving locally, anarchically, without centralization in anything but repression, will work out new ways of life for themselves, or whether they will be drawn into the festering tumult of a Europe where the system that is dying is only strong enough to kill in its death-throes all new growth in which there was hope for the future. (*TB* 30)

Whether Spain can find hope for the future or implicate itself in the slow death of a declining Europe, the narrator tries to see through it all by leaving his sympathies with Spain.

In *Rosinante* Dos Passos seeks a possible solution to the question of Spain's modernity, as he turns to the so-called "Generation of 1898," a group of young intellectuals who, upon the country's loss of its remaining colonies as a result of the Spanish-American War, "felt a pressing need to mount an all-out attack on the old governing establishment and all that it stood for" (Shaw 2).[25] Now that the old Spain was extinct, some young intellectuals embraced the opportunity to investigate the nature of the problem and the possible futures of their country. Dos Passos examines some members of this group. The novelist Pío Baroja, for example, challenges the system, in that "[h]is great mission is to put the acid test to existing institutions, and to strip the veils off them"[26] (*TB* 45), which seems to be in tune with Dos Passos's own literary aspirations. Dos Passos has high hopes those Spanish young intellectuals will lead the country and renew it by grappling with social and aesthetic questions. History, however, proves that their ambitions were not to be fulfilled. Although their attempts left firm impressions in modern Spanish literature, they could not revitalize Spain, which suffered the 1923 military coup by Miguel Primo de Rivera and his subsequent dictatorship through 1930, followed by the reign of the Second Republic, and the outbreak of the Civil War in 1936 (Pierson 117–33). Therefore, when Dos Passos was writing *1919* in the early 1930s, he could not afford the optimism imbued in *Rosinante* of a decade earlier and was clearly aware of Dick's limitations in idealizing Spain in *1919*.

Spain's atrophy and America's imperialistic advancement thus strike a sharp contrast. An ill-humored Spanish student suggests that it is to America that the "future belongs," while defining Spain as "'the most civilized country in Europe,'" whose very civilization is strangling people (*TB* 31). By way of contrast, the young Spaniard sees, on one end, the utmost civilization of Europe in Spain, while to the other extreme, the crudity of America. His measure is America's will and power to survive: "'[Y]ou are so vigorous and vulgar and uncultured. . . . From that crude animal brutality comes all the vigor of life. We have none of it'" (*TB* 31–32). The narrator can only confirm the fact that "America was the modern world," which he seems to find alarming (*TB* 19). As the world map shifted in the throes of early twentieth-century globalization, the US, after all, was the strongest force of modernity. While the narrator of *Rosinante* may have been suspect of the Orientalization of Spain,[27] Dos Passos in *1919* turns his critical eye to focus on the workings of the modern American empire.

DICK'S SURRENDER

The crude vitality of modernity lies at the center of US imperialism, and evidence of such force is well depicted in the account of Dick's surrender to the American empire. Launching his career as a second lieutenant in the army, Dick grows into the position. Setting sail again for France, he writes a letter to his friend mocking his advancement, though later carefully flushes it down the toilet to avoid trouble with authorities. Once in Paris, he becomes Captain Savage in the Post Dispatch Service and, capitalizing on his language skills, is promoted to be a courier at the Peace Conference. This position allows him to witness the political circus and to enjoy jaunts around Europe:

> The hub of this Paris was the hôtel de Crillon on the place de la Concorde, its artery the rue Royale where arriving dignitaries, President Wilson, Lloyd George and the King and Queen of the Belgians were constantly parading escorted by the garde republicaine in their plumed helmets; Dick began living in a delirium of trips to Brussels on the night express, lobster cardinal washed down with Beaune on the red plush streets at Larue's, champagne cocktails at the Ritz bar, talk full of the lowdown over a demie at the Café Weber; it was like the old days of the Baltimore convention, only he didn't give a damn any more; it all hit him cockeyed funny. (662)

Armed with the privilege of US sovereignty, Dick finds himself on the streets of Europe in chic hotels and elegant restaurants with men of high rank, exploiting these older civilizations deposed by the rising imperialist power. It reminds him of the time in 1912 when he had had passion for democratic politics to redeem the world, but had lost the sentiment thereafter and could no longer care less. He turns out to be a mouthpiece of the official government line rather than remaining loyal to his own position.

Dick's consciousness of his complicity with US imperialism, however, remains curiously ambivalent. He is acting as its agent, but at the same time is aware of the imperialistic exploitation therein—to echo the cynicism of Wilson's biographer. He is dismayed as one friendly Italian tries to entertain him with great enthusiasm but not without a touch of servility: "It was all asti spumante and Evviva gli americani and Italia irredenta and Meester Veelson who had saved civiltá and evviva la pace" (678). While declaring his support for America and Wilson for saving civilization and the peace, the man defines Italy as an "irredenta," a territory that has succumbed to US control. The Italian's unabashed acknowledgement of US imperialism unnerves Dick.

Dick also makes a point to degrade Wilson for disguising imperialism as philanthropic idealism. He speaks with Anne Elizabeth Trent, a Texan who works for Near East Relief, about a chance glimpse of the president in Rome and assails Wilson for his inhumane coldness, as one with "'a reptile's face, not warmblooded, or else the face on one of those old Roman politicians on a tomb'" (677). Furthermore, he denounces the hypocrisy of Wilson, who is yet admired as if he were a savior to war-torn Europe:

> "By God, Anne Elizabeth, it's terrible to think about it. . . . You don't know the way people feel, people praying for him in peasants' huts . . . oh, we don't know anything and we're grinding them all underfoot. . . . It's the sack of Corinth . . . they think he's going to give them peace, give them back the cosy beforethewar world. It makes you sick to hear all the speeches. . . . Oh, Christ, let's stay human as long as we can . . . not get reptile's eyes and stone faces and ink in our veins instead of blood. . . . I'm damned if I'll be a Roman." [ellipsis in original] (677–78)

While Anne Elizabeth is enthusiastic about Wilson, the callous-looking politician wholly disenchants Dick. He is disgusted with the illusions the president proffers to Europeans as he promises to restore their life and bring peace to the world. As he refers to "the sack of Corinth," which signifies the total destruction of the Greek city by the Roman Empire in BC 146, Dick is well aware of the overwhelming power and cruelty of US imperialism that would usurp Europe's autonomy for good.

Accurate as he is about the domineering drive of US imperialism in Europe, Dick is nevertheless unable to recognize himself as its instrument. He claims that he would rather be the conquered than the conqueror: "'[W]e're the Romans of the Twentieth Century'; he burst out laughing, 'and I always wanted to be a Greek'" (677). In spite of his abusive assessment of Wilson and US imperialism, however, we must not forget that Dick is serving the empire as a courier, carrying messages that serve to widen its power. Lacking perspective to identify the irony of his situation, Dick unwittingly reveals his private imperialist nature toward Anne Elizabeth, who as a frivolous and desperate Southern belle despairing her brother lost in a military plane crash, plunges into infatuation with him. After their conversation, Dick makes love to her, an act the pair does not actually enjoy and which subsequently causes her to bleed. Upon learning of her pregnancy, Dick abandons her, driving the heartbroken girl to suicide and his unborn child to obliteration. Although a mere agent of the powerful empire, Dick acts as if he is an exploitive conqueror and mercilessly ruins the conquered in his private sphere. Whereas he fails to recognize his own parallel actions, his alignment with this brand of national cruelty conspicuously proves the empire's penetrating force.

Dick's transformation from dissident to imperialist surfaces unmistakably in his relationships with old friends as well. He surprises his friends in the ambulance drivers' unit by his compliance with authorities. To a friend who speaks of revolution and dissatisfaction with the home country, Dick insinuates in French that such subversive attitudes might get him in trouble. When another friend becomes excited about the world revolution to come, he counters, "the Allies had things well in hand" and then claims, "'The war's over now and all these revolutions are just the war turned inside out . . . You can't stop war by shooting all your opponents. That's just more war'" [ellipsis in original] (690). His alliance with the government is so transparent that to his friend he sounds as if he is merely the deliverer of their message, if not an outright pawn. He further accuses another friend, an imprisoned conscientious objector, of foolishness. When he comments, "'Well, that comes of monkeying with the buzzsaw'" (684), Dick is repeating the very phrase of the Red Cross officer who denied individuality in the great system. He has shifted from one side to the other: the denied becoming the denier of independent thinking.

Dick's surrender to US imperialism is complete as soon as he becomes attached to JD Moorehouse, a powerful public relations expert who resembles George Creel, head of CPI in that era, and was dedicated to the advancement of US imperialism and trans-Atlantic capitalism. Having served the government during the war to mobilize the nation effectively, Moorehouse stands as a conspicuous figure at the Paris Peace Conference. His elite clients include American oil giants such as Standard Oil, which aimed to start business with Royal Dutch-Shell after the treaty was settled. Such an example clearly represents another form of promoting US imperialism in the expansion of its capitalist platform. Dick's involvement in the business of public affairs even stands as an outright betrayal of his former commitments.[28] If poetry is an expression of truth, beauty, and passion, the language of publicity pitches serves as a tool to influence people's minds and attract profit. Once a believer in the power of words to propel people toward idealism, Dick becomes a manipulator of words to sway public opinion in support of capitalists of the empire. His surrender to US imperialism attests to the defeat of the lost generation to the American empire.

Dos Passos ends Dick's narrative with a final gripping scene that characterizes the fate of these restless lost souls. Assembled at random at a party in a fancy Paris apartment, they are unable to initiate any substantive conversation with one another. They nervously flutter about, while apathy and loneliness retard their spirits. The scene continues on to the last newsreel that features the lines from the popular patriotic song: "*America I love you / You're like a sweetheart of mine*" (755). The irony in the juxtaposition of the numbness of the lost generation with such enthusiastic patriotism is poignant. The final line of the lyric, "*And there's a hundred million others like me*" (756) yields to the novel's penultimate section, "The Body of an American," which represents a synthesized biographical sketch of an unknown soldier of the lost generation. He is an anonymous Everyman whose life is sacrificed for the sake of scheming politicians and profit-seeking capitalists who run the great machinery of the empire.

While Dick Savage is lured away from the unspoiled terrain symbolized by Spain, thereby spelling the defeat of the lost generation to US imperialism, Dos Passos manages to keep his critical distance from the American empire and proceeds to explore the literary frontier on his own. Even though he would bid farewell to civil war–torn Spain, Dos Passos, as one of the Lost Generation writers, managed to keep a firm foothold on the unconquered terrain of his own imagination in his writing. By illustrating the European phase of US imperialism during and after World War I, *1919* chronicles the ethos of America and the proclivities of its youth in that era. In the early decades of the twenty-first century, Dos Passos's text remains a source to inform the precariousness of nations today.

NOTES

A portion of this article was originally presented at the 2nd Biennial John Dos Passos Society Conference in Madrid on June 3, 2016, and was supported by JSPS KAKENHI Grant Number JP17K02574.

1. For example, Matthew Josephson in 1932 writes of Dos Passos's refusal to "believe either in the benevolence of American capitalism or in the wonders of American prosperity," vis-à-vis his longing for "a socialist and proletarian state" (Pizer, *John Dos Passos's* U.S.A. 323); similarly, Malcom Cowley recognizes "a radical historian of the class struggle" (Pizer, *John Dos Passos's* U.S.A. 324). Early criticism often discusses narrative techniques and their effects, but more thematic analysis across the narrative modes followed in the mid-century.

2. In *Empire as a Way of Life*, William Appleman Williams traces the concept of American empire back to the colonial period, in that the US was "born and bred of the British empire" (23), and discusses how the US propagated its "way of life" up to the late twentieth century.
3. María de Guzmán analyzes the phenomenon of the Anglo-American Orientalization of Spain to solidify the imperial identity of the US around the time of the 1898 war.
4. *1919* is collected in *U.S.A.*, edited by Townsend Ludington.
5. Thomas Bender underscores that Wilson purported "[t]his liberal world would be very fit indeed, a veritable empire tailored to American ambitions and talents" (244). Emily Rosenberg also agrees with Levin, writing "[t]o Wilson, as to his predecessors, America's influence and global progress went hand in hand" (63).
6. Williams assesses Wilson as occupying "a central importance as one who practically and symbolically integrated all the elements of empire as a way of life" (127).
7. Akira Iriye emphasizes the cultural turn in Wilson's idea: "[I]in a way Wilsonianism was an agenda for putting culture at the center of international relations. . . . The emergence of the United States as an international player at the beginning of the twentieth century was significant not simply because the nation became the leading military and economic power, but also because it introduced cultural factors into world affairs" (72). Iriye subsequently points to the effectiveness of the Committee on Public Information instituted by Wilson "to inform America's wartime diplomacy" and operated abroad to dispatch "its own representatives to engage in public relations work" (49–50).
8. Rosenberg, in her inquiry into American economic and cultural expansion from 1890 to 1945, examines the comprehensive ways in which the US government initiated and supported the continuation and inauguration of both public and private agencies to spread US influence in the world during and after WWI (63–160). Accordingly, Frank Costigliola argues that "America's performance during the war, its financial strength, and its capture of popular imagination endowed American society with enormous prestige in Europe," which absorbed "American culture from doughboys, publicity campaigns, Herbert Hoover's relief teams, or private aid groups" (26).
9. Bender evaluates Wilson in a similar vein: "[H]e always carried a big stick, bigger in fact than Roosevelt's—and he used it more often" (236).
10. Discussion of Wilson's motivation and judgment here is an ongoing issue; see David Steigerwald and Brian McKercher, for example. In 2000, under the new condition of globalization after the end of the Cold War, Steigerwald noted the emergence of movement to reclaim Wilson's authenticity beyond the criticism campaigned by realists and revisionists (148–49).

11. Here we cannot help detecting echoes of "the Strenuous Life," the jingoistic speech delivered in 1899 by Theodore Roosevelt, then praised as the hero of the Spanish-American War and viewed as a prototypical advocate for US imperialism abroad. Roosevelt declared: "I wish to preach not the doctrine of ignoble ease, but the doctrine of the strenuous life, the life of toil and effort, of labor and strife," which Dos Passos quoted in the biographical sketch of Roosevelt in *1919* (481).
12. Thomas G. Paterson holds the Fourteen Points as a compendium of Wilsonianism: "The first five called for diplomacy in the 'public view,' freedom of the seas, lower tariffs, reductions in armaments, and the decolonization of empires. Points 6 to 13 appealed for self-determination for national groups in Europe. For Wilson, the last point was the most essential, the vehicle for achieving all the others: 'a general association of nations' or 'League of Nations'" (659).
13. Bender ranks Wilson as "the first American to be a world leader"; though "Washington and Lincoln had been greatly admired abroad," they are not comparable to Wilson's stature (241).
14. Dos Passos gives minute accounts of the enthusiastic welcomes Wilson received as he toured Europe in his biographical work, *Mr. Wilson's War* (446–57).
15. Hemingway served in the American Red Cross, Dashiell Hammett and Cowley in the American Ambulance Field Service, and e. e. cummings, along with Dos Passos, in the Norton-Harjes, to name a few. See Virginia Spencer Carr (129) and Charles A. Fenton (326).
16. For more details about Dos Passos's upbringing, see his biographies by Carr and Townsend Ludington as well as Dos Passos's memoir *The Best Times* and "Chronology" compiled in Dos Passos's *U.S.A,* edited by Townsend Ludington (1243–45).
17. Dos Passos's earliest writing on Spain, entitled "Young Spain," appeared in *Seven Arts* in August 1917 (473–88), which was incorporated in *Rosinante* with some revisions. The essay is reprinted in Pizer, *John Dos Passos* (39–47).
18. David Murad minutely chronicles Dos Passos's fascination with Spain through his diaries and letters from 1916 into the 1920s (141–86).
19. The essay was originally published in *Common Sense*, vol. 6, July 1937 (9–11), and reprinted in Pizer, *John Dos Passos* (183–86).
20. Ludington argues, "Spain was the most important factor among many in shaping Dos Passos's ideas and forming the way he saw the world" ("'I am so fascinated'" 313). He emphasizes that the importance of the writer's early immersion in the country was even more crucial than his contact with modern art and war experience.
21. Donald Pizer points out that "Dos Passos wished to depict in Savage what he believed to be the worst potential of his own background—that of a youth whose

Harvard aestheticism reflected both his superficial rebelliousness and his weak posturing and whose later experiences confirmed the uselessness of rebellion and the advantages of deception and conformity" (*John Dos Passos's* U.S.A. 248).

22. See Francisco Romero for Spanish conditions during World War I and an in-depth analysis of Spain's engagement in Moroccan affairs (33–52).
23. Dos Passos effectively renders a machine-like image of war in his second novel *Three Soldiers* (1921), which is collected in *Novels 1920–1925*.
24. *Rosinante* is included in the collection *Travel Books and Other Writings* (hereafter referred to as *TB*).
25. Gayle Rogers explains the significance of the incident for the nation concerning "the long-disputed question of . . . [t]he Two Spains—one reactionary and conservative, the other progressive and reformist" (17) and how the termination of the empire "intensified the centuries-old debates about *el Ser de España* or the very nature, or essence, of Spain and Spanishness" (16).
26. While then contemporary Spanish modernists tended to emphasize aesthetic renewal in their artistic attempts, the generation of 1898 aimed moreover to regenerate the national conscience (Shaw 6).
27. de Guzmán argues how "Anglo-American works (verbal and visual) have Orientalized, racialized, and primitivized Spain" (xxv).
28. John Lydenberg refers to Moorehouse and Dick Savage as "manufacturers of the all-pervasive lies busily at work, [where] we see the words being deliberately perverted" (106).

WORKS CITED

Bender, Thomas. *A Nation among Nations: America's Place in World History*. Hill and Wang, 2006.

Bogues, Anthony. *Empire of Liberty: Power, Desire, and Freedom*. Dartmouth College P, 2010.

Carr, Virginia Spencer. *Dos Passos: A Life*. 1984. Northwestern UP, 2004.

Costigliola, Frank C. *Awkward Dominion: American Political, Economic, and Cultural Relations with Europe, 1919–1933*. Cornell UP, 1988.

Cowley, Malcolm. *Exile's Return: A Literary Odyssey of the 1920s*. Viking, 1951.

de Guzmán, María. *Spain's Long Shadow: The Black Legend, Off-Whiteness, and Anglo-American Empire*. U of Minnesota P, 2005.

Dos Passos, John. *The Best Times: An Informal Memoir*. 1966. Signet, 1968.

———. *The Fourteenth Chronicle: Letters and Diaries of John Dos Passos*, edited by Townsend Ludington, Gambit, 1973.

———. *Mr. Wilson's War*. Skyhorse, 1962.

———. *Novels 1920–1925*, edited by Townsend Ludington, Library of America, 2003.

———. *Travel Books and Other Writings 1916–1941*, edited by Townsend Ludington, Library of America, 2003.

———. *U.S.A.*, edited by Townsend Ludington, Library of America, 1996.

Fenton, Charles A. "Ambulance Driver in France and Italy: 1914–1918." *American Quarterly*, vol. 3, no. 4, Winter 1951, pp. 326–43.

Hogan, Michael J., editor. *Paths to Power: The Historiography of American Foreign Relations to 1941*. Cambridge UP, 2000.

Iriye, Akira. *The Globalizing of America, 1913–1945*. The Cambridge History of American Foreign Relations, edited by Warren I. Cohen, vol. 3, Cambridge UP, 2015.

Josephson, Matthew. "A Sad 'Big Parade,'" edited by Donald Pizer, *John Dos Passos's* U.S.A, Dictionary of Literary Biography, vol. 274, Gale, 2003, pp. 321, 323.

Joyce, James. *Ulysses: The Corrected Text*, edited by Hans Walter Gabler and Bodley Head, Penguin, 1986.

Kazin, Alfred. *On Native Grounds: An Interpretation of Modern American Prose Literature*. 1942. Harvest, 1995.

Kennedy, David M. *Over Here: The First World War and American Society*. Oxford UP, 2004.

Levin, N. Gordon. *Woodrow Wilson and World Politics: America's Response to War and Revolution*. Oxford UP, 1972.

Ludington, Townsend. "'I am so fascinated by Spain': John Dos Passos, January 1917." *Nor Shall Diamond Die: American Studies in Honour of Javier Coy*, edited by Carme Manuel and Paul Scott Derrick, Universidad de València, 2003, pp. 313–19.

———. *John Dos Passos: A Twentieth-Century Odyssey*. Carroll & Graf, 1998.

Lydenberg John. "Dos Passos' *U.S.A.*: The Words of the Hollow Men." *Essays on Determinism in American Literature*, edited by Sydney J. Krause, Kent State UP, 1964, pp. 97–107.

McKercher, Brian. "Reaching for the Brass Ring." Hogan, pp. 176–208.

Murad, David. *American Images of Spain, 1905–1936: Stein, Dos Passos, Hemingway*. 2013. Kent State University, PhD Dissertation.

Paterson, Thomas G. "America at War, 1914–1920." *A People and a Nation: A History of The United States*, edited by Mary Beth Norton et al., 2nd ed., full-length ed., Houghton, 1986, pp. 648–77.

Pierson, Peter. *The History of Spain*. Greenwood, 1999.

Pizer, Donald, editor. *John Dos Passos: The Major Nonfictional Prose*. Wayne State UP, 1988.

———. *John Dos Passos's* U.S.A.: *A Documentary Volume*. Dictionary of Literary Biography, vol. 274, Gale, 2003.

Rogers, Gayle. *Modernism and the New Spain: Britain, Cosmopolitan Europe, and Literary History*. Oxford UP, 2012.

Romero, Francisco. "Spain and the First World War." *Spain and the Great Powers in the Twentieth Century*, edited by Sebastian Balfour and Preston Paul, Routledge, 1999, pp. 33–52.

Roosevelt, Theodore. *The Strenuous Life: Essays and Addresses*. Richards, 1903. *Hathi-Trust Digital Library*, https://catalog.hathitrust.org/Record/010939906. Accessed 27 Mar. 2018.

Rosenberg, Emily. *Spreading the American Dream: American Economic and Cultural Expansion 1890–1945*. Hill and Wang, 1982.

Shaw, Donald L. *The Generation of 1898 in Spain*. Benn / Barnes & Noble, 1975.

Steigerwald, David. "The Reclamation of Woodrow Wilson?" Hogan, pp. 148–75.

Suárez-Galbán, Eugenio. *The Last Good Land: Spain in American Literature*. Rodopi, 2011.

Tomlinson, John. *Cultural Imperialism: A Critical Introduction*. Continuum, 1991.

Tooze, Adam J. *The Deluge: The Great War, America and the Remaking of the Global Order, 1916–1931*. Penguin, 2014.

Whalan, Mark. *World War One, American Literature, and the Federal State*. Cambridge UP, 2018.

Williams, William Appleman. *Empire as a Way of Life: An Essay on the Causes and Character of America's Present Predicament along with a Few Thoughts about an Alternative*. 1980. Oxford UP, 2007.

3

GLENN SPOTSWOOD AS CANNON FODDER

Myth vs. Reality at the International Brigades

Rosa María Bautista-Cordero

> Naturally, the common people don't want war: neither in Russia, nor in England, nor for that matter in Germany. That is understood. But, after all, it is the leaders of the country who determine the policy and it is always a simple matter to drag the people along, whether it is a democracy, or a fascist dictatorship, or a parliament, or a communist dictatorship. Voice or no voice, the people can always be brought to the bidding of the leaders. That is easy. All you have to do is tell them they are being attacked, and denounce the peacemakers for lack of patriotism and exposing the country to danger. It works the same in any country.
>
> —Hermann Göring, Nuremberg 1945.

Initially published in 1939, and later included as the first part of the *District of Columbia* trilogy in 1952,[1] *Adventures of a Young Man* has frequently been regarded as one of John Dos Passos's weakest works. Its negative reception meant a turning point in the author's fame, with critics dismissing the novel both on political and literary grounds. Even though the novel is as anti-Stalinist as anti-fascist, it has been described as "Trotskyist agit-prop" and "inconceivably rotten" (Sillen), "the weakest novel he [Dos Passos] has written since *One Man's Initiation*" (Cowley), "distinctly antileft" (Woodcok), or "John Dos Passos's personal vendetta" (Yetter). Others were more positive, like James T. Farrell in his well-known 1939 review, or more recently critic Samuel Hux, for whom the novel is "as close as Dos Passos ever got to real classic tragedy, and deserves much better treatment than it has ever received" (par. 4). Written when Dos Passos was forty-three years of age, *Adventures of a Young Man* is often referred to as illustrative of his ideological journey from radicalism to conservatism. However, this view might be overly simplistic, since Dos Passos, in his self-proclaimed role as a chronicler, seemed to maintain a position of informed political skepticism throughout his life.

Regarding the objections on literary grounds, the dominant underlying message from the critics was that Dos Passos had lost the narrative strength he displays in his previous fictional work, the *U.S.A.* trilogy (cf. "John Dos Passos in the 1920s," Ludington 31). Since *Adventures* is a satire written with what Cowley denounces as "conventional technique" (qtd. in Maine 207), it hardly seems plausible that Dos Passos had all of a sudden ceased to be the genial writer who had conceived the ground-breaking *Manhattan Transfer* back in 1925. More likely, as other critics have suggested, his interests had changed. This time he was not interested in *formal* innovations. Perhaps what he wanted to *tell* was too grave to indulge in technical pirouettes, the world being on the verge of World War II. If the artistic avant-garde had been the inspiration for the narrative technique that characterized Dos Passos's earlier works, the architectural International Style of the 1930s that predominated from the Great Depression until after World War II, in which straight lines and planar surfaces are completely stripped of decoration and color, could serve as the visual metaphor to describe Dos Passos's technical choice for this novel.[2]

A product of the economic and social crises America was going through in the 1930s, Glenn Spotswood, the hero of *Adventures of a Young Man,* is unable to fulfill his ideals of social justice. In his search for a way to combat capitalism, he joins the Communist Party, only to be eventually expelled upon disagreement with the Party's treatment of striking miners in Harlan County, Kentucky.[3] In the final part of the novel, Glenn, lacking better prospects at home, enlists as a volunteer with the International Brigades to fight fascism in Spain during its civil war.

When, several years ago, I carried out my research on the effects of censorship in the Spanish translation of the final chapter, titled "Enemies of the Human Race," of *Adventures of a Young Man*, I focused on the novel's reception in Franco's Spain of the early 1960s. At the time, however, I did not concentrate on the details of the historical events that might have inspired Dos Passos during his visit to wartime Spain in the spring of 1937 and immediately after. Looking back, I realize that my views on the novel were permeated, to a great extent, by what seems to have been the general scholarly consensus: on the one hand, that Glenn Spotswood, the hero, is an idealist whose youthful radicalism echoes Dos Passos's, and on the other, that Spotswood's death at the end of the novel reflects the author's personal feelings of "disillusionment" upon the unlawful execution of José [Pepe] Robles Pazos, his translator-friend, likely by Soviet secret police.

The story of Robles's disappearance and likely death by execution at the hands of the Soviets has been dealt with at length by various authors, both in Spain and in America. Dos Passos and Robles first met when the former came to Spain in 1916, and, as *The Best Times* explains, the two became "fast friends" (32–33).[4] In 1920, Robles took up an instructorship, and later a professorship, of romance languages at Johns Hopkins University, where he was employed until he returned to Spain at the outbreak of the Spanish Civil War.[5] A sympathizer of the loyalist cause, he did not hesitate to enlist with the Republican army to carry out administrative tasks. Because of his knowledge of languages, he worked as a translator with the Russian delegation in Madrid and later in Valencia, where one day he was arrested by a group of men in plain clothes who took him away when he was at home after a day's work (cf. Martínez de Pisón 32). Although his execution was never confirmed officially, it has become accepted that he was killed by the Russians under the dubious charge of espionage.

In general agreement with other scholars' views, I had assumed that Dos Passos had written *Adventures of a Young Man* as a fictional recreation of his own repudiation of leftist ideology, and that the hero's manipulation by the communists during the Spanish Civil War at the end of the novel merged Dos Passos's "own perceptions of the Communists' covert action with what he had learned of Robles's fate at the hands of the party" (Nanney, *John Dos Passos Revisited* 214). Townsend Ludington, for example, argues that the purpose of the final scene in *Adventures of a Young Man* "was to portray the kind of treachery he [Dos Passos] believed had killed José Robles" (*Twentieth-Century Odyssey* 393). Similarly, Malcolm Cowley's 1939 *New Republic* review of the novel signals Robles's death as the reason for not only Dos Passos's political disillusionment, but also the novel's diminished quality.

For my earlier analysis of how Glenn Spotswood's Spanish *adventure* had been translated under Franco's censorship, I then focused on the first and only Spanish translation by Planeta, published in 1962.[6] In those days, censors were concerned about attacks against the Catholic Church, the morals (mostly regarding sex), and/or the "Regime" (that is, Franco and his cronies). Interested in the political element, in order to find evidence of censorship based on "attacks against the Regime" in the Spanish translation of *Adventures of a Young Man*, I looked for explicit political references. More specifically, I looked at how Franco, the Republicans, and the International Brigades are portrayed.[7] Overall, after my research into the censorship of *Adventures of a Young Man*, I concluded that the censored segments were qualitatively significant.[8] Specifically throughout the final chapter, "Enemies of the Human Race," references to Franco are avoided—as are references to Italian and German intervention to support his army; as a result, the ideological reasons for the hero to join the International Brigades are blurred, and "the Spanish Glenn Spotswood appears naïve, equivocal: he is an international brigader who is an anti-communist, but is fighting some fascists who have nothing to do with Franco" (Bautista 156).

Further research into Dos Passos's works as "contemporary chronicles" has led me to a reconsideration of my previous approach to *Adventures of a Young Man*. As the author himself declared in his famous 1969 interview with David Sanders, his interest had always been in writing "for the record," and he claimed that there was nothing "necessarily inartistic in being the historian" (in Pizer 241). In that same interview, when asked about the hostile American reception of *Adventures of a Young Man*, he said, "I think they were wrong . . . because I don't think my position was so much changed. Politically it was, but from a human point of view I don't think it was so different" (246). In his various letters and essays just after his return from Spain, Dos Passos had always been consistent in affirming his duty to report what he had witnessed and offer a concrete and conflicted "human point of view." The hero's fate was probably personally biased, as critics had suggested, since the shadow of Soviet intervention looming over Robles's death surely influenced Dos Passos's choice of subject matter. Yet, were there also grounds to argue that Dos Passos was *chronicling* the participation of the International Brigades in the Spanish Civil War? In this new light, I analyzed Glenn Spotswood not as a direct reflection of Dos Passos's ideological diatribe against his former leftist impulses, but as a historic type, rife with contradictions and ambiguities.

In this current analysis, I therefore set out to explore the extent to which Glenn Spotswood's Spanish "adventures" may be read today as fictionalized historical reportage, and not as either "Trotskyst [sic] propaganda"[9] or as the author's personal disillusionment with the Left. Against the historical background of the Spanish Civil War, and more particularly in the historical context of the International Brigades and the testimonies of real-life Brigade veterans, Spotswood emerges as representative of those whose abstract ideals collapsed in the face of the concreteness of a war in which, as Dos Passos chronicled, fascism was the main enemy, but not the only one. The first challenge the brigaders had to face was poor military training and inadequate weapons and munitions; the initial reluctance of the Spanish administration had kept the international volunteers in separate brigades, independent from the Republican army structure and reporting to the Comintern. Only a minority of their officers-in-command had a professional military background. Extremely high casualties were the norm in their ranks; chances of success in combat were slim. Furthermore, linguistic and cultural barriers made it difficult for International Brigaders to communicate effectively and also prevented them from feeling the shared abstract identity common to most armies. Finally, as Glenn's experiences also show, foreign volunteers in the International Brigades did not escape Stalin's thirst for control of those fighting on the loyalist side not willing to abide by Communist Party discipline.

THE PRELUDE TO THE SPANISH CIVIL WAR

Young Dos Passos was irresistibly attracted to Spain since the first of his various visits there during the years 1916–1937. He dove into Madrid's cultural life, travelled extensively, and learned about Spanish history, art, and literature. Spain inspired not only his poetry, travel essays, and historical reflections, but also his art, in the form of beautiful watercolors (cf. Pizer et al., *The Paintings and Drawings*). He also made life-time friends, Robles chief among them.

From an aesthetic perspective, those were fascinating times in Spain. The period 1917–1939, known as the *Edad de Plata*, bustled with cultural life. It was peopled by extraordinary writers, artists, and philosophers, such as García Lorca, Pío Baroja, Antonio Machado, Pablo Picasso, Salvador Dalí, Antonio Miró, Miguel de Unamuno, José Ortega y Gasset, Manuel de Falla, and Luis Buñuel, to name a few. Dos Passos had the opportunity to meet some of them. However, this explosion in the arts and in scholarly life was taking place in agitated times. "The twentieth century had admittedly seen an astonishing reawakening of the Spanish spirit: the political volatility of the years between 1898 and 1936, and most intensely between 1931 and 1936, was the expression of a vitality which extended through most spheres of national life" (Thomas 180). In the spring of 1936, as García Lorca was completing his masterpiece *La Casa de Bernarda Alba*, Spain had reached "the culmination of a hundred and fifty years of passionate quarrels" (Thomas 181).

Indeed, since the end of the War of Independence against Napoleon's army and the proclamation of the first Spanish Constitution in 1812, Spain had been immersed in a series of political fights, civil strife, revolutions, military uprisings, and assassinations by various radical groups. The short periods of relative stability and economic growth found throughout this long span of time did not translate into real development for the deprived classes, however. Spanish monarchs and political leaders of the nineteenth and early twentieth centuries failed to provide their people with truly robust and reliably democratic institutions. The situation became particularly critical during the worldwide economic and political crises of the 1930s, including the proliferation of radical movements of fascists, Marxists, and anarchists across Europe. A number of factors in Spain contributed to deep social and political instability, all quite complex and difficult to analyze in just a few lines. To provide a general overview, I will focus on the historical events that historians have identified as crucial for a better understanding of the events that led the country to civil war.

One of the most serious social tensions had a religious root. Those eager to modernize Spain saw the Catholic Church, which had accumulated much power and wealth through the centuries, as a major enemy of their ideal modern state. Some extremists, in turn, translated that anti-clerical sentiment into violence against priests, nuns, and later even ordinary church-goers.[10] The burning of churches and convents, which began as early as 1931, fractured the initial widespread enthusiasm among Spaniards in support of the Second Republic. But religion was just one of the problems. Other major issues worried voters: Catalan and Basque nationalisms, agrarian reforms, the rising unemployment rate, and the increasing street violence that fed on the revolutionary narratives of both right and left extremist political leaders. Some of these tensions, such as the dramatic episode of Casas Viejas,[11] were recorded by Dos Passos in his nonfictional work "The Republic of Honest Men," written during his stay in Madrid in the summer of 1933.

The inability of the socialist administration, led by President Manuel Azaña (one of the "honest men" in Dos Passos's account), to handle the social tensions prompted Azaña's resignation in September of 1933. He was succeeded by Alejandro Lerroux, leader of the Radical Republican Party (a centrist party despite its name), both provisionally upon Azaña's resignation, and later as the democratically elected president after the November elections. The Republican government was then led by the Spanish Confederation of Autonomous Rights (CEDA), a coalition of mostly Republican centrist and right-wing parties, who defined themselves as Catholic-democrats. The newly established vote for women, championed by Clara Campoamor, was initially opposed by the socialists, who argued it might contribute to the rise of the Catholic parties.[12] Cases of corruption, once brought to the public's attention, badly weakened the government. The months that followed did not see an improvement in the social scene, culminating in the labor disturbances and riots known as the 1934 October Revolution. For Paul Preston, "because the 1933 elections had given the power to the CEDA, the left decided to take through violence what they couldn't get through votes" (*We Saw Spain Die* 131).

The October Revolution resulted in the polarization of the political scene. "The tensions ended up with the hopes of those few republicans who were struggling to uphold the Rule of Law" (Jackson 157). Prominent socialist and Marxist politicians were arrested as leaders of the revolt, among them former President Azaña and Francisco Largo Caballero. From then on, "a revolutionary mentality of the right and of the left clearly dominated all parties" (Vicens-Vives 179). For Hugh Thomas, "after the revolution of October 1934 and the manner in which it had been quelled, it would have required a superhuman effort to avoid the culminating disaster of civil war" (137).

With the threat of war in Europe and fascism growing, the Soviet Union "had a good reputation in Spain and elsewhere among left and progressive people. The great Russian experiment did not seem to have betrayed its ideals" (Thomas 117). Street protesters and workers' leaders would cheer '*Viva Rusia!*' across Spanish cities and towns. In the broader European context, the myths of empire and national regeneration on the one hand, and anti-fascism on the other, were unstoppable. The February 1936 elections in Spain gave a narrow victory to the Popular Front left coalition over the right coalition of the National Front. Along with the rising unemployment rate and the virulent, radicalized political discourse on both sides of the political spectrum, the election resulted in extremely serious disturbances that "might be interpreted as having many characteristics of a raid by unemployed *pistoleros*, of both sides of the political spectrum, on the lives and possessions of the salaried" (Thomas 180). Spain was virtually a failed state.

Under this set of circumstances, a group of angry ultra-conservative militaries led by General Emilio Mola began planning a coup d'état in the spring of 1936. Their aim was to appoint General Sanjurjo—in exile in Portugal after his failed coup in 1932—as head of a military dictatorship. In the group was also the initially reluctant General Francisco Franco, who at the orders of Mola would eventually lead the first war movement from Morocco, where Spain still kept some territories. Their insurrection ignited the Spanish Civil War in July 1936.

DOS PASSOS IN CIVIL WAR SPAIN

John Dos Passos's famous picture on the front cover of *Time* magazine dates from August 1936. He was considered then to be one of the most influential American writers, after the success of the third novel of the *U.S.A* trilogy, *The Big Money,* that had been published earlier that year. Despite this moment of fame, the outbreak of the Spanish Civil War deeply concerned him. He joined the American Committee to Aid Spanish Democracy, a gesture that would be identified with activism in defense of human rights by today's standards. Furthermore, in an effort to raise awareness about the urgent need to aid the legitimate Republican government, Dos Passos, Hemingway, Lillian Hellman, and Archibald MacLeish, among others, set up the Contemporary Historians. The idea behind the organization was to produce a documentary film about the Spanish Civil War. For the project, they hired Dutch filmmaker Joris Ivens, a committed communist (Carr 362). Hemingway and Dos Passos would finally meet in Madrid in the spring of 1937 for the filming.[13] Dos Passos was convinced that "unless the American government intervened, the country was, in effect, handing Spain over to fascism as well as to Communism" (Carr 357–58).

When Dos Passos arrived in Spain, he was utterly concerned about the news of the disappearance of his best Spanish friend, Pepe Robles. The whole matter of Robles's death, once it became known, deeply affected Dos Passos. He was distressed to the point of totally altering his plans in Spain for the time being, and he ultimately reacted against the leftist political "cause" that had once moved him. That event dramatically changed Dos Passos's views not only of the Spanish Civil War, but also, consequently, of the way in which American critics and old party friends saw him from that moment on.

When in 1939 Dos Passos described Robles's story as "only one story among the thousands in the vast butchery that was the Spanish civil war," he was right. Indeed, from a twenty-first-century perspective, we now know more about the collective history of the "vast butchery" that was the war, and historians have documented the illegal arrests and summary executions, the violence, and the revenge that made the abstract unreconcilable with the concrete. Political ideology, in other words, led ordinary people to fight in a war that took thousands of innocent lives and at times for reasons that had little or nothing to do with ideals. In a speech at Madrid's Ateneo in 2007, on the celebration of the seventieth anniversary of the Antifascist Writer's Congress held in Valencia in 1937, Spanish writer Andrés Trapiello described the atmosphere of fear among Spanish intellectuals that spring, when Soviet control was at its fiercest. His speech was based on one single photograph taken in Valencia, in which a group of young Republican artists of García Lorca's circle appear in their bathing suits, as if the war had stopped for a moment. They had gathered in Valencia to produce a stage show in memoriam of the recently killed young writer:

> At the time this photograph was taken,[14] one of the young men in it [stage designer Vitín Cortezo] had already been arrested by the

> dreadful Service of Military Security, under the charge of espionage, and although he was released after a horrid night, some of his friends lived those hours in alarm. They all know that one night is much more than the few minutes that it takes to make anyone disappear forever, or appear the next morning lying dead by the cemetery walls. . . . Many have been killed that way in Madrid and in other parts of Spain in less time. The city of Valencia, far from the operations theatre of the war, was no less dangerous or even more so than the battlefront, because the bullet that might put an end to anybody's life could come from your back.[15](2)

The atmosphere in Valencia described by Trapiello is consistent with Dos Passos's impressions on the "blind intolerance" that the communists had brought to Spain (quoted in Ludington, *Twentieth-Century Odyssey* 383). Dos Passos left the country "soured by foolish bravado, secrecy, treachery, and, as he saw it, a vast waste of courage on the side of the Loyalists who were being undercut by the communists" (Ludington *Twentieth-Century Odyssey* 372). His name never appeared on the credits of the documentary *The Spanish Earth*, whose production had brought him to Spain, although he did spend a few days in Fuentidueña de Tajo to learn from the locals about the irrigation project that is featured prominently in the film.

Spain 1—the John Dos Passos Papers—Call Number MSS 5950-Co. Permission by Lucy DP Coggin, Dos Passos Literary Estate.

His essays on the Spanish Civil War were collected in "Introduction to Civil War," which comprises a section of *Journeys Between Wars* (1938). In them, Dos Passos portrays the impact of the war on the ordinary people in Madrid, Fuentidueña, Valencia, and also in Barcelona, where he met George Orwell briefly and whose views of the conflict were so close to his own. These writings have stood the test of time remarkably well. Shortly afterwards, in 1939, Dos Passos published *Adventures of a Young Man*. The public manifestation of his political disillusionment, which had a negative impact on his literary career in the United States, has not influenced the Spanish reception of his works.

GLENN SPOTSWOOD AND THE INTERNATIONAL BRIGADES

As Australian scholar M. W. Jackson notes, "The Spanish Civil War is one of the mythic events of the twentieth century. One main part of that myth is the International Brigades" (105). In an unprecedented movement in history, thousands of volunteers from many different parts of the world—fifty-two countries in all—came to Spain to fight against fascism. Recruitment of volunteers took place at a time when it could not have drawn more sympathizers. "Powerful symbols were invoked," Jackson adds (111). Numerous books with testimonies of the veterans, fictional accounts by popular writers, and more serious historical approaches by academics have been published on the matter. Although their fight took place in Spain and for Republican Spain, not many Spanish scholars other than Jesús González de Miguel have dealt with their history in depth. Who were these young volunteers, and what made them fight? According to Hugh Thomas, "many Italian, German and other exiles from fascist or right-wing authoritarian régimes . . . longed for the outbreak of a real war against fascism" (440). Estimates are that there were about thirty-five thousand volunteers in the Brigades in total. No more than eighteen thousand of them were in service at any one time (Thomas in M. W. Jackson 106). The British, Canadian, and Americans amounted to 15 percent of the Brigades. Of them, approximately three thousand were American volunteers, of whom only 250 were Communist Party members. (Thomas in M. W. Jackson 108). George Orwell proclaimed in 1937, "The International Brigade is in some sense fighting for all of us—a thin line of suffering and often ill-armed human beings standing between barbarism and at least comparative "decency" (in Preston "George Orwell's SCW" par.12).

In *Adventures of a Young Man*, Glenn Spotswood is not a party member when he enlists as a volunteer with the International Brigades. When his prospects at home in America seem to have exhausted themselves, jobless and broke, he takes the bus to an address for someone listed as Lopez. The man who answers the door with a foreign accent asks if he is "volunteer or mercenary" before letting him in. Indeed, as in every war, mercenaries came to Spain to fight on both sides. In his book *Le Mercenaire*, International Brigade veteran Nick Gillain admits that "war in sunny Spain seemed a better prospect than another dreary winter in Brussels" (quoted in M. W. Jackson 110). However, the majority of them were ordinary men. Though books abound on what led volunteers to fight, diaries and testimonies of veterans cite motivations that fit Spotswood's reason. For many, it was about ideals, "no matter what prompted them to seek one"; for others "restlessness and loneliness" were the common denominators (M. W. Jackson 110). For M. W. Jackson, though, "it is safe to assume that all of them were anti-fascist, it is not safe to assume that anti-fascism meant the same thing to all of them. . . . One British volunteer candidly admitted that he used the slogans of anti-fascism to fend off awkward questions about his motivations in volunteering" (107–08). Among the idealistic types, some were intellectuals, others were workers with nothing to lose. In the case of American volunteers, historians have identified that they were, like Spotswood, the economically displaced of the Great Depression, for "[t]he card file in NYC shows that nearly half of the 1800 men listed gave no occupation" (M.W. Jackson 109).

Greeted by Lopez with "Come in, comrade" and a salute, Spotswood replies he is not a party member, and then he is led to Dr. Wiseman, dressed in a Russian tunic. This scene recreates a common procedure that those wanting to enlist had to go through: "where the volunteer was not a communist, he was investigated by a NKVD representative and by a communist doctor" (Thomas 440). Significantly, Dr. Wiseman uses the expression "Haha, more cannon fodder" in a grim premonition of Glenn's fate, a premonition that proved true for half of the total number of volunteers in the International Brigades in Spain, with an estimated "3 percent of the Brigaders coming through totally unscathed" (Castells 383). Dr. Wiseman warns Glenn: "You know it's no picnic over there." Indeed, it was no picnic. According to historian Vincent Brome, "volunteers were invariably used as shock troops by the Republic, first into fire and last out of it" (quoted in M.W. Jackson 113).[16]

In the next scene, we find Spotswood getting off a train from Paris, in the company of three other men under cover. A boy is waiting at the station; he greets Glenn with the words "Abraham Leencoln" (311). They all get in a black car headed for the Spanish border. When Dos Passos travelled to Spain in 1937, the International Brigades, and more particularly the 15th English-speaking

Lincoln Brigade,[17] had recently suffered one of their worst defeats, at the battle of the Jarama River, which occurred on February 12–14. In the bleak essay "The Fiesta at the 15th Brigade," collected in *Journeys Between Wars*, Dos Passos provides a very personal account of the banquet offered as a homage to those fighting with the Lincoln Brigade in which Hemingway broke the news to him that Robles had been killed. The banquet was held at the Castle of the Duke of Tovar, the improvised International Brigades headquarters on the Sierra de Guadarrama. It marked the creation of a new brigade formed by the few remaining English-speaking members of the old 15th, with the addition of other foreign men and officers (cf. Ludington, *A Twentieth-Century Odyssey* 370). It is estimated that approximately 2,500 members of the International Brigades lost their lives in that single February battle of the Jarama River, one of the fiercest of the war. On the so-called Suicide Hill, a name given by the combatants after the bloody fight that took place there on February 12, 1937, of the roughly four hundred members of the Lincoln Brigade, an estimated three hundred were killed in seven hours (cf. González de Miguel 176–90). Its location was barely eighteen miles from Fuentidueña de Tajo, the filming site where Dos Passos spent some of his time in Spain in April 1937. For Lisa Nanney "the International Communist Party . . . gave the troops a conspicuously patriotically American name that deflected attention from the party's role in the organization" (*Dos Passos and Cinema* 162). As Payne notes, "there was a minority of naive non-Communist idealists who probably did not understand all this at first. Even some of the Communist majority may not at first fully grasped the situation." (4)

In August 1936, both the presence of leftist "uncontrollables," made up of anarchist groups that did not follow communist discipline, and the failure of the Republicans to stop the occupation of Extremadura by Franco's army had triggered the plan to centralize the recruitment of volunteers through the French Communist Party. President José Giral's administration resigned on September 4, 1936, and socialist Francisco Largo-Caballero took over, reorganizing the chief staff and creating the Republican Army. By then, a number of Russian officials had arrived too. On October 15, 1936, the first shipment of Russian tanks arrived in Valencia aboard the *Komsomol.*

Just as mineral ore and other goods were paid in exchange for German, Italian, and Portuguese aid to Franco's army (apart from financial support by bankers such as Juan March), Russian deliveries of men and materials were not a friendly contribution to the revolutionary cause. Spain had at the time the world's fourth largest gold reserve, which was shipped to Russia on October 25. Three days earlier, on October 22, the Spanish prime minister Largo-

Caballero had reluctantly passed a law whereby the International Brigades were made official, he but kept them separate from the Spanish Brigades. He felt it was "a price he had to pay" in exchange for the Russian weapons, but he was not happy about it (cf. Alpert 229). For Thomas, none of the Spanish political leaders "were enthusiastic about the idea, but thought that at least the publicity would be good." Illustrating this point, Thomas quoted Italian exile Emilio Lussu: "We had a greater need of going to Spain than the Spanish Republic had need of us." The central recruiting office of the Brigades was in the Rue Lafayette in Paris (440–42).

Like Spotswood, Brigaders crossed the French border into Spain with the help of the Communist Party. The Italian Communist youth leader "Gallo"—who had been around in Spain since before the outbreak of the war—started the International Brigades' training camp in Albacete (cf. Alpert 229). In the case of the hero of *Adventures of a Young Man*, the government delegate who welcomes him and other Brigade members across the Spanish border says he has come "to greet the brave American fighters for democracy in the name of the Spanish Republic and the workers of hand and brain of the Spanish masses who were fighting for their lives against a double fascist invasion and the perfidy of the other socalled democratic states of Europe" (321). Significantly, in the Spanish version, the "double fascist invasion" used by the government delegate in the English original becomes "*invasores fascistas*," avoiding reference to Italian and German intervention on behalf of Franco. Likewise, no reference is made in the Spanish version to the "masses," a word perhaps with too strong a communist connotation for the censors' taste. Dos Passos's characteristic lack of enthusiasm toward government officials is made clear in his description of the Spanish delegate: a "bland little man with somewhat slippery English" that tires the American volunteers with his "rounded and oddly accented remarks" (321). This depiction contrasts with the author's sympathetic references to Spanish villagers: young peasant boys being trained as militiamen (324), country people driving mules and donkeys, and the "great jungling twowheeled carts" (329); women and children fleeing as the front draws closer (330).

The following morning, Glenn has a key encounter with an old friend from Horton, Frankie Perez. That single encounter is the origin of the suspicions that lead to Glenn's eventual imprisonment by his own mates, as Frankie is a trade union leader and probably a Trotskyist, though Glenn does not know this. They talk like old friends, and Frankie learns that Glenn has joined the *Brigadas.* Immediately Frankie asks, "Communist party?" Glenn shakes his head, and so Frankie confides to him: "Here several kinds of war. We fight

Franco but also we fight Moscow . . . if you go to the Brigada you mustn't let them fight us" (305). In the Spanish translation, Franco's name is replaced with "*los nacionales*"—meaning "the nationals"—hence, the dictator is not identified as the enemy. Furthermore, the segment "you mustn't let them fight us" becomes, in Spanish, "*no les dejes que luchen con nosotros*" (don't let them fight *with* us). What this dialogue between Frankie and Glenn is recreating—the internal fights among the Loyalists upon disagreement on Communist Party discipline—has been recorded by historians as a nightmarish issue looming over the International Brigades. For M. W. Jackson as well as the terror and privations that are common to every soldier at the battlefront, "they had their own private hell" originated by political animosities in the Republican camp. They often would be ordered "to undertake attacks 'at all costs.'" And he adds:

> Emotional blackmail was standard operating procedure . . . there were rumours of nocturnal purgations of Trotsky demons carried out by the NKVD. The nominee of the French Communist Party who ran the base camp in Albacete, Andrè Marty, used to brag about having ordered 500 executions. Though some attribute these killings to Marty's madness, others like Ludwig Renn acknowledge the role of the NKVD. (113)

After his encounter with Frankie Perez, Spotswood is taken to training camp on a truck with other American recruits. There, he feels "strange and lost, wishing he'd stayed at home where he understood the language, where he had some way of doping out what things were about" (324). His feelings are like those described by other nonfictional veterans, such as Winston Churchill's nephew Esmond Romilly: "However strongly I sympathized with the Spanish people . . . I should have gone no further than sympathy" (in M. W. Jackson 110). At the camp, Glenn meets the newly installed battalion commander Jed Farrington, another old friend from America who is a party member. Incidentally, Glenn drops the name of Frankie Perez, and the initially friendly face of his counterpart fades. Farrington refers to Perez as an "uncontrollable" and warns Glenn not to "monkey around them." Totally focused on the tactics of the war, Farrington says: "The minute the fascists are cleaned out we'll have to clean out those boys" (326). Farrington's statement is historically consistent with political commissioner André Marty's remarks in his report to the Comintern of October 1936, in which he states that a short-term agreement with the anarchists was necessary (their militias being heavily armed), but action against them would be needed later (cf. Preston *El holocausto español* 342). Farrington's motivation to combat in Spain is anti-fascist, like Glenn's. "We can't turn this place over to the wops and the squareheads," Farrington says. But for Glenn, it is a war that must be won by the Spanish workers, and not by the party, which operates from abstract notions of purity. Furthermore, Glenn speaks his mind and says he is in Spain to try to help, but not to "tell other guys to get their heads blocked off." Farrington then tests Glenn's "loyalty to the cause" and asks what he would tell if he got back home: "You wouldn´t try to make out these damn uncontrollables were martyrs of the working class?" (327). Glenn's honest hesitation expressed through silence is enough evidence for Farrington to conclude he is a traitor and sentences him: "[T]hey shouldn't have let you come."

The next day, Glenn is given a transport order and sent up the line to Jack Stern, a man who runs a repair shop and a gas station. His relationship is initially good, but soon Glenn notices some whispering about him from guys coming through, until one day he hears Stern referring to him as a "Trotzkyist." The smells and the colors of the rural Spain Dos Passos describes in *Rosinante to the Road Again* (1923) or in letters to his friend Rumsey Marvin (cf. Ludington *The Fourteenth Chronicle*) may still be traced in Glenn's impressions: the smells of coffee, bread, olive oil, flowers; and the red, green, and yellow of the landscapes. Mules, dogs, chickens, and sheep play their part too. Blue skies, sunny expanses of yellow country, green pastures and olive trees are reminiscent of other Dos Passos writings on Spain. But this time, war has altered the villagers' lives, which Dos Passos had been so fond of in youth:

> There began to be traffic on the road from that direction, trucks full of civilians, buses jammed with women and children, and then countrypeople driving loaded mules and donkeys, little handcarts stacked with crates of chickens, and household furniture, droves of steers, flocks of sheep and goats, old people painfully dragging bundles, staggering under heavy sacks, lost children. The guns sounded nearer. (330)

As an offensive comes closer, day by day the guns from the front sound nearer. Life and work seem to go on as usual as traffic to and from the frontline grows. And then one day, two "German comrades" come to the shop where Glenn works and announce he is wanted for questioning at the special brigade. Glenn is not surprised: "He couldn't shake off a funny feeling that he was going through a play that he had rehearsed many times" (331). Here Dos Passos's portrayal of Glenn's detention is consistent with historical research on the covert action by Soviet secret police. In his book *El holocausto español*, Paul Preston refers to Stalin's paranoia in demanding that all dissident foreign communists in Spain must be eliminated, commissioning such a task to Aleksander Orlov, chief of the Soviet secret police, whose name has also been associated with Robles's disappearance (540).

In the final section of the novel, Glenn is locked in a cell set up in some partly destroyed barracks, where the next day three party members interview him. The group is formed by a German, an American, and a man by the name of Peter, "who didn't seem to understand any known language" (333), whom Glenn had met as he crossed the border into Spain. According to Paul Preston, Aleksander Orlov's main duty as chief of the NKVD in Spain was to keep dissident foreign communists under control. Suspected Trotskyists were imprisoned at the convent of Santa Úrsula, in Valencia, where they were usually interviewed by Russian, German, and eastern European Party members (Preston, *El holocausto español* 540). In the novel, these three men let Spotswood know about the grounds for his arrest: "We are informed that you represent the Trotzky counterrevolutionary organization in America and were one of the channels of communication engaged in actively preparing the Barcelona uprising" (333). Dos Passos is referring here to the revolution of May 3–7 in Barcelona, in which security forces of the Republican government on one side, and workers' and anarchist groups on the other, fought for control. It cost an estimated five hundred to a thousand lives. One month later, Anarchist leader of the Partido Obrero de Unificación Marxista (POUM), Andreu Nin disappeared, and it is assumed he was killed by the secret Soviet police. Like Robles's, his body was never found.

Spotswood is further accused by this foreign communist "court of inquiry" of keeping a diary as the basis for an attack on party leadership, but none of the charges has any grounds. Glenn has nothing to confess, and insists on his innocence, but he is nevertheless put "back on ice for a couple of weeks" so that he may remember something. Days go by; having been victimized by abstract notions of political purity, Glenn's life has now been reduced to its most concrete immediacy of "a routine of hunger and meals" (337). One day the sound of machine guns is so near that he is released. He is finally given the chance to take an active role in the fight: his first mission is to take water to the comrades in the trenches. He never made it. Again, there is a historical truth behind Dos Passos's depiction of Glenn's death. According to M. W. Jackson, the Internationals "would literally stand up to machine gun fire. Once." (112).

International Brigades Memorial on the Site of the Battle of the Jarama River—Reproduced with permission of Jorge Rosenvinge©.

For Spanish historian Jesús González de Miguel, the Internationals had come to fight for their ideals, but felt they were being used as cattle led to the slaughterhouse (705).

Looking at *Adventures of A Young Man* through the eyes of Franco's censors, Dos Passos's criticism of fascism in the novel became more visible—those subtle though major manipulations of every anti-fascist reference acting as a magnifying glass over the writer's political position: fervently anti-communist, but nonetheless anti-fascist. Dos Passos's political views on the Spanish conflict as depicted in this novel show his commitment to stand up for the rights and freedoms of the ordinary people, rather than to party politics; "[T]he Spanish workers have got to win it," Glenn says. The novel is critical of fascism *but* against Soviet intervention.

The fact that Dos Passos's manifestations of political disillusionment after his civil war experience provoked sour reactions from the critics in the United States but not in Spain may be an indication that his criticism of communist methods was better understood by the people who actually experienced it concretely in first person. Regarding Soviet intervention during the war, I have found no evidence of accusations against Dos Passos by any Spanish critic or scholar for having manipulated what he had observed in Spain, where he has ever remained the loyal friend of the Spanish Republic.[18]

No doubt Robles's inexplicable death was a blow for Dos Passos, and inevitably his disappearance during the Spanish Civil War must have been in his mind and heart when he wrote *Adventures of a Young Man.* However, when Glenn Spotswood's fictional experience in Spain is read in light of the history of the International Brigades, the novel may be reassessed and understood from a different perspective: as a *chronicle* of a complex and often contradictory political situation in which concrete lives could not be easily reconciled to abstract theories. As Lisa Nanney notes, "Idealistic Americans serving voluntarily in the Abraham Lincoln battalion, who were sent into battle with outdated Soviet weapons and inadequate supplies, came to the conclusion that the Soviets had exploited the idealism of those who fought and that 'Communist enforcers' were covertly policing them, as many later attested" (*Dos Passos and Cinema* 161–62).

Historical accounts show that Dos Passos may have been less personally biased when he wrote *Adventures of a Young Man* than critics have suggested. Perhaps Dos Passos was damned for unveiling a political truth that some were not yet ready to believe back in 1939: as Franco's army was ravaging Spain, the ideals that had led thousands of foreign volunteers to fight fascism had materialized as a reactionary force at a time when the Communist Party under Stalin was proving to be equally inflexible.

ACKNOWLEDGMENTS

I would like to express my heartfelt gratitude to my co-editor Aaron Shaheen for his constant support, generosity, and camaraderie along the way in the making of this volume. Furthermore, his encouragement, advice, and critical readings have been fundamental in shaping this essay. I have learnt so much. *Gracias, amigo.*

NOTES

1. It must be noted that the two English editions of *Adventures of a Young Man* (1939 and 1952) are not identical. The latter was published as part of the *District of Columbia* trilogy, and the difference lies in the insertion of brief, nonfictional pieces before each chapter and at the end of the novel in said 1952 edition. The content of those fragments is political, and they also provide a historical context to the events in the novel. Page number references in this article belong to the 1952 edition of *District of Columbia*, published by Houghton Mifflin.
2. The term "International Style" "was first used in 1932 by Henry-Russell Hitchcock

and Philip Johnson in their essay titled *The International Style: Architecture Since 1922*. Major FIG.s included Le Corbusier in France, and Richard Neutra and Philip Johnson in the United States." For further reference, see "International Style," *Encyclopedia Britannica.*

3. The Harlan County War was a series of coal mining-related skirmishes, executions, bombings, and strikes that took place in Harlan County, Kentucky, during the 1930s.
4. Dos Passos himself provides an account of the tragic event in his reply to Malcolm Cowley's critique of *Adventures of a Young Man* in June 1939 (Pizer 193–95). In *The Best Times,* Dos Passos describes Robles as "an ironic man who was always willing to laugh at anything"—an extraordinary talker whose spirits were closer to Baroja's characters than to his mates' at the Institución Libre de Enseñanza. Dos Passos and Robles had the chance to go on trips to the Sierra madrileña or to the bullfights (32–33).
5. Dos Passos and Robles kept in touch until the breakout of the Spanish Civil War. During their time in America, the two frequently wrote to each other, and Pepe and his wife Márgara, who translated *Rosinante to the Road Again* into Spanish in 1930, would visit Dos Passos in New York whenever they had the opportunity to do so, particularly on their way to, or back from, Spain, where they continued to spend their summer holidays.
6. The Spanish Civil War stalled the publishing industry, and it was not until 1962 that *Adventures of a Young Man* was published in Spain, censored, as part of the *District of Columbia* trilogy. It has never been republished in Spanish since the 1970s, so no uncensored translations are available in this country.
7. My findings were unexpected: whereas references to fascism and communism in the original were respected in the Spanish version, references to Franco, and to Italian and German support of Franco's army, were deleted in every case.
8. The translation of twelve politically sensitive fragments in the final chapter of the novel show signs of censorship. In five instances, the "critical" elements were eliminated, whereas in seven others, various reformulations took place.
9. See Yetter, Michael K. "John Dos Passos and the Individual." Northern Illinois University, 2016 (Unpublished PhD dissertation)
10. An estimated 6,770 clergymen and nuns were killed in raids on churches and convents during the war. Source: "Delenda est ecclesia. De la violencia anticlerical y la guerra civil de 1936." Paper delivered by José Luis Ledesma (Universidad de Zaragoza) during the José Ortega y Gasset Seminar held at Universidad Complutense de Madrid, June 2009.
11. The Casas Viejas incident takes its name from the Andalusian hamlet close to the village of Benalup, where the Republican security forces massacred anarchist

activists and their families, including nineteen men, two women, and one child, in the context of the so-called Anarchist Revolution of 1933. The highly controversial action by the security forces was taken after two civil guards had been wounded during a workers' demonstration. For Dos Passos's account of the matter, see "The Republic of Honest Men" in *Journeys Between Wars*.

12. Clara Campoamor was a member of Congress with the Partido Republicano Radical, which, despite its name, was ideologically a centrist party. They defended the Republic as a form of government, and a laic state. The Spanish socialists were initially opposed to granting women the right to vote, as they feared doing so might contribute to a rise of the Catholic parties. Campoamor's famous counterpart in the socialist benches of the Spanish Congress was Victoria Kemp. Before 1933, women in Spain could be elected members of parliament, but could not vote.
13. For a full account of Dos Passos's role in the filming of *The Spanish Earth*, see Nanney, *Dos Passos and Cinema*, chapter 7.
14. The photograph Trapiello describes, on which he based his speech, is a joyful, pretty picture of three women and three men, arm in arm, running in their bathing suits, and was taken during the days of the Valencia congress. The second year of the war was about to begin. They were all members of a drama group that was to perform their friend García Lorca's play *Mariana Pineda* as part of the program for the congress. Also by Trapiello, see *Las armas y las letras*.
15. My own translation of a Spanish original.
16. See Brome, *International Brigades* 266.
17. The International Brigades were numbered xi to xv (numbers i–x corresponded to the Spanish Brigades). They were grouped according to languages. Brigade xi spoke German; Brigade xii, Italian; Brigade xiii, a variety of Balkan languages; Brigade xiv, French; Brigade xv spoke English. According to testimonies, chaos was frequent due to linguistic and cultural barriers (Alpert 233).
18. For an in-depth analysis of the Spanish reception of John Dos Passos, see Bautista Cordero, "A Descriptive Analysis."

WORKS CITED

Alpert, Michael. "Una trompeta Lejana. Las Brigadas Internacionales en la guerra de España: Una reconsideración sesenta años después." *Espacio, Tiempo y Forma, Historia Contemporánea*, vol. 12, 1999, pp. 225–38.

Bautista Cordero, Rosa María. "*Adventures of a Young Man* vs. *Las aventuras de un joven*." *New Approaches to Translation, Conflict and Memory*, edited by Lucía Pintado Gutiérrez and Alicia Castillo Villanueva, Palgrave MacMillan, 2019, pp. 143–60.

———. *A Descriptive Analysis of the Spanish Translation of* Manhattan Transfer *and Their Role in the Spanish Construction of John Dos Passos.* 2016. PhD dissertation. *Biblos-e Archivo*, UAM_Biblioteca.

Brome, Vincent. *The International Brigades.* Morrow, 1966.

Castells, Andreu. *Las Brigadas Internacionales de la Guerra de España.* Ariel, 1974.

Dos Passos, John. *Adventures of a Young Man.* Harcourt, Brace, 1939.

———. *The Best Times, an Informal Memoir.* The New American Library, 1966.

———. *The Big Money.* Harcourt, Brace and Company, 1936.

———. *District of Columbia.* Houghton Mifflin, 1952.

———. *Journeys Between Wars.* Harcourt, Brace, 1938.

———. *One Man's Initiation.* George Allen & Unwin Ltd, 1920.

———. *Rocinante vuelve al camino.* Translated by Márgara Villegas. Cenit, 1930.

———. *Rosinante to the Road Again.* George H. Doran, 1922.

"International Style." *Encyclopedia Britannica.* Web. 3 Feb. 2019.

Jackson, Gabriel. *La república española y la guerra civil (1931–1939).* Barcelona: Crítica, 1976.

Jackson, M. W. "The Army of Strangers: The International Brigades in the Spanish Civil War." *Australian Journal of Politics & History*, vol. 32, no. 1, 1986, pp. 105–18.

Ledesma, José Luis. "Delenda est Ecclesia: De la violencia anticlerical y la Guerra Civil de 1936." Paper. Seminario de Historia, Instituto Universitario Ortega y Gasset. Madrid, June 25 2009. ucm.es/data/cont/docs/297-2013-07-29-4-09.pdf. Accessed March 20, 2020.

Ludington, Townsend. "John Dos Passos in the 1920s." *Ilha do Desterro*, no. 23, 1990, pp. 31–41.

———. *John Dos Passos, A Twentieth–Century Odyssey.* E.P. Dutton, 1980.

Ludington, Townsend, ed. *The Fourteenth Chronicle.* Gambit, 1973.

Maine, Barry, ed. *Dos Passos: The Critical Heritage.* Routledge, 1988.

Martínez de Pisón, Ignacio. *Enterrar a los muertos.* Barcelona: Seix Barral, 2005.

Nanney, Lisa. *John Dos Passos and Cinema.* Clemson UP, 2019.

———. *John Dos Passos Revisited.* Twayne Publishers, 1998.

Payne, Stanley. *The Spanish Civil War: A New Take.* Myles Kantor interview, 11 March 2004. Web, 3 Feb. 2021.

Pizer, Donald, ed. *John Dos Passos, The Major Nonfictional Prose.* Wayne State UP, 1988.

———. *Toward a Modernist Style: John Dos Passos.* Bloomsbury, 2013.

Pizer, Donald, Lisa Nanney, and Richard Layman. *The Paintings and Drawings of John Dos Passos.* Clemson UP, 2017.

Preston, Paul. "George Orwell's Spanish Civil War Memoir Is a Classic, But Is It Bad History?" *The Guardian*, 7 May 2017, www.theguardian.com/books/2017

/may/06/george-orwell-homage-to-catalonia-account-spanish-civil-war-wrong. Accessed 13 Oct. 2019.

———. *El holocausto español: Odio y exterminio en la Guerra Civil y después*. Debolsillo, 2013.

———. *We Saw Spain Die: Foreign Correspondents in the Spanish Civil War*. Constable, 2009.

Sillen, Samuel. "Misadventures of John Dos Passos." *New Masses,* vol. xxxii, 4 July 1939, pp. 21–2.

Thomas, Hugh. *The Spanish Civil War*. Penguin, 2003.

Trapiello, Andrés. *Las armas y las letras: Literatura y Guerra Civil (1936–1939)*. Barcelona: Destino, 2010.

———. "Una fotografía." *Lecture given at Madrid's Ateneo on the occasion of the 70th Anniversary of the 2nd Anti-Fascist Writers Conference held in Valencia in 1937*. 19 Sept. 2007, published in *Clarín, Revista de Nueva Literatura* , 10 June 2010, par. 8, revistaclarin.com/5/andres-trapiello-una-fotografia/#more-5. Accessed 20 Nov. 2019

Yetter, Michael K. "John Dos Passos and the Individual." Northern Illinois University, 2016 (Unpublished PhD dissertation). commons.lib.niu.edu/bitstream/handle/10843/21247/Yetter_niu_0162D_12722.pdf?sequence=1&isAllowed=y. Accessed 25/04/2020

PART 2

CHRONICLING AMERICAN COMMERICAL CULTURE: *MANHATTAN TRANSFER*

4

THE HAT IN *MANHATTAN TRANSFER*

A Jazz Age Tale of the Man in the Straw Hat and the Arrow Collar

William Brevda

> Crowds of men and women attired in the usual costumes,
> how curious you are to me!
> —Walt Whitman, "Crossing Brooklyn Ferry"

Hat historian Neil Steinberg writes that "[t]he mid-1920s were the high-water mark for hat fashion in this country, their zenith and thus, by definition, the beginning of the decline" (220). Coincidentally, the mid-1920s were also a high-water mark for literary modernism. Men's hat fashion played a key role in a number of modernist works published in these years, two of the most significant being James Joyce's *Ulysses* (1922) and John Dos Passos's *Manhattan Transfer* (1925). In both these works, the straw hat or "boater" figures prominently.

The straw boater is a stiff oval hat with a narrow brim and a flat-topped crown that has a band around it. The vogue of the boater as a fashionable and popular summer hat for men in Europe and America lasted from the 1880s through the 1920s. Every spring, men put away their felt hats and pulled out their boaters. Despite the nautical name, the boater became associated with the urban masses. A "sea of boaters" was an appropriate metaphor for city crowds in these decades. Like the bowler, the boater was also associated with the middle classes and modern times. In his study of the history and iconography of the bowler, Fred Miller Robinson maintains that "no other single item of fashion in this period has evolved a semantics complex enough to be regarded as a 'sign' of its times" (7). But the boater can also be read as a sign of "modern," "middle class," and "modernist" life, as can other items of clothing, such as the Arrow collar and the "Modern(ist) Mackintosh" (Marshik). With a tip of the hat to Robinson's *The Man in the Bowler Hat*, I propose that the man in the straw hat was also an iconic figure. The hat in *Manhattan Transfer* is another example of the modern in *modern*ism and the *transfer* of something iconic into something ironic that modernist writers liked to effect. In "The Modern(ist) Mackintosh," Celia Marshik writes that "[t]he case of the mackintosh suggests that modernist writers used clothing to advance subtle analyses of both specific psyches and group behavior—to communicate, often quietly, a profound disquiet about the way bodies were imprinted by forces beyond their control" (44). I would argue that the case of the boater makes a similar suggestion. Dos Passos once stated, "The basic tragedy my work tries to express remains monotonously the same: man's struggle for life against the strangling institutions he himself creates" (qtd. in Gurko 59). In *Manhattan Transfer*, one of these institutions is the Fashion system. Dos Passos uses the straw hat and Arrow collar to symbolize conformity, standardization, Americanization, and the power of the Fashion system to turn anything into its sign. He sets up a straw man of his own to confute the system's sham man (and woman) of fashion.

During the 1920s, men's fashions were as ritualized as the seasonal myths described in *The Golden Bough* and as regimented as the soldiers during the Great War, an irony not lost on Lost Generation writers. Anticipating Roland Barthes, these writers discerned that "fashion obeys the law of myth in its attempt to present its conventions as natural facts" (Culler 75). Straw hat season began in the spring on Straw Hat Day, May 15, and ended on Felt Hat Day, September 15, when a man had to stop wearing his boater or risk offending the

Louis Bonnotte, "From Summer to Autumn." Private Collection, The Stapleton Collection/ Bridgeman Images.

gods of fashion and gangs of marauding hat-smashing hooligans. Do I dare to wear a straw hat out of season?

In the opening montage of the 1921 avant-garde documentary film *Manhatta* by Paul Strand and Charles Sheeler, a ferry is shown approaching Manhattan, followed by shots of a crowd pouring off of it. The camera is positioned above their heads, or rather, their hats. The people are wearing derbies, fedoras, and other dark hats, so it must be fall or winter. Yet in the next crowd shot, everyone is wearing a straw hat, so it must be spring or summer. The juxtaposed images evoke the seasons of the city by the fashion of the hats. In "Crossing Brooklyn Ferry" (1856), Walt Whitman created the prototype for the "day-in-the-life-of-a-big-city" genre and the inspiration for *Manhatta* (a silent film that uses quotations from Whitman as intertitles).

In the first stanza of "Crossing Brooklyn Ferry," Whitman positions himself on the Fulton ferry crossing to Manhattan. "Crowds of men and women attired in the usual costumes, / how curious you are to me!" he exclaims (308; sec. 1). The costumes strike Whitman as "curious," even though he must be similarly attired, because of the poet's transcendental vision of future generations on this crossing ferry seeing and feeling as he does. Only the "usual costumes" will have changed. How "curious" fashion becomes when we look through it. In *Sartor Resartus* (1838), Thomas Carlyle uses metaphors of "The World in Clothes" (Book I, Chapter 5) and "The World out of Clothes" (Book I, Chapter 8) to stand for the material and spiritual worlds respectively. American transcendentalists agreed with Carlyle that "[t]he beginning of all Wisdom is to look fixedly on Clothes . . . till they become *transparent*" (52; Carlyle's emphasis).

Like *Manhatta*, Dos Passos's *Manhattan Transfer* begins with a ferry arriving in Manhattan and crowds streaming out of it:

> Three gulls wheel above the broken boxes, orangerinds, spoiled cabbage heads that heave between the splintered plank walls, the green waves spume under the round box as the ferry, skidding on the tide, crashes, gulps the broken water, slides, settles slowly into the slip. Handwinches whirl with jingle of chains. Gates fold upwards, feet step out across the crack, men and women press through the manuresmelling wooden tunnel of the ferryhouse, crushed and jostling like apples fed down a chute into a press. (3)

The wheeling gulls connect the novel to "Crossing Brooklyn Ferry" and the "slow-wheeling circles" of sea-gulls that Whitman watched "high in the /

air floating with motionless wings, oscillating their / bodies" (309; sec. 3). The same gulls float timelessly over the fast-paced, broken world of Jazz Age Manhattan, "The World in Clothes" (Carlyle). They symbolize unity, the center that holds "The World out of Clothes" and function as unifying devices to shore up this fragmented novel, reappearing five more times (see 246, 251, 289, 290, 302).

On the ferry is a fugitive from upstate New York named Bud Korpenning. "Say, friend, how fur is it into the city from where this ferry lands?" Bud asks "a young man in a straw hat wearing blue and white striped necktie" (3–4). The man glances at Bud, noting the shabby condition of his shoes, coat, and "broken-visored cap," a sign of Bud's working-class status (4). The fashionably dressed man replies, "That depends where you want to get to" (4). Bud responds: "How do I get to Broadway? . . . I want to get to the center of things" (4). The man in the straw hat replies: "Walk east a block and turn down Broadway and you'll find the center of things if you walk far enough" (4). Thus begins Bud Korpenning's hapless search for the mythical Broadway, the center that does not hold.

When the ferry docks, Bud is "pushed forward among the crowd through the ferryhouse" (4). At a lunch wagon, the counterman offers him some crucial advice that sums up the theme of *Manhattan Transfer*: "It's looks that count in this city" (5). In other words, it is fashion that counts in this city. The reader will later learn that Bud killed his abusive father before fleeing to the big city, where "it'd be like lookin for a needle in a haystack to find yer" (123). Every time Bud sees a "man in a brown derby," he fears a detective is watching him (43). In *Manhattan Transfer*, detectives can be identified by their derby hats (see also 342). (A derby is the American name for a bowler.) Bud hopes to disappear into the crowd. What he does not realize is that he met the 1920s *man of the crowd* on the ferry when he met the *man in the straw hat*.

In Edgar Allan Poe's story "The Man of the Crowd," the "*man of the crowd*" represents "the type and the genius of deep crime" (264; Poe's italics). In *Manhattan Transfer*, the deep crime is what Roland Barthes terms the "Fashion system" and the man in the straw hat represents what the social psychologist Gustave Le Bon calls the "collective mind" of the crowd (Le Bon 4). Dos Passos uses the straw hat as a sign and symbol of the psychological process that Le Bon describes in his 1895 book, *The Crowd: A Study of the Popular Mind*. Through "suggestion" and "contagion," the Fashion system effects the transformation of the individual into a member of the crowd (Le Bon 8). "[The individual] is no longer himself, but has become an automaton who has ceased to be guided by his will" (Le Bon 8). Dos Passos also uses the straw

Unknown Artist, Illustration of Four Men Wearing Boaters. Private Collection, Photo © GraphicaArtis/ Bridgeman Images.

hat as a sign and symbol of the semiotic process that Barthes analyzes in *The Fashion System* (1967). He anticipates Barthes's view that "the institution of the Fashion sign is a tyrannical act" that conceals the sign's arbitrariness by rationalizing and naturalizing it (Barthes 216). Dos Passos uses the unwritten law that governed straw hat season to illustrate this tyranny.

Variations of the "young man in a straw hat" appear throughout *Manhattan Transfer*. This recurring figure of Jazz Age Manhattan's generic man-in-the-street functions, like the gulls, as a unifying device. However, the gulls symbolize "The World out of Clothes," the transcendental sphere; and the men in straw hats symbolize the "World in Clothes," the "sphere of blind Custom" that Carlyle said "doth make dotards of us all" (196). Like the man in a macintosh in *Ulysses*, the nameless "young man in a straw hat" is identified only by what he wears, and the connotations of this item of dress are what define him. Celia Marshik's analysis of the "modern(ist) mackintosh" is applicable to the boater: "While the mackintosh was commercially and popularly aligned with positive traits, . . . writers of the period would emphasize the garment's less flattering connotations, including violence, anonymity, and the paralysis of individuals dwarfed by economic and social structures they could not transcend" (44). The violence of straw hat fashion will become apparent later in the novel.

Standardization was, of course, one of the major themes of the 1920s. In his 1922 symposium on the state of *Civilization in the United States* (1922),

Harold Stearns cites "the pressure of standardization" as a problem in American intellectual life (149). Most famously, in *Babbitt* (1922), Sinclair Lewis satirizes the "Standardized American Citizen" (188). What is perhaps forgotten today is that the straw hat became a symbol of standardization for writers and intellectuals. The author of one of the essays in *Civilization in the United States* wrote that a traveler from Mars, when asked to give his impressions of America, would reply:

> You Americans more and more seem to me to be essentially alike. . . . And in nothing are you so alike as in your universal desire to be alike–to be inconspicuous, to put on straw hats on the same day, to change your clothes in Texas in accordance with the seasons in New York, to adopt the opinions a weekly digests for you from the almost uniform opinions of the whole of the daily press, in war and peace to be incontestably and entirely American. (109–10)

Even travelers from England were struck by the average American's lack of independence. "The Americans—who are rapidly becoming as 'standardised' as Ford cars—usually remove their straw hats on Sept. 15," one Brit observed (Withington 247).

In 1925, President Coolidge's defiance of "the unwritten law banning the wearing of straw hats after Sept. 15" became a front page news story ("Discard Date"). The *New York Times* reported that "Yesterday, which was close and hot, he wore his straw hat on a late afternoon stroll, and today he again appeared in the tabooed headgear" ("Discard Date"). The president's bold action gave new meaning to his slogan "Keep cool with Coolidge." Because he was accompanied by a secret service man, nobody tried to smash his hat.

Collars also symbolized standardization for Dos Passos and other writers of the 1920s who might have drawn inspiration from Whitman's line in "Song of Myself" about "The little plentiful manikins skipping around in collars and tail'd coats" (235, sec. 42). Whitman dresses down in "Song of Myself," but self-fashioning in the 1920s demanded dressing up, and the most plentiful manikins skipped around in Arrow collars and straw hats.

In his 1926 play *The Garbage Man: A Parade with Shouting* (a later version of *The Moon is a Gong* [1923]), Dos Passos refers to young men "with Arrow Collar faces" (32) and describes marchers in the Prosperity Day parade "walking lockstep, shackled in Arrow Collar shackles" (32, 140). Collars in general and Arrow collars in particular became tropes for faceless, "lockstep" conformity during the 1920s because of the popularity of the Arrow Collar Man advertisement. Fashion illustrator J. C. Leyendecker created the Arrow Collar Man in 1905 for Cluett, Peabody & Company of Troy, New York, and the company grew to control 96 percent of the shirt and collar market (Cutler 74). The best known literary reference to the Arrow Collar Man occurs in the Plaza Hotel scene in *The Great Gatsby* when Daisy inadvertently reveals her love for Gatsby by praising his "cool" look and resemblance to "the advertisement of the man" (125). Nowadays we remember how Fitzgerald transformed an iconic image of male fashion into an ironic one, but we may have forgotten that other writers did this too. Writing in defense of Sacco and Vanzetti, Dos Passos describes immigrants as being under "the bootheels of the Arrow Collar social order" (*Facing* 45). Dos Passos implies that a Fashion system that dictates conformity could turn into a fascist system that dictates *uniform*ity. Indeed, in 1928, Mussolini decreed that Italians were required to wear straw hats from April 1 to October 1 (Steinberg 169).

After Dos Passos came to New York in 1920, he wrote to a friend, "New York is rather funny—like a badly drawn cartoon—everybody looks and dresses like the Arrow-collarman" (To John Howard Lawson 299). This simile informs Dos Passos's theme that the American Dream of Thomas Jefferson has been trivialized. Freedom's just another word for nothing left to choose: "[O]ne of two unalienable alternatives: go away in a dirty soft shirt or stay in a clean arrow collar" (365–66). Many of the stream of consciousness passages in *Manhattan Transfer* imply sociologist Georg Simmel's idea that "fashion exercises such a powerful influence on our consciousness . . . that the great, permanent, unquestionable convictions are continually losing strength, as a consequence of which the transitory and vacillating elements of life acquire more room for the display of their activity" (Simmel, "Fashion" 303).

All men are created equal in an Arrow collar and straw hat. As the "trickle-down" theory explains, fashion is imitation. The "lower grades have sought to raise themselves into the grades above, by assuming their distinctive mark," to quote Herbert Spencer (qtd. in Carter 30). Two such marks that promised to erase the boundaries of class were inexpensive collars and boaters. In several of Leyendecker's advertisements, the Arrow Collar Man is wearing a straw boater. See for example the 1909 "Tremont," the 1910 "Concord," and the 1912 "Belmont." The names refer to collar styles. The Arrow Collar Man illustrated four hundred collar styles before he was retired in 1930 (Schau 28). In *Manhattan Transfer*, the "young man in a straw hat wearing a blue and white striped necktie" who told Bud Korpenning that he would find the "center of things" if he turned down Broadway and walked "far enough" is a simulacrum of the Arrow Collar Man (4). Call him "Tremont." The "young man in a new straw hat" wearing "a red, green, and blue striped tie" who tries to pick up Ellen Thatcher just before she walks through the revolving doors in her final appearance in the novel is also a simulacrum of the Arrow Collar Man (399). Call him "Concord." Was the "young man in a straw hat" (137) who tried to lure Ellen into his Stutz roadster in an earlier scene Tremont or Concord? Or was he "Belmont"? (In *Ulysses*, the man in the mackintosh is called M'Intosh.) The "Anglo-Saxon" features of the Arrow Collar Man tie in with Dos Passos's depiction of the nativist fervor that led to conviction of Sacco and Vanzetti in 1921, the passage of the Immigration Act of 1924, and the deportation of "undesirable aliens" (353). In *Manhattan Transfer*, an immigrant can be identified by his "foreignlooking cap," and wearing a straw hat is implied to be a form of Americanization (395). It's looks that count in this country.

All the anonymous young men in their straw hats who keep appearing throughout *Manhattan Transfer* can be interpreted as simulacra of the Arrow Collar Man: "the young men in straw hats . . . three deep along the soda fountain" at the Columbus Circle drugstore (161); the "Men running to cover with their straw hats under their coats" in the rain (207). (Rain is bad for straw hats but good for rebirth in the spiritual waste land of Manhattan.) Sometimes only the "glances of eyes under straw hats" are seen (153). Sometimes only the hats are seen. Walking in the streets, Ellen sees "people in Sunday clothes, strawhats, sunshades" (137). From the window of the Fifth Avenue bus, Ellen, who is also wearing a straw hat, sees "Sunshades, summer dresses, straw hats" (136). In "The Metropolis and Mental Life" (1903), Georg Simmel describes the problem "of the individual . . . being leveled, swallowed up in the social-technological mechanism" (52). Dos Passos depicts this metropolitan loss of individuality by abstracting people into metonymic images of hats and articles of clothing, as Joyce had done in *Ulysses*. After Jimmy Herf rejects Uncle Jeff Merivale's offer to launch him on a career in business, Herf retrieves his hat from the hatcheck girl: "she hands Jimmy his hat that looks squashed, flat and soiled and limp among the big bellied derbies and the fedoras and the majestic panamas hanging on the pegs" (120). Having turned down an opportunity to "Get a taste of how it feels to make a living, like a man in a man's world," Jimmy's insecurity is reflected in this description of the hats (119).[1]

Manhattan Transfer is not the first work in which Dos Passos identifies characters by their hats. In *The Garbage Man*, the dramatis personae include The Girl in the Red Hat, The Man in the Stovepipe Hat, The Man in the Panama Hat, and Two Men in Brown Derbies. Other characters are described by their hats in the stage directions, such as the "Young Men With

Cold Cream Faces in straw hats" and the "Four Real Estate Men with black derby hats" (82, 137). In the final scene of the play, an Orwellian radio voice decrees "That there shall be a list made of all dissenters knockers reds carping critics nonchurchgoers wearers of straw hats out of season nonfordowners loafers discontented persons readers of foreign languages divorcees advocates of free love the eight hour day subversive doctrines" (149).[2] Dos Passos correlates the Red Scare with "Straw Hat Fear," a phenomenon identified in a 1929 book *The Psychology of Dress* (Hurlock).

The arrest and conviction of Sacco and Vanzetti demonstrated this link between unwritten laws of fashion and politics. In *Facing the Chair: Story of the Americanization of Two Foreignborn Workmen* (1927), Dos Passos attributes the arrest of Sacco and Vanzetti for a payroll robbery and murder in South Braintree, Massachusetts, on April 15, 1920, to the "Red Delirium" that made immigrant radicals suspect and undesirable (46). In a futile attempt to save Sacco and Vanzetti from the electric chair, Dos Passos argues that they had been framed, and he shows how hats played a role in convicting them for a crime they did not commit. Vanzetti had been brought to trial for an earlier holdup in Bridgewater. At the preliminary hearing, one witness identified "a man with a dark face, moustache and dark soft hat, who 'seemed like some kind of a foreigner'" (76). Yet at the trial, the prosecution suppressed this testimony "that Vanzetti had worn a hat" (76). The chief justice "exhibited in court a cap, which he claimed to have taken from Vanzetti's home; then he produced a witness . . . who said he thought he saw this cap on the shotgun man's head on December 24" (76). Today, this distinction between a "hat" and a "cap" would not be meaningful. But in the 1920s, cloth caps were worn by the working class or by radicals who wished to express solidarity with the working class (Crane 84–85, UHP 1–3). After the Russian Revolution, Lenin stopped wearing a homburg hat and began wearing a flat cloth cap, a "workers' cap" (UHP 1). As discussed at the trial for the South Braintree crime, a "dark brown cap" was found near the slain paymaster's body. The prosecution claimed that this cap belonged to Sacco even though it did not fit him in court, and a witness testified that it was not Sacco's cap. Sacco owned a "pepper-and-salt cloth" cap; whereas the "'bandit cap' was fur-lined and had ear-laps" (105). The "if it doesn't fit you must acquit" defense worked better for O. J. Simpson.

After Sacco and Vanzetti were executed in 1927, Dos Passos published a poem in the *New Masses* portraying the members of the governor's advisory board that rejected clemency as spiritually dead elites clad in the sartorial style of the previous century: "The white collar dead; the silkhatted dead; the frockcoated dead" ("They are Dead Now"). Since black frock coats and silk toppers became obsolescent in the 1910s–20s, replaced by modern business suits (Shannon 123, 176–78, 219), Dos Passos's metonymic images suggested that an anachronistic aristocracy of old men killed Sacco and Vanzetti. "The black automatons have won" ("They are Dead Now").

In *Manhattan Transfer*, it is "the hat that makes the man." Dos Passos was probably familiar with Max Ernst's surrealist collage *C'est Le Chapeau Qui Fait L'homme* (1920), in which pictures of hats cut from a catalog have been assembled into machinelike figures that resemble robotic hat racks. Werner Spies interprets Ernst's images as depicting "The human being as a robot enchained by self-created categories" (58). Similarly, Dos Passos portrays human beings as little more than catalog cut-outs and suggests that they have been imprisoned by their own systems of meaning that they have reified and deified.

Yet the hat buyer for Lord and Taylor's department store regarded buying a hat as an act of free will, the final expression of male individuality in dress since the "Great Masculine Renunciation" of the late eighteenth century made uniformity the norm and "the man in the gray flannel suit" the future (see Flugel 111–12; Wilson). When a man buys a business suit or a pair of shoes, he finds little variation, and his ties were probably bought for him by his wife. "But his *hat* is his own choice. He picks it out himself; and he has a wide range . . . to choose from" (Crowell 43; Crowell's emphasis). However, window displays in department stores supported Dos Passos's view that hats were signs of a herd mentality. Articles about window dressing in 1910s–20s issues of *American Hatter* offer a window into history that reveals the rigidity of American hat customs. In "The Window in May," the author advises window workers to restrain "that fatal annual tendency to rush the straw hat season," since "[b]efore the 15th of May no one, except the notoriety-seeker, will publicly wear a straw hat" (57). Although these articles featured the "many unique and clever ways with which 'the man in the street' is informed that it is straw hat time," the displays that they show-cased communicated a message of conformity. The window display in a 1921 Denver department store was praised for attracting attention: "The frame, representing the calendar form, was covered with straw and each day was represented by a hat, on the crown of which was placed a card bearing the date of the month. Felt hats were used up to twenty, when straws took the place of the felts, thus graphically telling the public that the twenty-first was the day on which to blossom forth in a nice new straw" ("And Here's" 87). If this display did not "forcefully impress upon the mind of the public the fact that the twenty-first was THE DAY" (87), then the threat of violence for wearing a hat out of season might have. Two window displays for straw hat day deemed "just right" by *American Hatter* were featured in a

1910 illustrated article. The display in a Kansas City department store window included nearly two hundred boaters with a mirror background that made it seem like even more. In a window trimmed for a Cincinnati store, dozens of straw hats were set upon pedestals and decorated with canes, ribbons, and hat bands ("The Window" 57–58). Such disembodied hats in store window displays might have inspired writers like Dos Passos and Joyce to metonymically reduce characters to their hats or other articles of clothing.[3]

Throughout *Ulysses*, Blazes Boylan is primarily identified by his straw hat and trendy clothes: "a skyblue tie, a widebrimmed straw hat at a rakish angle and a suit of indigo serge" (254). Bloom laments that Molly would be attracted to a "type like that" (92). Boylan is "the modern fashion machine incarnate," to quote Garry Leonard (8). Dos Passos was impressed by Joyce's experimental urban novel, which he read on his way back from Europe in spring 1922 ("Contemporary" 239). In *Manhattan Transfer*, Dos Passos created a variety of his own urban "types." He felt that "Joyce was knocking established ideas on the novel into a cocked hat with his *Ulysses*" ("What Makes" 270). Dos Passos's metaphor captures his own interest in hats as well as Joyce's. Because the cocked hat was *the* hat of the eighteenth century (the top hat was *the* hat of the nineteenth century), Joyce pulled his new ideas on the novel out of bowlers (the hat that Bloom wears) and boaters, *the* hats of modern life.

Dos Passos was clearly influenced by Joyce's theme of how "advertising and commodity culture . . . is an invisible form of production that makes one's identity intelligible to one's 'self' and others" (Leonard xi). The modern Ulysses is an advertising canvasser who walks around Dublin thinking how "[a]ll kinds of places are good for ads" (153). Bloom's final thought each night before falling asleep is "[o]f some one sole unique advertisement to cause passers to stop in wonder" (720). Such an ad, he realizes, must be "congruous with the velocity of modern life" (153). Dos Passos took these ideas and developed them. Manhattanites are walking advertisements. Manhattan is a spectacular advertisement of itself. Like Bloom's ideal ad, a modernist novel must be "congruous with the velocity of modern life" (and it did not hurt to advertise yourself as a modernist like the famous Joyce). Leopold Bloom would have loved the signs of Times Square that advertise the "center of things" in Dos Passos's novel (4). But individual canvassers were being replaced by agencies even in 1904 (Wicke 126–27). Bloom would not have found a place in a 1920s Fashion system like the one in *Manhattan Transfer*.

The modern Fashion system creates the discourse of Fashion, the rhetoric of "written clothing" (Barthes 3). As Barthes explains, "In order to blunt the buyer's calculating consciousness, a veil must be drawn around the object—a veil of images of reasons, of meanings" (xi). Thus, a man does not buy a "real" hat; he buys a "represented" hat, a "simulacrum of the real object" created by the system (xii). In *Manhattan Transfer*, Dos Passos rewrites "written clothing" by making the straw hat a metonym for the human being as a robot, duped by discourse, enchained by simulacra, and he makes "the man who would wear a straw hat out of season" express the novel's basic tragedy (402). The protagonists of *Manhattan Transfer* are drawn in opposite directions by the energy of the novel. Ellen Thatcher moves centripetally toward "the center of things" and a job as a fashion magazine editor (368). Jimmy Herf moves centrifugally away from the "center of things" that the Fashion system invents, breaking free from its magnetic pull at the end of the novel.

Ellen's final scene in the novel begins with her buying an evening dress at Madame Soubrine's shop. Suddenly, a fire breaks out in the backroom where the working class girls sew the dresses for the rich Women of Fashion. Anna Cohen is terribly burned, and Ellen flees into the street. Here she encounters "[a] young man in a new straw hat [who is] looking at her out of the corners of his eyes, trying to pick her up. She stares him blankly in the face. He has on a red, green, and blue striped tie" (399). The fate of the Straw Woman of Fashion is to be hit on by the Straw Man of Fashion.

In the final scenes that precede Jimmy Herf's escape from New York, Dos Passos exposes the violence of fashion, the "murder it commits of its own past" every season (Barthes 273). Herf keeps thinking about a man who was killed for wearing a straw hat out of season that his friend Bob Hildebrand tells him about:

> "Say Herf did you read about the man in Philadelphia who was killed because he wore his straw hat on the fourteenth of May?"
>
> "By God if I was starting a new religion he'd be made a saint."
>
> "Didn't you read about it? It was funny as a crutch.... This man had the temerity to defend his straw hat. Somebody had busted it and he started to fight, and in the middle of it one of these street-corner heroes came up behind him and brained him with a piece of lead pipe. They picked him up with a cracked skull and he died in the hospital."
>
> "Bob what was his name?"
>
> "I didn't notice."
>
> "Talk about the Unknown Soldier.... That's a real hero for you; the golden legend of the man who would wear a straw hat out of season." (401)

Dos Passos's source for this incident was probably a September 14, 1924, article in the *New York Times* "Straw Hat Prank Has Fatal Ending." If so, he altered a few facts. The real-life incident occurred on the lower east side of New York the evening of September 13, which means that the assailants jumped the gun, since Felt Hat Day was September 15. The victim was set upon by "a gang of whooping youngsters" who knocked his hat off with "long sticks." He gave chase, caught one of them, began to spank him, at which time one of the older boys, who were there to protect the younger ones, rushed in, words were exchanged, and a fight ensued. The man was killed when his head struck the curbstone after he was punched. "Silent sentinels of his death were the near-by light poles decorated with broken straw hats taken by the neighborhood youngsters," according to the article. The victim was "an unidentified man": "He wore a dark suit, white shirt with green stripes, green tie, black socks and tan oxfords," wrote the *Times* reporter, whose description of the anonymous well-dressed corpse might have inspired Dos Passos's satirical idea of the Unknown Soldier of Fashion ("Straw Hat Prank").

Why did Dos Passos change the season of the violation of the convention that mandated when straw hats must be donned or discarded? According to a 1923 article in the *American Magazine* titled "Human Nature in a Hat Store," the closing date of straw hat season, September 15, known as Felt Hat Day, was more "religiously adhered to" than the opening date, May 15, known as Straw Hat Day (Crowell 188). This is not to say that rushing Straw Hat Day did not have its perils. Recall that an article in *American Hatter* stated that "[b]efore the 15th of May no one, except the notoriety-seeker, will publicly wear a straw hat" ("Window in May" 57). Dos Passos probably changed the season to spring to reinforce the ending of the novel that ironically juxtaposes traditional rebirth against Fashion's usurpation of the mythology of spring.

A September 13, 1925, article in the *New York Times Magazine* titled "Good-Bye to the Straw Hat" by a writer identified as "E. A. J." provides another hint why Dos Passos might have altered the season:

> The man who is guilty of wearing the last straw is bound to find his position less romantic than that of the pioneer who parades a brand-new straw earlier than the day prescribed by herd law. To the pioneer attaches a kind of glamour. You may set him down as a foolish personification of bravado: you may hoot at his tender just-hatched straw and invoke the winds to blow it into the nearest puddle; yet you cannot but admire, if secretly, his hardihood. (SM20)

Dos Passos added several more layers of irony to the idea of a man killed for wearing a straw hat out of season as a romantic and a pioneer. Herf thinks of him as a Revolutionary War hero (the possible reason for the change of setting from New York to Philadelphia): "Give me liberty, said Patrick Henry, putting on his straw hat on the first of May, or give me death. And he got it" (402). Herf also thinks of the man as a religious martyr: "It's the funeral of Saint Aloysius of Philadelphia, virgin and martyr, the man who would wear a straw hat out of season" (401). Spring is the season for Christian martyrs.

But fall was the bloodier season for straw hat violence, and America was the country where not removing a straw hat on a fixed date was most likely to lead to violence. In 1899, a British traveler to Philadelphia at the end of September was warned not to buy a straw hat despite the hot weather because he was "liable to have it knocked off [his] head" ("Hat Wearing Customs" 281). In 1911, a Memphis man was shot to death for destroying another man's out-of-season boater ("Killed in Straw Hat Row"). In September, 1922 straw hat riots broke out in New York City. On the first night of disturbances, the *New York Times* reported that "thousands of skypieces" were wrecked and "straw hat bonfires were started." Seven of the "wreckers" were convicted of disorderly conduct for their role in a "hat-smashing saturnalia" ("Straw Hat Riots"). On subsequent nights, the rioting spread. "Straw Hat Smashing Orgy Bares Heads From Battery to Bronx" screamed the headline in the *New York Tribune*. "City Has Wild Night of Straw Hat Riots," shouted the headline in the *New York Times*. "Gangs of Young Hoodlums With Spiked Sticks Terrorize Whole Blocks." A favorite method of the "hat-hunting hoodlums" was to arm themselves with sticks that had nails at the end to hook the straw hats off the heads of their victims who were made to "run the gauntlet" ("Straw Hat Smashing Orgy," "City Has Wild Night"). Mobs in the hundreds, as many as a thousand on Amsterdam Avenue, smashed and trampled hats throughout the city. The streets "were strewn with broken straw hats" ("City Has Wild Night").

Fortuitously, the magistrate before whom many of the rowdies were brought who received a lot of press attention for upholding "the inalienable right of a man to wear a straw hat in a snowstorm" was named Peter A. Hatting ("Straw Hat Riots"). Dos Passos must have been aware of the straw hat riots because he was living in New York at the time. He might have even derived his line about "one of two unalienable alternatives: go away in a dirty soft shirt or stay in a clean Arrow collar" from the cynical reporter's paraphrase of Magistrate Hatting's defense of Jeffersonian principles (366). Most men endured the humiliation of losing their hats with little resistance. The few who fought back were cited in newspaper accounts ("City Has Wild Night"). In some precincts, the police crackdown did not begin until plainclothes detectives were assaulted ("City Has Wild Night").

What would motivate gangs of boys and young men to want to knock a man's hat off? Did the impulse spring from class resentment? Did the bourgeois symbolism of the straw hat arouse the ire of the masses? Was it oedipal rage that drove the rioters to want to mock or ridicule or emasculate their elders by removing their hats? Did the rowdies interpret the slang term for a straw hat, "straw basher," as an invitation? Were the straw hat rioters participating in a modern version of a saturnalia, an "annual period of license . . . when the darker passions find a vent which would never be allowed them in the more staid and sober course of ordinary life"? (Frazer 641). On the other hand, maybe the passions vented by the revelers were not the darker ones. Maybe "a hat on the move was a free comic spectacle, a joyful, unifying public event," at least for those who had not lost their hats (Steinberg 118). The author of a 1925 *New York Times Magazine* article titled "Straw Hat's Rigid Conventions" suggested that "[s]omething of the street arab lurks in the most sedate of grown men" (20). The question of straw hat violence is—or used to be—a vexing one. If doffing one's hat indicated deference to authority, did smashing someone's hat indicate defiance of authority? Were the straw hat rioters the unwitting or witting tools of the hat makers and merchants? "Stores Do Thriving Business," noted the *New York Tribune* headline (*Straw Hat Smashing Orgy*). Were they paid off or encouraged by the Fashion system to enforce the specious reasons and spurious seasons of the Fashion sign (straw hat = summer) (straw hat in summer = fashion)? Was there something about the vulnerability of the straw hat itself, as the *Times Magazine* author suggests? "It can be knocked off with such facility" ("Straw Hat's Rigid Conventions" 20). Or was it "the freemasonry of the streets," to quote the author of "Human Nature in a Hat Store," that would cause "boys and young men to feel they have the privilege of smashing a straw hat worn after the official closing date" (Crowell 188).

In *Manhattan Transfer*, the man who is killed for wearing his straw hat out of season gains what Faulkner's Mr. Compson calls "the reducto absurdum of all human experience" (76). (In *The Sound and the Fury*, Quentin Compson worries about being seen without a hat on the way to his suicide.) "'It's the funeral of Saint Aloysius of Philadelphia, virgin and martyr, the man who would wear a straw hat out of season,' said Herf" (401). Herf refers to Saint Aloysius Gonzaga (1568–1591), the patron saint of youth. Aloysius's life provides an ironic commentary on the lives of Jay Gatsby, Clyde Griffiths, and the anonymous fashion martyr of *Manhattan Transfer*. The son of a rich Italian nobleman, Aloysius was raised in a castle. When he was seventeen, Aloysius renounced his patrimony—the castle, the wealth, the title of marquis—and entered the religious order of the Society of Jesus. He took vows of poverty and chastity and began theological studies to become a Jesuit priest. During his fourth year of study, Aloysius contracted the plague as a result of tending the sick in the streets and hospitals of Rome. He died on June 21, 1591, at the age of twenty-three. Aloysius was beatified in 1621 and sanctified in 1726. In 1729, he was declared the patron saint of youth. "Saint Aloysius, pray for the youth, the future of our world, pray for us" (qtd. in "Gonzaga"). In religious art, the attributes of Aloysius are a lily (symbol of innocence), a cross (symbol of sacrifice), a skull (symbol of early death), and a rosary (symbol of devotion to the Virgin Mary) ("Gonzaga").

In Dos Passos's art, Saint Aloysius is a symbol of irony. The plague of the 1920s is "irony, the Holy Ghost of this later day," as Fitzgerald (ironically) calls it (*Beautiful* 3). "'Don't you know about irony and pity?'" Hemingway (ironically) wrote. "'They're mad about it in New York'" (*Sun* 119). "By gum if I were a painter, maybe they'll let me paint in the nuthouse, I'd do Saint Aloysius of Philadelphia with a straw hat on his head instead of a halo and in his hand the lead pipe, instrument of his martyrdom, and a little me praying at his feet," thinks Jimmy Herf as he waits for the ferry to leave mad New York (403). (Joyce also alludes to Saint Aloysius in *Ulysses*, as does Hemingway in *The Sun Also Rises*.[4]) "The golden legend of the man who would wear a straw hat out of season. Jimmy Herf is walking along Twenty-third Street, laughing to himself" (402). This allusion is to *The Golden Legend*, or *Lives of the Saints*, a medieval collection of hagiographies compiled by Jacobus de Voragine (1230–98). *The Golden Legend* is organized by the saint's day of the year, as for example, June 21 Saint Aloysius Gonzaga. *The Great Gatsby*, *An American Tragedy*, and *Manhattan Transfer* are all ironic golden legends about the youthful worship of false idols: "St. Aloysius Gonzaga, pray for Jay Gatsby, Clyde Griffiths, and 'the man who would wear a straw hat out of season,' the future of our world, pray for us."

As Jimmy Herf leaves Manhattan on a ferry at the end of the novel, "[h]e keeps trying to explain his gayety to himself" (403). The variant spelling of "gaiety" allows Dos Passos to imply a contrast between the happiness of the "'Gay White Way'" (a variant of Broadway as the "Great White Way"), and a different kind of happiness that Herf seeks (78). Herf's departure on a ferry completes the circle that began with the ferry's arrival at the beginning of the novel and completes the larger circle that connects the novel spiritually to Whitman's "Crossing Brooklyn Ferry." "Our life is an apprenticeship to the truth that around every circle another can be drawn," wrote Emerson ("Circles" 168). Perhaps the transcendentalist themes of Carlyle, Emerson, and Whitman are behind Herf's feeling of gayety. "He sits smoking happily. He can't seem to remember anything" (403). As Emerson wrote: "In nature every moment is new; the past is always swallowed and forgotten; the coming only is sacred" (177). In fashion, the same could be said. But what is happening to Herf is different from Ellen's "sudden pang of something forgotten" (400) and escape into "the euphoria of fashion" (Barthes 261) that enables her to forget her troubles by becoming a "walking talking doll," an "Elliedoll" who exits the novel "smiling" (399, 301, 400). She will probably marry George Baldwin, the new district attorney who has proposed to her. Baldwin is last seen through Ellen's eyes "in a tan felt hat and a light tan overcoat, smiling like some celebrity in the rotogravure section of a Sunday paper" (374). There is no reason to believe that the smiling Ellen will remain faithful to the smiling George even if he succeeds in becoming the next mayor of Manhattan. As the Woman of Fashion, Ellen represents the infidelity of fashion. Loyalty ends with the new style, or the latest lover.

What Herf seems to be experiencing is the "universal HERE" and "Everlasting NOW" of the "World out of Clothes" (Carlyle 198). Herf "stands with his hat off at the rail and feels the river wind in his hair. Perhaps he's gone crazy, and this is amnesia, some disease with a long Greek name" (403). Still crazy like a transcendentalist after all these years: "The one thing which we seek with insatiable desire is to forget ourselves, to be surprised out of our propriety, to lose our sempiternal memory and to do something without knowing how or why; in short to draw a new circle" ("Circles" 178). Herf "laughs aloud so that the old man who came to open the gates gave him a sudden sidelong look" (403). Maybe Jimmy just wanted to draw a new circle. Maybe he just wanted to take his hat off.

Herf has not told his friends where he is going and probably does not know himself. "I wish Jimmy would tell us where he expected to go on his mysterious travels," Alice had teased him (361). In the same scene, Martin Schiff describes Jimmy as having "no money, . . . no pretty wife, no good conversation, no tips on the stock market, a useless fardel on society. . . . The artist as fardel on society" (361). To which someone (either Jimmy or Alice) responds: "That's not so Martin. . . . You're talking through your hat" (361).

When Herf "stands with his hat off at the rail," he becomes the "you" Whitman addresses in "Crossing Brooklyn Ferry": "Just as you stand and lean on the rail, yet hurry with the swift current, I stood yet was hurried" (309). Whitman must have taken his hat off, because when he saw a reflection of himself in the river, he "Look'd at the fine centrifugal spokes of light round the / shape of my head in the sunlit water" (309). The removal of the hat stands for the shedding of the social self that it represents. Whitman now has a halo over his head instead of a hat. In Whitman's poem, as in *Manhattan Transfer*, "the hat functions as a barrier between the public identity and the private self; it ultimately serves to fragment the self or to reduce the self to a metonymy" (Faison 6). Since Herf does not want to be reduced to a "man in a straw hat" or to a "Saint Aloysius of Philadelphia with a straw hat on his head instead of a halo," he flees the city (403).

For a while Jimmy is alone on the ferry, but then "a brokendown spring-wagon loaded with flowers" comes aboard (403). "Jimmy Herf walks around it; behind the drooping horse with haunches like a hatrack the little warped wagon is unexpectedly merry, stocked with pots of scarlet and pink geraniums, carnations, alyssum, forced roses, blue lobelia" (403). Perhaps the rebirth symbolism explains why Jimmy is also unexpectedly merry. Perhaps the hatrack haunches of the horse (a clotheshorse) and "[t]he driver [who] sits hunched with his hat over his eyes" explain Jimmy's gayety.[5] Everything is becoming *transparent*.

A novel that began with the question "How do I get to Broadway?" (4) ends with the question, Why am I laughing? Is it because a cryptic meaning of "Manhattan Transfer" has been discovered? Manhattan is where the men transfer their hats on May 15 and September 15 in a man hat transfer. Is that why you are laughing, Jimmy? When Herf gets off the ferry, "he stops to look back. He can see nothing but fog spaced with a file of blurred arclights" (403–04). Manhattan, or, if you prefer, Man Hat Island, has disappeared. Although Dos Passos titles his final chapter "The Burthen of Nineveh" and portrays a tramp named Jonah prophesying the destruction of Manhattan, the novel does not conclude with apocalyptic Biblical weather. As in the final lines of T. S. Eliot's 1925 poem "The Hollow Men," the world of *Manhattan Transfer* ends anticlimactically, as befits people undone by the straw man of fashion, their "Headpiece filled with straw" ("Hollow Men" 82, 79). The world in clothes ends not with a bang but a boater.[6] Is that why you are laughing, Jimmy?

NOTES

1. An object of Dos Passos's satire of sartorial correctness is Herf's clothes-conscious cousin, James Merivale. In a scene at a Brooks Brothers store, Merivale is more concerned that he bought the same suit as Cunningham, his sister's fiancé, than that Cunningham is already married: "'People'll think it's a uniform'" (335).

2. As Landsberg comments, "the straw hat out of season deserves special notice, for in *Manhattan Transfer* it reappears more prominently as a symbol of non-conformity" (112). Landsberg quotes a 1920 article about the Red Scare in the *Atlantic Monthly*: "Just now, in popular parlance, a Bolshevik is anybody, from a dynamiter to the man who wears a straw hat in September" (112). The author of a 1925 article in the *New York Times* also sarcastically wrote that someone wearing a straw hat after September "may even be a Bolshevik, a communal enemy, a potential subverter of the social order" ("Good-bye" 20).
3. A pioneer in the field of window display was L. Frank Baum. After founding the trade journal *The Show Window: A Journal of Practical Window Trimming for the Merchant and the Professional* in 1897, Baum wrote *The Art of Decorating Dry Goods Windows and Interiors* (1900). That same year Baum's *The Wonderful Wizard of Oz* was published. We're off to see the wizard, the wonderful wizard of window display.
4. In *The Sun Also Rises*, expatriate Jake Barnes reads his mail from the States, and one letter is a wedding announcement: "Mr. and Mrs. Aloysius Kirby announce the marriage of their daughter Katherine–I knew neither the girl nor the man she was marrying. They must be circularizing the town. It was a funny name. I felt sure I could remember anybody with a name like Aloysius. It was a good Catholic name" (38). As the scene develops, Jake also uses the word "funny" to refer to the war wound that has forced him to practice celibacy (Stoneback 63). It is a good Catholic joke that Jake, a practicing Catholic, shares with the reader. Hemingway was probably remembering his friend Dos Passos's ironic use of Saint Aloysius in *Manhattan Transfer*. Dos Passos, in turn, might have been influenced by Joyce's ironic reference to the patron of "holy youth" in *Ulysses* who is among the mock religious procession that enters Barney Kiernan's pub in the "Cyclops" episode (339). When he was a choir boy, Joyce chose Aloysius as his saint's name (Ellmann 29). After an issue of the *Little Review* serializing the "Cyclops" episode was confiscated and burned, Joyce joked, "I hope I will pass through the fires of purgatory as quickly as my patron S. Aloysius" (qtd. in Ellmann 517). It was inevitable that a model of holy youth would become an ironic reference in a decade that worshipped unholy youth. After all, as William James writes of Aloysius in *The Varieties of Religious Experience*, he represents "a type of excess of purification .... to a point which we cannot unreservedly admire" (272).
5. The horse's hatrack haunches recall an earlier reference to "the staghorns of the hatrack" at Mrs. Sunderland's, upon which hang "Straw hats, silk eveningwraps, and a couple of men's dress overcoats" (130). Hatracks are also important in *Ulysses*. In "Circe," Bloom's feelings about being a cuckold are exposed when he imagines that Blazes Boylan *"hangs his hat smartly on a peg of Bloom's antlered head"* (565;

Joyce's italics). In "Penelope," Molly thinks about what a man looks like with his "thing hanging down out of him or sticking up at you like a hatrack" (753).

6. "The Hollow Men" ends as follows:

    This is the way the world ends
    This is the way the world ends
    This is the way the world ends
    Not with a bang but a whimper. (82; italics in original)

   Because the epigraph of "The Hollow Men" reads "A Penny for the Old Guy," the poem's straw image is usually understood to be an allusion to Guy Fawkes effigies:

    We are the stuffed men
    Leaning together
    Headpiece filled with straw. Alas! (lines 2–4)

   However, these lines can also be interpreted as a reference to the straw hats worn by the crowd-men of 1925. Such a meaning would have worked better for an American reader. In 1920s America, the word "guy," although it originally derived from Guy Fawkes, did not refer to the "Old Guy." It was an affectionate term that girls used to refer to their boyfriends. When a flapper talked about "my guy," she was seeing a young guy in a straw hat (Flexner 115).

WORKS CITED

Allen, Irving Lewis. *The City in Slang: New York Life and Popular Speech.* Oxford UP, 1993.

"And Here's Another One!" *American Hatter*, July 1921, p. 87.

Barthes, Roland. *The Fashion System.* Translated by Matthew Ward and Richard Howard. U of California P, 1990.

Baum, L. Frank. *The Art of Decorating Dry Goods Windows and Interiors.* The Show Window Publishing Company, 1900.

Carlyle, Thomas. *Sartor Resartus.* 1838. Oxford UP, 2008.

Carter, Michael. *Fashion Classics from Carlyle to Barthes.* Oxford UP, 2003.

"City Has Wild Night of Straw Hat Riots." *New York Times.* 16 Sept. 1922, search-proquest-com.cmich.idm.oclc.org/hupnewyorktimes/docview/100155831/55DD5B34.

Crane, Diana. *Fashion and Its Social Agendas: Class, Gender, and Identity in Clothing.* U of Chicago P, 2000.

Crowell, Merle. "Human Nature in a Hat Store." *American Magazine*, March 1923, pp. 186–96.

Culler, Jonathan. *Roland Barthes*. Oxford UP, 1983.

Cutler, Laurence S., and Judy Goffman Cutler. *J. C. Leyendecker: American Imagist*. Abrams, 2008.

"Discard Date for Straw Hats Ignored by President Coolidge." *New York Times*, 20 Sept. 1925, p. 1, search.proquest.com/hnpnewyorktimes/docview/103456654/3E8944C4686D4D38.

Dos Passos, John. "Contemporary Chronicles." *John Dos Passos: The Major Nonfictional Prose*, edited by Donald Pizr, Wayne State UP, 1988, pp. 238–40.

———. *Facing the Chair: Story of the Americanization of Two Foreignborn Workmen*. 1927. Da Capo Press, 1970.

———. *The Garbage Man: A Parade with Shouting*. Harper & Brothers, 1926.

———. *Manhattan Transfer*. Houghton Mifflin, 1925.

———. "They are Dead Now." *New Masses*, Oct. 1927, p. 7.

———. "To John Howard Lawson." 12 Sept. 1920. *The Fourteenth Chronicle: Letters and Diaries of John Dos Passos*, edited by Townsend Ludington, Gambit, 1973, pp. 299–300.

———. "What Makes a Novelist." *John Dos Passos: The Major Nonfictional Prose*, edited by Donald Pizer, Wayne State UP, 1988, pp. 268–75.

Dreiser, Theodore. *An American Tragedy*. 1925. NAL Penguin, 1981.

E. A. J. "Good-Bye to the Straw Hat." *New York Times*, 13 Sept. 1925, p. SM20, search-proquest-com.cmich.idm.oclc.org/hnpnewyorktimes/docview/103491647/DF87B1AE.

Eliot, T. S. "The Hollow Men." *Collected Poems 1909–1962*. Harcourt, Brace & World, 1970, pp. 79–82.

Ellmann, Richard. *James Joyce*. Oxford UP, 1972.

Emerson, Ralph Waldo. "Circles." *Selections from Ralph Waldo Emerson*, edited by Stephen E. Whicher, Houghton Mifflin, 1957, pp. 168–78.

Ernst, Max. *The Hat Makes the Man*. 1920. Collage and water color. Museum of Modern Art, *Ernst*, edited by Ian Turpin, Phaidon Press, 1979, p. 38.

Faison, Elisa. "The Hat Trick: The Fluid Symbol of the Hat in James Joyce's *Ulysses*." 2011, dspace.sewanee.edu/handle/11005/267.

Faulkner, William. *The Sound and the Fury*. 1929. Vintage, 1990.

Fitzgerald, F. Scott. *The Beautiful and Damned*. Scribner's, 1922.

———. *The Great Gatsby*. 1925. Collier, 1992.

Flexner, Stuart Berg. *I Hear America Talking*. Touchstone, 1979.

Flugel, J. C. *The Psychology of Clothes*. Hogarth, 1930.

Frazer, Sir James. *The New Golden Bough*. 1922. Edited by Theodor H. Gaster, New American Library, 1959.

Gonzaga, St. Aloysius. *Wikipedia*. En.wickipedia.org/Aloysius_Gonzaga.

Gurko, Leo. "John Dos Passos' *U.S.A.*: A 1930's Spectacular." *Proletarian Writers of the Thirties*, edited by David Madden, Southern Illinois P, 1968, pp. 46–63.
"Hat Wearing Customs in the U. S. A." *Notes and Queries*, 16 April 1927, p. 281.
Hemingway, Ernest. *The Sun Also Rises*. Scribner's, 1926.
Hurlock, Elizabeth B. *The Psychology of Dress: An Analysis of Fashion and Its Motive*. 1929. Arno Press, 1976.
James, William. *The Varieties of Religious Experience*. 1902. New American Library, 1958.
Joyce, James. *Ulysses*. 1922. Vintage, 1961.
"Killed in Straw Hat Row." *New York Times*, 9 Oct. 1911, p. 11, search.proquest.com /hnpnewyorktimes/docview/97211191/404FCBA8B5F24AO4F.
Landsberg, Melvin. *Dos Passos' Path to U.S.A.* The Colorado Associated UP, 1972.
Le Bon, Gustave. *The Crowd: A Study of the Popular Mind*. 1895. Dover, 2002.
Leonard, Garry. *Advertising and Commodity Culture in Joyce*. UP of Florida, 1998.
Lewis, Sinclair. *Babbitt*. 1922. Signet Classics, 2007.
Ludington, Townsend, editor. *The Fourteenth Chronicle: Letters and Diaries of John Dos Passos*. Gambit, 1973.
Manhatta. Directed by Paul Strand and Charles Sheeler. 1921. Film. Youtube.com. Accessed 26 March 2021.
Marshik, Celia. "The Modern(ist) Mackintosh." *Modernism/modernity*, vol. 19, no.1, Jan. 2012, pp. 43–71.
Poe, Edgar Allan. "The Man of the Crowd." *Introduction to Poe: A Thematic Reader*, edited by Eric Carlson and Scott Foresman, 1967, pp. 257–64.
Robinson, Fred Miller. *The Man in the Bowler Hat*. U of North Carolina P, 1993.
Schau, Michael. *J. C. Leyendecker*. Watson-Guptill, 1974.
Shannon, Brent. *The Cut of His Coat: Men, Dress, and Consumer Culture in Britain, 1860–1914*. Ohio UP, 2006.
Simmel, Georg. "Fashion." 1904. *On Individuality and Social Forms*, edited by Donald N. Levine, U of Chicago P, 1971, pp. 294–323.
———. "The Metropolis and Mental Life." 1903. *Modernism: An Anthology of Sources and Documents*, edited by Vassiliki Kolocotroni, Jane Goldman, and Olga Taxidou, U of Chicago P, 1998, pp. 51–60.
Spies, Werner. *Max Ernst Collages: The Invention of the Surrealist Universe*. Translated by John William Gabriel, Harry N. Abrams, 1988.
Stearns, Harold, editor. *Civilization in the United States: An Inquiry by Thirty Americans*. Harcourt, Brace, 1922.
Steinberg, Neil. *Hatless Jack: The President, the Fedora, and the History of an American Style*. Plume, 2004.
Stoneback, H. R. *Reading Hemingway's The Sun Also Rises*. Kent State UP, 2007.

"Straw Hat Orgy Bares Heads from Battery to Bronx." *New York Tribune*, 16 September 1922, chroniclingamerica.loc.gov/Icon/sn83030214/1922-09-16/ed-1/seq-3.

"Straw Hat Prank Has Fatal Ending." *New York Times*, 14 Sept. 1924, p. 28, proquest.com/hnpnewyorktimes/docview/103326681/C19F9644508042E7F.

"Straw Hat Riots Embroil East Side." *New York Times*. 14 Sept. 1922, proquest.com/hupnewyorktimes/docview/99394433/C2DC2AEE3552447EF.

"Straw Hat's Rigid Conventions." *New York Times Magazine*, 21 June 1925.

UHP Staff. "History of the Worker's Cap." *The Ultimate History Project*. ultimatehistoryproject.com/making-a-statement.

Whitman, Walt. "Crossing Brooklyn Ferry." *Walt Whitman Poetry and Prose*. Library of America College Editions, 1996, pp. 307–13.

———. "Song of Myself." *Walt Whitman Poetry and Prose*. Library of America College Editions, 1996, pp. 188–247.

Wicke, Jennifer. *Advertising Fictions: Literature, Advertisement, & Social Reading*. Columbia UP, 1988.

Wilson, Sloan. *The Man in the Gray Flannel Suit*. Simon and Schuster, 1955.

"The Window in May." *American Hatter*, May 1910, pp. 57–58.

Withington, Robert. "Hat-Wearing Customs in the United States." *Notes and Queries*, 2 April 1927, pp. 247–48.

5

BETWEEN A NOVELIST AND A CHRONICLER

John Dos Passos in *Manhattan Transfer*

Lauro Iglesias Quadrado

John Dos Passos was never a writer to escape his times. Always opinionated in public life, he wrote books featuring a wide-ranging documentary impulse. He came to embody the "man-of-the-world attitude," present in assorted fronts and causes; he was frequently involved in major social and political events of a given time, traveling to witness things *in loco*, involved in protests and public discussions. He wanted, as he described in his own words, to "get firsthand knowledge" of things (*Best Times* 165). He was never afraid of participating in, reflecting on, and writing about what was happening in the world around him, and his approach to novel writing bordered on nonfictional reportage.

In his fiction, Dos Passos sketches a wide variety of characters, thus stimulating readers and critics to take part in a challenging exercise of categorization of his novels within literary systems. Investigations into the work of Dos Passos are likely to be filled with contradiction as an elemental feature of the writer himself as a person and as a writer. His work challenges literary theory and critique, since it is not an easy task to place his writing into a single category; his journalistic-like register of novels adds to the far-from-univocal puzzle of labels and discussions around his oeuvre.

In general, scholars and critics have long considered Dos Passos's elaborate manner of narrating under diversified critical lights. Some of this work relates to the points I explore in this essay. In "Artfulness and Artlessness, the Literary and Political Uses of Impersonality in John Dos Passos's *U.S.A.* Trilogy," for instance, Alice Béja (2011) examines how the disappearance of narrative voices in Dos Passos functions as a way of criticizing American society.[1] Elsewhere, Simon Stevens affirms that the exaggeration of focus on the extra-literary—or the "extra-aesthetic," as he puts it—is "the gift of 'bad' criticism and much 'contemporary comment' to reveal this process more clearly"

(226). Stevens's assertion attacks a type of uncommitted criticism that, he explains, regards Dos Passos's books as political propaganda, as pamphlets that hedge too strongly on partisanship. Stevens therefore argues that Dos Passos's literature should be read not as "contemporary comment," but as works of fiction. Ranging from the "proletarian literature" exposed by Barbara Foley (1993) to the "naturalistic fiction" category under Donald Pizer (1982), Dos Passos remains more commonly recognized as a modernist writer. As a result, the scholarship identifies him as an author well-rounded enough to fit all these categories—even if not completely to fit any one of them.

This essay examines some of Dos Passos's idiosyncrasies in an effort to reconsider his role as a writer of fiction: a novelist or, as he called himself, a "contemporary chronicler." Thus I propose a discussion of theoretical and critical terms that have been applied to Dos Passos's literature, a matter of relevance given that the author has had an oscillating presence in literary scholarship. I will cover some of the critiques of his work—the novel *Manhattan Transfer* (1925), in particular—for my argument centers on Dos Passos's creative choices in the novel that inaugurated plenty of his most recurrent forms of narrative experimentation. I will analyze the work with regard to the notion of a "complex novel," a term coined by Granville Hicks, and under Walter Benjamin's formulation of the terms "storyteller" and "chronicler." As Hicks and Benjamin will serve as the main references for my proposition, I shall investigate how the notions of "chronicler" and "contemporary chronicler" may be actively recognized in Dos Passos's writing through critical close reading of specific scenes in *Manhattan Transfer*. To complement my analysis of Dos Passos's writing *per se* and the innovative style of his audiovisual and collage techniques, I refer to works by Michael North and Tom McEnaney. Both of them contextualize Dos Passos's fiction in a historical era of major change in technical possibilities for mass-communication media and audiovisual experimentation.

READING DOS PASSOS

The different layers of text in *Manhattan Transfer* as a novel entice the reader on various sensory levels: visual, auditory, olfactory. Released in 1925, the book resonates strongly with technical audiovisual novelties of the time. The author ventured into experiments that approximated written literature to visual assemblages, photography, popular music, and editing tricks found in cutting-edge filmmaking. These creative strategies—found not only in *Manhattan Transfer* but also in the *U.S.A* trilogy (1930, 1932, 1936), mainly in the

Newsreel and Camera Eye sections—paralleled techniques and technological innovations being developed at the time, such as cinematic montage and/or radio broadcasts.

The sensuous quality in Dos Passos's writing unfolds in a mixture of genres and registers. His fiction embodies and feeds on kinds of speech found in journalism and advertisement. Readers are introduced to an intricate form of novel writing that presents dozens of characters, many of whom only pop up in short, apparently incomplete scenes. No single protagonist is clearly highlighted, nor is there a main character around whom all fictional events revolve. In *Manhattan Transfer*, what stands out is the city of New York, the unquestionable epicenter of action. "As soon as everything is sufficiently blotted out . . . I shall start knocking together a long dull and arduous novel about New York and go-getters and God knows what besides," said Dos Passos ahead of drafting the novel in the 1920s (qtd. in Ludington 224).

Remarkably idiosyncratic, *Manhattan Transfer* is widely esteemed by critics as Dos Passos's first distinctive work: it presents recognizable traits of his fiction that would endure until the end of his career. It is also a strong manifestation of his satiric approach to literature, a lens that Dos Passos greatly treasured. It was ultimately with the release of *Manhattan Transfer* that the writer became regarded as an experimental modernist, as the book features similar innovations to those being practiced in artistic endeavors since the last years of the nineteenth century.

Around the time the author was writing this book and preparing for its release, he had significant contact with *The New Masses*, a magazine closely linked to leftist and Marxist ideals in the United States. Dos Passos was an intermittent contributor to a number of its editions and a member of the executive board. The author generated a following among critics and essayists, among them Granville Hicks, a literary critic who was one of the editors of *The New Masses* and who identified *Manhattan Transfer* and the *U.S.A.* trilogy as what he called "complex novels." Hicks's ideas are developed and published in the magazine itself, and his thoughts helped broaden the discussion on the works of Dos Passos. Hicks contrasts "complex novels" with "collective novels," the latter being an attempt to treat a collective entity as an individual consciousness. The complex novel, on the other hand, has no single protagonist, collective or individual. Hicks argues that collective novels are at times depictions of an illusory solution of commitment to a particular group all at once working in idealized wholeness. Hicks also articulates how collective novels are deceptive images of traditional novels, those in which the protagonist, usually a single individual, is carefully built and deepened by the narrative:

"[T]he problem of creating credible individuals without destroying the sense of group unity is the great problem of the collective novel" (23). Hicks recognizes that a group is built on individuals from different walks of life and diversified conceptions, and a collective novel reinforces the independence of a certain group as a whole unit, even if resorting to a single individual to capture that group character. In the complex novel, however, "the various characters do not compose a collective entity; they may or may not have a factual relationship, but they do not have the psychological relationship that would entitle them to be called a group" (23).

The way *Manhattan Transfer* organizes and distributes legions of characters in countless scenes and fragments may present a challenge for a more traditional, plot-oriented reader or critic. When the author says in the aforementioned quotation that he wanted to write a book featuring New York and its errant people, he is establishing a scenario for developing individual stories. There is no moment in all of the narratives of specific characters that a certain fictional body is depicted as having the "group mind." *Manhattan Transfer*'s seemingly disconnected characters struggle for readers' attention, and, when their stories do not overlap, their thematic unity is based on what Hicks calls the "magnificent variety of New York" (24). Their factual relationship lies in the sense of diversity presented in the modern metropolis.

It is not surprising that the book, when released in 1925, simultaneously faced critical acclaim and scorn. *Manhattan Transfer* is not only arranged in a variety of literary techniques but also a novel that does not commit to a single ideological agenda. On the one hand, it was applauded for its modern approach: Henry Longan Stuart said that it countered the "older writers" in a manner that fought "that old-fashioned device—a plot," as Dos Passos gave the text "a mechanical impartiality . . . allow[ing] the senses their momentary function" (65). Yet Dos Passos was accused of being too pessimistic and cynical, of lacking a more sympathetic reading of the world. His machinelike narratives were, for some, an automated passionless text: "[H]e has not yet found the faith of Walt Whitman in the American masses," said *New Masses* founding editor, Michael Gold (117).

Oddly enough, when a significant number of critics censured Dos Passos for not being a skilled novelist—or for not being a novelist at all—they voiced how the author himself perceived his own fiction. Decades after publishing *Manhattan Transfer*, Dos Passos claimed that he did not see himself purely as a novelist, but instead as a chronicler: "I've been calling my novels contemporary chronicles, which seems to fit them better" (*Writers at Work* 74). In his attempt to coin a kind of aesthetics of his own and to set his writing apart from other fiction writers, his choice of words, if read carefully, reveals an interesting conflict. Dos Passos acknowledges to some extent that his texts are somewhere between novels and contemporary chronicles; after all, he still refers to his books as novels—"I call my *novels* contemporary chronicles." The author's provocation is appealing—and it allows room for further reflection on the way he organizes his prose.

Walter Benjamin's *The Storyteller* offers a way to understand Dos Passos's remarks, above all when read alongside much of his fiction, and how he assesses his own role as a writer. Benjamin asserts:

> [T]he earliest symptom of a process whose end is the decline of storytelling is the rise of the novel at the beginning of modern times. What distinguishes the novel from the story . . . is its essential dependence on the book. . . . What differentiates the novel from all other forms of prose literature—the fairy tale, the legend, even the novella—is that it neither comes from oral tradition nor goes into it. . . . The novelist has isolated himself. The birthplace of the novel is the solitary individual. (364)

Dos Passos was interested in writing about individuals, not so much in their singularity as distinguished people, but as members of a collective experience, in a constant conflict between objectivity and subjectivity. This approach situates Dos Passos in an unstable position as a novelist: indeed, *Manhattan Transfer* does not focus on single heroes; the novel's "solitary individual," as formulated by Benjamin, is never alone in Dos Passos, for his characters are always immersed in crowds and in the immensity of the city. Personal isolation does not take the shape of a self-imposed exile, for it is otherwise a component of metropolitan life enforced by the urban modern narrative. Characters are never left alone even when they are indoors or at home.

Dos Passos's literature has a documentary style that flirts with both journalism and journalistic satire. Apart from this quasi-nonfictional register, his fiction has a strong display of oral tradition, manifesting especially in the transliteral registers of characters—"the speech of the people" on the page, as Dos Passos famously puts it in the preface to the *U.S.A.* trilogy (*U.S.A.* 3). He wanted to convey the "speech that clung to the ears" (2). Closeness to vernacular language and reportage are constant features in Dos Passos's writing; according to Benjamin, those would be traits of stories not novels: *Manhattan Transfer* opens up urban twentieth-century oral tradition into writing, along with a decentralized experience of individuality. In this manner, John Dos

Passos is a name on the list of writers who, according to Hicks, "are intensely conscious of the instability and artificiality of formal social relationships . . . [T]hey wish to do justice to more than one aspect of experience" (24). Thus a consistent deviation from the traditional novel takes shape precisely in the way that "the complex novel permits a writer to make use of his knowledge of bourgeois life without restricting him to that life" (25). In this case, the image of the novelist as the solitary individual as drawn by Benjamin is dramatically challenged. Dos Passos is the embodiment of the "complex novelist," the bourgeois individual who is an avid traveler, a man of the world constantly in search of action and major events and public discussions.

Dos Passos's characters display little of their subjectivities as they are diluted in communal social environments. In a complex novel such as *Manhattan Transfer* they adhere to the general framework delineated by Benjamin, even reaching a point at which Dos Passos can be considered, following the German thinker's terms, a "history-teller" instead of a storyteller. Benjamin connects history-telling to chronicling and, in doing so, exercises a comparison similar to the one Dos Passos makes between the novelist and the chronicler. "In the broad spectrum of the chronicle," Benjamin explains, "the ways in which a story can be told are graduated like shadings of one and the same color. The chronicler is the history-teller" (370).

Manhattan Transfer's innumerable characters share spaces and circumstances with one another in a confusing urban scenario. Considering that universe, John Dos Passos himself revealed how he sensed characters' expectations in his introduction to one edition of the book: the author writes that characters are all asking the same "unspoken question . . . : what shall I do to become a whole man?" ("Special Collections"). This common motivation for most characters in the novel favors a movement where the book once again borders on the realm of more conventional perceptions of the novel. If the search for spiritual and emotional "wholeness" can be comfortably taken as a motif for twentieth-century Existentialist novels—Jean-Paul Sartre remarkably regarded Dos Passos as "the greatest writer of [their] time" (175)—it can also work for more traditional approaches to novel writing. Looking for "completeness" is a common motif in kindred subgenres of novels such as the *Bildungsroman* and the *Künstlerroman*, which both focus on how individuals achieve internal discovery in their own journeys. So here we return to the novelist side of Dos Passos.

Nevertheless, we should still consider the writer's assertion of himself as a contemporary chronicler as a guideline for deepening this discussion. His constant practice of refraining from establishing clear-cut limits between fiction and nonfiction meets a strong parallel in the following formulation by Benjamin, who comments on the larger-than-life quality of a chronicler's tale:

> The historian is bound to explain in one way or another the happenings with which he deals; under no circumstances can he content himself with displaying them as models of the course of the world. But this is precisely what the chronicler does, especially in his classical representatives, the chroniclers of the Middle Ages, the precursors of the historians of today. By basing their historical tales on a divine plan of salvation—an inscrutable one—they have from the very start lifted the burden of demonstrable explanation from their own shoulders. Its place is taken by interpretation, which is not concerned with an accurate concatenation of definite events, but with the way these are embedded in the great inscrutable course of the world. (370)

Here—and in the whole of *The Storyteller*—Benjamin differentiates between schools of narratives. Dos Passos's writing lies in the middle of a challenging gap, as what is referred to as storytelling and history-telling, taking Benjamin's terms, are frequently intertwined under his pen. Dos Passos is aptly described by English writer and editor Robert McCrum (2014) as "[a] novelist with the instincts of a journalist, and a fictional reporter with the insight of a storyteller." Dos Passos's work demonstrates how boundaries of fiction and nonfiction can be confronted with the very foundation the genres share: narrative.

In *Manhattan Transfer*, characters are usually depicted straightforwardly, their deeds connected as if chained one to the other, leaving no room for longer annotations on thoughts and feelings in narration itself; these are only conveyed through characters' dialogues. Their fictional lives are narrated as if they were stories in the daily newspaper, in a factual and aloof language. This quality evokes an anecdote by Jean-Paul Sartre in which he has an epiphany when he reads about Charlie Chaplin's retirement on the news: the informational tone of the article reminds him of Dos Passos's language. The American writer's approach to literature is derivative of blunt news language; Sartre realizes: "Dos Passos reports all his characters' utterances to us in the style of a statement to the Press. Their words are cut off from thought, and [they] become pure utterances, simple reactions that must be registered as such, in the behaviorist style" (172). If Dos Passos's fictional people are commonly attacked for being unlike humans and more like robots, it is because they represent a reflection of what "comes from afar," as Sartre puts it (172). These automaton-like beings represent seemingly immutable conditions in the established social structures, which manifest in the firmly tied fabric of the text. Unlike the medieval chroniclers mentioned by Benjamin, who rely on revelations or plans of salvation in an attempt to explain the inscrutable in social life, Dos Passos's contemporary chronicle is a blunt register of the "inscrutable course of the world" as based on mechanical reproduction, relating both to machines and interpersonal relations. In an interesting choice of words, when Dos Passos affirms that his chronicles are *contemporary*, he is highlighting that, in a twentieth-century scenario, the medieval illusion of salvation got lost in history.

An avid traveler and observer, Dos Passos presumably had a constitutional craving for the taxonomy of sociopolitical engineering. The international, itinerant experience made him aware of different lifestyles. The same experience was responsible for exposing him to different government and economic models. Such exposure seemed to have been conclusive in the reiterated nomadic component of his fragmentary characters. If considered a distant observer with an acute sense for perception and difference in organizational systems, the writer still had the heart to scrutinize human beings' behaviors, agonies, and passions. In his words:

> As the correspondent for a labor paper I wasn't much of a success. Though I was thoroughly interested in syndicalism and socialism and trade union matters, I was continually distracted by scenery and painting and architecture and the *canto hondo* and the grave rhythms of flamenco dancing. And the people, the people, the infinitely tragical, comical, pathetic and laughable varieties of people. (*Best Times* 81)

As if taking his cue from these remarks, Benjamin concludes *The Storyteller* by highlighting once more how storytellers—or novelists, following traditional literary critique nomenclature—are committed to the search of human values and of greater self-comprehension. He writes that "the storyteller [is] the man who could let the wick of his life be consumed completely by the gentle flame of his story. . . . The storyteller is the figure in which the righteous man encounters himself" (378). This passage takes us back to *Manhattan Transfer*'s characters and their quests for wholeness amid the "tragical, comical, pathetic and laughable" aspects of living. Economic and social misery play a vital role in fueling these fictional bodies' intensity and despair toward life. And those who can only perceive Dos Passos's creations as automatons—as some of his most severe critics do—are missing the essence of the author's treatment of language, as he satirizes the speeches of journalism and makes the "righteous man encounter himself" through escape.

As British writer D. H. Lawrence maintained, "*Manhattan Transfer* is still a greater ravel of flights from nowhere to nowhere. But, at least, the author knows it" (75). The image Lawrence creates is enticing: he might be talking about actual flights, possibly journeys taken by airplanes that would have neither a clear departure point nor a specific destination; another possible reading is that of a complicated tangle of stairs, flights of stairs that share the same space, as in the case of an apartment complex or in street alleys. Either way, the provocation is resolved, in the sense that Dos Passos is a conscious pilot or architect, and the simultaneity of apparently disconnected information is one the characteristics of his literary brand. Dos Passos nullifies potential tragic significance by denying clear climaxes and remarkable plot twists. Such reading of the apparent lack of passionate zeal with the novel's plot matches with what Michael Gold wrote about it: "[T]he result is not tragedy, which may be clean and great, but bewilderment, which is smaller" (74). Frustration seems to be evidently connected to fictional events in the book, as idealism winds up a dead-end street.

French *nouveau roman* writer Nathalie Sarraute critically affirms that relying on sensuous layers of literary perception rather than traditional plot-driven structures can be a powerful engine for literature. She makes claims for an anti-climactic literary craft. Sarraute borrows the term "tropism" from biology as she relates to the "interior movement that [she] wanted to show" ("Art of Fiction") in characters toward their surroundings, in the same way a plant responds to stimuli in the environment through a physical reaction. Sarraute's tropism is a way to assess Dos Passos's language and what is explicitly and implicitly uttered. Clear-cut dialogues and thorough descriptions are not the only resources in literary texts: the whole person has a more demanding sensorium.

Dos Passos denies a defined ending for *Manhattan Transfer* plot-wise. Instead, he relies once more on characters' sensations to communicate meaning and perceptions, exploring the tools that literature has to offer. The author mixes different writing styles, playing with traditional plot resources such as diegetic deaths, but mixing them with run-of-the-mill descriptions, bereft of emotional drama as in a news story. And the looming presence of New York City is amplified in the outcome of the book's narratives. Dos Passos's biographer Townsend Ludington affirms that

> the more he wrote, the more the work became a "collective" novel about the city, where individuals were less the central concern than the city itself, which overwhelmed and sometimes killed them—as

> it did the vagabond Bud Korpenning and the playboy Stan Emery—sometimes turned them into stiff, porcelain figures like Ellen Thatcher, or sometimes drove them out, as Dos Passos had planned from the start it would Jimmy Herf. (229)

Ludington is likely not referring to "collective" in the same way Granville Hicks does, but rather as a composite view of New York City whose inhabitants cannot be placed on a singular ideological trajectory. Nonetheless, these New Yorker characters are similar in their inability to achieve their hearts' lasting desires. The sort of anti-climax expressed by Sarraute—or the "dead-end street" type of scene—is essentially what happens in the very last scene of *Manhattan Transfer*. Jimmy Herf, right after having finally left New York, wanders about the streets of an unnamed place located at the very end of the ferry's route. Dos Passos finds no need to be specific about Herf's whereabouts, and finishes the book pointing the man's fate in the same unknown direction. Narration is able to approximate the character's perception to that of the reader, who can notice that no conclusive plot element is needed to convey what matters for Herf at that diegetic point. It is a classic *Manhattan Transfer* moment: he is lost, does not know where he is heading, but is inwardly satisfied; he encounters himself through escape. The final dialogue makes his moves explicit: "'Say will you give me a lift?' he asks the redhaired man at the wheel. 'How fur ye goin?' 'I dunno . . . Pretty far'" (404).

The novel's title is to be considered as well, for it makes a clear reference to the action of trains in the city and the way this action is connected with the stories collected in the book. "Manhattan transfer" is the line uttered by officials in the train station to warn passengers they have reached a point where they have to leave their own train, only to hop on another one to get to or away from Manhattan. It is a situation of a constant state of movement, a constant change of destinations: "They had to change at Manhattan Transfer. . . . The wheels rumbled on [their] head, saying Man-hattan Tran-sfer. Man-hattan Tran-sfer" (116–17). Stations—the ferry station, the train station, the bus station—have always served metaphorically as tangible representations for states of transition or transience. What makes Dos Passos extend a well-known device in literature is the focus on the journey itself, made even more intense and fleeting inasmuch as it relates to a specific state between two displacements, declared in the echoing sound of the informative sentence. Such a fusion of signifiers perfectly suits a few of the literary aspects that make *Manhattan Transfer* so peculiarly appealing: feeble characters, fractional plots, variable language.

The conceptualization behind the novel's title continues in its first section, whose initial chapter is "Ferryslip." Besides being the first display of Dos Passos's clear hate for apostrophes and hyphens—and love for made-up compound words—the name focuses on the very material structure that receives the ferry. It corresponds to the idea of the title of the book itself, as it references both the place for transit and the act of moving. The ferry slip is the threshold for the immigrant characters to enter New York; it is a name that also attracts attention to the fabric of the city, its skyline and natural landscape, and first sensory contacts; it is a facility that is responsible for receiving both these fictional people and readers alike. "Ferryslip" sets the tone of the opening section of the book with its clear focus on machinery and systems of industrial production; following chapters are appropriately named "Metropolis," "Dollars," "Tracks," and "Steamroller": masses of people, lack of (and need for) money, transport, and hard mechanical-industrial work.

The table of contents foresees familiar, collective stories in the life of international workers. "Ferry" and "metropolis" are both words that invoke images of crowds. Before them, the book's epigraph paints a large picture: an urban snapshot with spoiled food and jingling sounds along with a group of people, a crowd of undistinguishable faces, that makes up a swarm of immigrants squeezed into the ferry station. Following this epigraphic scene—which could have easily been translated into a Sergei Eisenstein movie—the novel opens with a character being born. It is an unnamed baby, another recurrent symbol of attempting universality in fiction. In typical Dos Passos fashion, narration takes allegory to a level of satire as the story of the toddler unfolds into uncertainty for the parents: "'How can you tell them apart nurse?' 'Sometimes we cant'" (7). The agony of not knowing who the actual child is is emblematic of the lack of interest of institutions in the lives of regular citizens. As the author tends to mock formal coalitions in search of power and control—above all, governmental institutions such as the army or parties that sustain the partisan political system—it comes as another blow to civilization's alleged organization.

Dos Passos would resort to similar kinds of structure and satirical scenes, which permeate other narrated scenes both in this novel and throughout other pieces of his long literary career. He claimed for himself "the cultivated pose of sidewalk proletarian" (*Best Times* 146), a title indicating both his elite education and his lack of attachment to a specific social cause. Paradoxically, his cultivated attitude, to some extent a counterfeit, at the same time provoked in him an outlet for disputing institutional violence and displays of power against masses and personal liberties. Dos Passos's satirical demeanor and language manifested the author's constant battle for individual freedom of thought and action. As Townsend Ludington explains, he "clung to satire and to a style that went at characters from the outside rather than treating them in depth. . . . It was not that Dos Passos characterized incompletely. Rather his intention was to define by actions and surfaces, not to present psychological studies . . . [he chose] that abstraction called society as the focus of his fiction" (64).

A TWENTIETH-CENTURY OUTLOOK

John Dos Passos has remained a modernist writer in the eyes of the general public, mostly familiar with his best-known novels. However, his constant change of attitudes and opinions about all sorts of subjects, world facts, and political positions has puzzled part of his readership. If anything, he had a life and a career that symbolized the turmoil of changes in major facts of the early and mid-twentieth century, and both his fiction and nonfiction stand as testaments to the dynamics of those decades.[2] The author used a number of facts and references that spoke directly to the readers of his time. Some instances will be analyzed here in an effort to both understand and challenge reception and criticism of Dos Passos. To this end, the above-mentioned notions of contemporary chronicles and complex novels come as suitable concepts.

The pretexts for and implications of World War I offer pertinent ways to begin this discussion. At the time of the war's outbreak in 1914, the United States was receiving immigrants from opposing sides of the conflict and had to manage many inner disagreements when it came to effectively acting on the battlegrounds in Europe. The social consequences of World War I unfold through a number of motifs in Dos Passos's fiction. The Great War provides, for instance, the background story for the second novel of the *U.S.A.* trilogy, *1919*, a volume almost entirely revolving around the absurdity of societies and their indifference toward the horrors of war. Likewise, his early works reveal the violent, destructive side of the conflict, as made explicit in *One Man's Initiation: 1917* (1920) and *Three Soldiers* (1921). Besides that, the conflicts of World War I were a stage for technological innovations and new mechanical possibilities.

In *Manhattan Transfer*, a noteworthy example of the imminent presence of war in the novel is a rowdy scene in which George Baldwin, a lawyer in search of big money, is having an argument with his wife Cecily at the breakfast table. The newspaper—*The New York Times*—initially appears as a stone-cold physical obstacle between the couple. Annoyed by George's indifferent silence, Cecily destroys the piece of paper that stands in the way of their problems, and the couple starts arguing. Soon after the beginning of the quarrel, their housekeeper comes with a tray of bacon and eggs, and they feel compelled to stop talking, pausing their altercation: "They sat silent looking at each other." Cecily begins to cry, as George "[sits] staring at the headlines in the paper. ASSASSINATION OF ARCHDUKE WILL HAVE GRAVE CONSEQUENCES. AUSTRIAN ARMY MOBILIZED" (183). There is a speechless war going on between these characters, and the narrative makes that explicit in clearly alluding to the 1914 Sarajevo assassination that gave World War I its kick-start.

Dos Passos brings attention to the social role of newspapers throughout the whole novel. Narration periodically displays a collage of news as a striking visual presence, as the text inserted in the novel has different font types and sizes (as in the example above, when the headlines are all in capital letters) on a single page, even when their contents are not explicitly connected with each other. Journalism expands beyond the medieval concept of chronicling, as it has been described by Walter Benjamin. The twentieth-century approach to spreading and documenting current facts opposes the medieval way in a central aspect: there is no spiritual search. Dos Passos, in his attempt to associate his literature with chronicles, recovers the unfathomable factor that is present in any narrative, fictional or not. Narrative is mediated by the popular written registers of a time, in this case by the massive presence of news journalism. Thus, the relevance of journalistic speech, in the shape of news stories or in satires of journalism's particular kind of language, complement the chronicling aspect in Dos Passos's novel writing.

The author himself perceived, reporter-like, that a thematic unity could hold together a fictional narrative that expands from world events to the individual realm. Sonia Tercero, film director and producer who made the documentary *Robles: Duelo al Sol* (2015), affirms that, for Dos Passos, "what mattered was how big events in the history of the world affected individuals, the people. That was what he loved to scrutinize and experiment with, what he liked to write about" ("Entrevista"; my trans.). Her impression comes very close to Granville Hicks's idea of the complex novel, as it stands for the recognition of Dos Passos's unique ability to deal with individuality amid a greater collective event. The author's special care for the masses makes his approach to characters distinct from that of either the traditional novel, which usually focuses on a certain individual, or of the historical novel, which aims to reconstruct a certain epoch that is often far removed from the reader's present time. In his contemporary chronicle, he is documenting the life and speech of present-day people.

That is the case of *Manhattan Transfer*'s innumerable immigrant characters. They hold characteristics in common, as they are working-class people facing xenophobia, poverty, or unemployment; when working, they suffer from small pay and tyrannical bosses. In his memoir, Dos Passos comments on excruciating instances of xenophobia and intolerance in the United States during the 1920s, when immigration was at its peak:

> In college and out I had personally felt the frustrations that came from being considered a wop or a guinea or a greaser. It is hard to explain to people who never lived through the early twenties the violence of the revulsion against foreigners and radicals that went through the United States after the first world war. . . . The spring of 1920 saw the height of the delirium of arrests and deportations of alleged radicals instigated by Woodrow Wilson's Attorney General. (*Best Times* 166–67)

Dos Passos's sympathy for and—to some extent—identification with immigrant life in the United States is evidenced and documented in *Manhattan Transfer*. Adding to that scenario, minority immigrant groups were, in the early twentieth century, involved in embryonic versions of entertainment industries—such businesses were then considered immoral or degenerate by dominant classes, which did not want to have their names connected with filmmaking or vaudeville shows. As is perceptible throughout the novel, popular culture is a constant element of the mosaic of stories of *Manhattan Transfer*, in references to the growing popularity of American movies and musical revues (these were early manifestations and incipient displays of massive phenomena such as Hollywood and Broadway musicals as we know them nowadays).

Different plots of *Manhattan Transfer* explore the world of theater in multiple layers. Characters and narrative references reveal Dos Passos's repertoire of theatrical experiences, both in his personal and direct interest in theater as a playwright and stage director, and on Ellen Thatcher as one of his fictional creatures, a performer involved in musical revues, as a central character in the novel. In a 2016 article, Alix Beeston draws attention to the American theatrical creation—including vaudeville shows and musical revues—in the 1920s, which reached its historical peak in number of productions (640). The universe of *Manhattan Transfer* straightforwardly absorbs the dilemmas, social conundrums, and mechanical aspects of the world of spectacles on the stages of New York City. If cinema was surely a popular interest of the time, it was always paralleled and even surpassed by theatrical shows: "[T]he uneven development of the cinema in the early twentieth century in the United States was intimately caught up with the theater, with which it shared its exhibition context and, to some extent, its segmented arrangement" (Beeston 640).[3]

The intersection of creative choices and contexts of diverse technologies and art forms constitute Dos Passos's project for his literature, something that Beeston, when referring to modernism, calls "socialized and technologized mechanisms of writing" (638). Dos Passos experimented with changes in the cycle of production and reception of cultural objects and spectacles, experimentations that distanced him and his contemporaries from nineteenth-century writers (who did not have the opportunity of living under the significant change in the audiovisual markets as it happened at the turn of the century). Béja refers to that as a "peculiar blending of artfulness and artlessness," a challenge to the "illusions of objectivity" (40), which is based on the incorporation of the most varied stories and techniques—in cinema, in theater, in music, in recording technologies—that were taking shape in the 1920s.

Michael North, in his book *Camera Works*, is another scholar who hears the echoes of early twentieth-century technical and technological features in the modernist experimentation of Dos Passos. North focuses on the exploration of the altering visual culture of the time, which involved observations made by the novelist about the increase in the number of shop windows, cinemas, and modernist art shows, all of them elements "that extended and provoked a visual appetite that had barely existed at the turn of the century" (141). North imagines the characters of *U.S.A.* as moviegoers—an analogy I am applying to *Manhattan Transfer*. The symbolism is strong, given the outline of Dos Passos's characters and their behavior; according to him, "the conditions of moviegoing already prevent individuals from seeing one another or conversing. The contradictory and yet necessary relationship between loneliness and conformity is thus cemented more firmly into place by visual habits that the camera has made pervasive" (North 152–53). If in fact the experience in a movie theater may be alienating or individualized, it is at the same time a shared experience: a room hosts a crowd that barely communicates with each other verbally—audible conversation is actually discouraged—up until the end of the movie. It is not hard to imagine or remember our experiences as moviegoers and the kind of comments, gestures, or tame reactions we tend to make when watching a film along with hundreds of strangers. Ultimately, if we follow North's image, we can perceive the relationship and dialogues between characters in Dos Passos as those which take place in a screening room: simultaneous, incomplete, fractured.

It is tempting but also risky to say that the very position adopted by the narrators in Dos Passos is analogous to that of a person holding a camera. The well-known "camera-eye narrator"—which would be literally sponsored by its writer in *U.S.A.*—is a piece of a world seen through the eye of a lens. In the narratives of *Manhattan Transfer*, the social life portrayed in the novel has a dynamic that indeed feels as if mediated by a technical device. Pizer refers to Dos Passos's brand of fiction as "panoramic social novel[s]" (40), another reference to camera movements or photographic shots: the panorama as a composite form; a camera, photographic or filmic, needs an operator to command it, and its limitations and possibilities of range and framing are features of Dos Passos's writing. Nevertheless, he was not an eyecentric writer, and the consideration for the visual side is one more aspect to compose his holistic approach to human sensorium. To quote North, "there is something structurally isolating in eyesight itself, something that the camera exaggerates by separating the other senses from the visual, physical presence from the act of seeing, and one moment in time from every other"[4 (146).]

If Dos Passos handles the limitations of certain media and of eyecentrism, he is also aware of the confines of the written word. The potentialities of words on the printed page are nevertheless an area treasured by the writer's maneuvers. His prose is reliable on *effect* to two ends: both in the creative process, as an attempt to recreate a reflection of life; and on readers' reactions. North is once more of relevance in this analysis: "Dos Passos is not as interested in representing the appearance of the visual, a rather difficult matter for a book in any case, as he is in representing the effects of it on social life" (144).

Acknowledgment of the technical side of Dos Passos's fiction easily expands from the visual, especially when we consider the possibilities of effects of simultaneity in literature that sound provides. Before all else, *Manhattan Transfer* was written in an era of aural excitement. Experiences with sound changed in an unheard-of way on a daily basis. Music played on phonograph records, urban noise, and the sound of various languages provided by unprecedented waves of immigrants who kept coming to the United States were, among others, all elements in this sonic blend. At the time when the novel was being conceived and published, the general response to new sonic possibilities was one of awe and incomprehension. "Chaotic" was a label instantly applied to this new experience, one of instability and lack of perception: "[Dos Passos] was interested in rendering the staccato rhythms of the city and also, through words, in conveying the visual images that were part of its chaotic life" (Ludington 202). Correlations between machinery and sonic agitation have led to spirited experimentations in artistic creation, especially since the dawn of modernist days. Dos Passos, by transliterating the speech of immigrants and working-class people (here, their speech is taken as sonic material, as "noise" to ears that do not recognize the semantics of words spoken in a foreign language or accent), was able to assemble the sonic panorama of social life in New York in the first decades of the 1900s. The author recognizes the potential of music-recording and music-playing devices and explores the emerging music market as a literary tool. He capably assembles, in fiction, one of Theodor Adorno's most notable aphorisms: "[T]he downtrodden gramophone horns reassert themselves as proletarian loudspeakers" (52). If Dos Passos's characters stand for sonic material, narrative in general stands for a recording phonograph (Adorno's gramophone); his books' everyday registers are paralleled to daily chronicles, documents of wider approach, of general public life and domain.

"Writers . . . used sound to ask big questions about their cultural moments and the crises and problems of their time," announces sound scholar Jonathan Sterne (3). If the appeal of narrators holding cameras, or characters as moviegoers who dwell in society may be visual, author Tom McEnaney's provides the hearing counterparts to the sensorial analysis of Dos Passos. In *Acoustic Properties*, McEnaney observes the importance of sound (not only) in literature, of the radio as a medium, and of radio networks as multi-territorial entities. The scholar appreciates the wide social penetration of radio transmissions as a characteristic phenomenon of early twentieth century, mostly commenting on the simultaneity of content, as audiences would be exposed to genres as varied as popular songs, hard news, *radionovelas*, and weather forecasts. "For just as audio engineers developed new ways to record, edit, and transmit sound, writers—often learning from those very engineers—developed techniques to work with sound according to the specificity of their medium" (McEnaney 5).

These techniques are reflected in Dos Passos's fiction as he frames registers of modern sound that can be as varied as music, urban noise, or different languages. Eisenstein once wrote that "the modern urban scene, especially that of a large city at night, is clearly the plastic equivalent of jazz" (98). I take that as a rich audiovisual approach that contemplates the Dos Passos reading experience in many of its remarkable features: urban life in a big city, visual experimentation, music represented by jazz, the musical genre of simultaneity. The representation in writing of this experience has earmarks of a radio broadcast, or a radio network. What I propose next is to analyze examples, via close reading, of scenes in *Manhattan Transfer* that display this intermedial connection in a complex novel.

One episode with characters Ruth Prynne and Jimmy Herf offers a good example of how narration moves diegetically along with acoustics, representing a chronicling quality. Jimmy comes to the pension where Ruth lives and invites her out. Amid plenty of interference from other characters, they leave the tenement building and start a faulty conversation as "an Elevated train shattered the barred sunlight overhead. He could see Ruth's mouth forming words. 'Look,' he shouted above the diminishing clatter. 'Let's go have brunch at the Campus and then go for a walk on the Palisades'" (134). Jimmy can see that Ruth is trying to say something, but only by looking at her; he cannot apprehend anything due to the dominating acoustic presence of the train. The characters keep walking, attempting to establish a meaningful and logical conversation, only to be disrupted repeatedly by the sound of trains. The text keeps giving hints of that, with fragmented narratives and frequent appearances of incomplete sentences clearly cut from a longer utterance. They seek refuge in an indoor place, presumably with different acoustics: "'Jimmy you shock me . . . She keeps losing her false teeth, began Ruth; an L train drowned out the rest. The restaurant door closing behind them choked off the roar of wheels on rails" (135). Narration of their lines uses ellipses as surrounding sound goes up and down. The moment they walk in the restaurant and escape the street noise they are welcomed by "an orchestra playing *When It's Appleblossom Time in Normandee*" (135), a well-known song of the early twentieth century composed by Mellor Giffore and Trevor (see Giffore et al.). Using popular music and surrounding metropolitan sounds, the narration sets the soundtrack for the scene and highlights the presence of the singular acoustic experience at the time Dos Passos was writing. This sonic panorama, at most times incomprehensible, can be read in the novel as the modernist analogue to medieval chronicles. Popular music is also a relevant element when reading Dos Passos's work as a complex novel, for the reception of music embodies the relation of individuals to the society around them. The experience of listening to music in a group is simultaneously individual and collective, and the mechanical reproduction of records multiplied this possibility, with direct cultural consequences.

In the universe of *Manhattan Transfer*, this new auditory experience is exemplified by the case of Madame Rigaud and Emile, two French characters who use music to communicate symbolically. According to Mark Greif, songs can elaborate on "things that are inarticulable in social speech because they are too delicate or ideologically out of step, and things that should not be articulated because they are selfish, thoughtless, destructive, and stupid" (29). The two immigrant characters use American songs to convey their implicit and inarticulate desire to belong to a new setting. The music they learn is a strategy used by the narration to enhance the construction of characters, providing them with new layers of social and subjective meaning and complexity. Readers experience Rigaud proudly uttering to her lover and eventual husband, Emile: "I've learned a new American song . . . C'est chic vous savez" (59). In singing, comprehending, and ultimately enjoying the music that is being produced now in America, the French couple reveals their ambition for prestige and wealth. It is not a coincidence that Rigaud's performance of an American song is what ultimately ties her to Emile; it makes these two foreign people who, so far, had felt lost in New York, able to finally start a new life. There is a representative expansion of repertoire, a symbolic trade: from chanson to jazz, from cabarets to speakeasies, from France to the United States.

In the words of McEnaney, "Dos Passos pursues a narrative mode whose simultaneous interiority and exteriority transforms personal experience into collective experience without attending to the pluralism within that collective"[5] (50). The peculiar sense of collectiveness in *Manhattan Transfer* and in the complex novel is, according to Hicks, "not only communicated to the readers as an objective fact; it is also shown as a psychological reality for the members of the group" (23). If Rigaud and Emile are examples of foreign characters who are mentally trying to adhere to the New World experience, characters Mrs. Cohen and Anna Cohen provide another perspective on Dos Passos's chronicling of immigration. The Cohens are mother and daughter in a Jewish immigrant family, and the two are often depicted having intense arguments about money problems and social posture. Having talked back to her mother "like a goy," as Mrs. Cohen says, Anna is finally expelled from the house (356). Leading up to that expulsion, Anna complains that her mother cannot countenance a girl working independently, making her own money, and not being subordinate to a man. Anna is experiencing a professional life in New York, and it is the disruption of tradition caused by the capital of modernity that causes the reluctant cry of the Jewish mother, expressed in the following scene: "[F]rom the kitchen came the old woman's fierce monotonous sobbing" (356). The sobbing of the mother is a direct opponent to the "goy language" of the daughter; here, we find a clear confrontation with established traditions. Once more, Hicks's evaluation of complex novels is applicable to *Manhattan Transfer* and Dos Passos: "[A]uthors are intensely conscious of the instability and artificiality of formal social relationships, and they wish to do justice to more than one aspect of experience" (24). And, once again, Walter Benjamin's history-teller, the one that relies on oral language, manifests in Dos Passos, as the altercation between mother and daughter is narrated through their distinctive verbal descriptions—the new is literally speaking against the traditional.

FINAL WORDS

Theoretical and critical discussion around John Dos Passos's *Manhattan Transfer* benefits from the applied reading of the literary theory developed by Granville Hicks and Walter Benjamin. In "The Revolution and the Novel," Hicks's ideas of varied psychological realities and plurality of aspects of existence in complex novels are analogous and complementary to medieval chroniclers' practices described by Benjamin in *The Storyteller*. Dos Passos manifests these formulations in his work, for his main concerns are not just the solitary characters—or, for that matter, the lonely novelist. When reading Dos Passos, the reader is introduced to collective scenarios supporting his position as a "contemporary chronicler." The author, however, explores those scenarios with subjective issues as core questions, once again moving closer to a position of novelist and to the realm of the novel, as the search for the understanding of human wholeness and growth has been constant in this literary genre.

This essay also values Dos Passos's intermedial work with language, considering the multiple and cutting-edge technologies of the 1920s that were assimilated into his fiction. This mosaic of elements and rich intertextual relations, along with different conceptual categorizations created and supported by critics, are proof of the plurality of techniques, themes, and resourcefulness in Dos Passos's oeuvre. Moreover, the findings in this essay indicate a route for new assessments of his fiction.

NOTES

1. Béja focuses on the analysis of narrative and its political implications, via the apparent impersonal trait given by the author to his characters. According to her, impersonality provides a way out from such dichotomies as sophistication versus naiveté, or literature and politics, implicitly built in the opposition between modernism and radicalism.
2. John Dos Passos fluctuated between extremes of the political spectrum and published his views on diverse public debates on a regular basis. His shift from leftist radical to right-wing conservative—from the defense of Sacco and Vanzetti to the defense of McCarthyism—is expressed especially in his nonfictional work. Dos Passos's life story is accurately exemplified by Townsend Ludington's subtitle to the writer's biography: "a twentieth-century odyssey." On a similar note, Granville

Hicks affirms that "no American novelist has written more directly about change, the great social changes, the characteristic and revolutionary changes of the twentieth century, than Dos Passos. He has been student and reporter and often poet of change" ("Politics of Dos Passos" 85).

3. Beeston challenges the historically traditional critique on Dos Passos, which frequently analyzes his prose as an extension of cinematic montage. Beeston proposes that *Manhattan Transfer* is, in its transmedial approach, closer to a theatrical novel than it is to a film-like narrative. Beeston sees Dos Passos as one of the exponents of high modernism in literature, and the scrutiny given to chorus girls in *Manhattan Transfer*—and other show women in *U.S.A.*—is a symptom of how "revues contributed to the redefinition of spectatorial entertainment in modernism" (642).
4. British filmmaker Peter Greenaway—well known for his use of painting-like colors in the palette of his movies—is vocal on the artificiality of screening rooms: "[T]he screen in my film is divided and is subdivided into squares. And that is just the beginning. It is ridiculous to expect the audience to sit there for two hours looking straight ahead. Life is everywhere, above, below, in front, behind . . . cinema is just in front. We need to create cubist cinema where the screen is everywhere" (Bogani 3). The attempts to develop an intermedial conversation in his cinematic work are remindful of those of Dos Passos in literature.
5. McEnaney and Foley are two scholars who criticize the lack of sympathy or even consciousness about racial and ethnic differences in the works of Dos Passos. The shallow sketches of non-whites in his books are other elements to challenge any notion of complete universality that a few critics intend to apply to the novelist's catalog.

WORKS CITED

Adorno, Theodor W. "The Curves of the Needle." Translated by Thomas Y. Levin, *October*, vol. 55, Winter 1990, pp. 48–55.

Beeston, Alix. "A 'Leg Show Dance' in a Skyscraper: The Sequenced Mechanics of John Dos Passos's *Manhattan Transfer*." *PMLA*, vol. 131, no. 3, May 2016, pp. 636–51.

Béja, Alice. "Artfulness and Artlessness, the Literary and Political Uses of Impersonality in John Dos Passos's *U.S.A.* Trilogy." *Revue Française d'Études Americaines*, vol. 1, no. 127, 2011, pp. 34–46.

Benjamin, Walter. "The Storyteller: Reflections on the Works of Nikolai Leskov," translated by Harry Zohn. *The Novel: An Anthology of Criticism and Theory 1900–2000*, edited by Dorothy J. Hale, Blackwell Publishing, 2006, pp. 361–78.

Bogani, Giovanni. "Peter Greenaway—Director: Towards Cubist Cinema." *Cineuropa*, 24 May 2003, https://cineuropa.org/en/interview/30444/.

Dos Passos, John. "John Dos Passos." Interview by David Sanders. *Writers at Work: The Paris Review Interviews Writers*, edited by George Plimpton, introduced by Wilfrid Sheed, Penguin Books, 1977, pp. 67-89.

———. *Manhattan Transfer*. Houghton Mifflin, 1925.

———. "Manhattan Transfer—Manuscript Draft of 'Introduction' Text to Portuguese Translation." *Papers of John Dos Passos 1865–1998*. Special Collections, University of Virginia Library, 1960.

———. *U.S.A.* 1938. The Library of America, 1996.

Eisenstein, Sergei. *The Film Sense*. Translated by Jay Leyda, Meridian Books, 1957.

Foley, Barbara. *Radical Representations: Politics and Form in U.S. Proletarian Fiction, 1929–1941*. Duke UP, 1993.

Giffore, Mellor, Trevor. "*When It's Apple Blossom Time in Normandy*." *Library of Congress*, Notated Music, Jerome H. Remick & Co., New York, 1912, www.loc.gov/item/ihas.100006224/.

Gold, Michael. "Review." 1926. *Dos Passos: The Critical Heritage*, edited by Barry Maine, Routledge, 1988, pp. 72–73.

Greif, Mark. "Radiohead, or the Philosophy of Pop." *Radiohead and Philosophy: Fitter Happier More Deductive*, edited by Brandon W. Forbes and George A. Reisch, Open Court, 2009, pp. 15–32.

Hicks, Granville. "The Politics of Dos Passos." *The Antioch Review*, vol. 10, no. 1, Spring 1950, pp. 85–98.

———. "Revolution and the Novel." *The New Masses*, 10 Apr. 1934, pp. 23–25.

Lawrence, D. H. "Review." 1927. *Dos Passos: The Critical Heritage*, edited by Barry Maine, Routledge, 1988, pp. 74–76.

Ludington, Townsend. *John Dos Passos: A Twentieth-Century Odyssey*. Carroll & Graf Publishers, 1998.

McCrum, Robert. "The 100 Best Novels: No 58—*Nineteen Nineteen* by John Dos Passos (1932)." *The Guardian*, 27 Oct. 2014, www.theguardian.com/books/2014/oct/27/100-best-novels-john-dos-passos-nineteen-nineteen-1919-usa-trilogy.

McEnaney, Tom. *Acoustic Properties: Radio, Narratives, and the New Neighborhood of the Americas*. Northwestern UP, 2017.

North, Michael. *Camera Works: Photography and the Twentieth-Century Word*. Oxford UP, 2005.

Pizer, Donald. *Twentieth-Century American Literary Naturalism: An Interpretation*. Southern Illinois UP, 1982.

Sarraute, Nathalie. Interview with Shusha Guppy and Jason Weiss. "Nathalie Sarraute, The Art of Fiction No. 115." *The Paris Review*, Issue 114, Spring 1990, www.theparisreview.org/interviews/2341/the-art-of-fiction-no-115-nathalie-sarraute.

Sartre, Jean-Paul. "John Dos Passos and *1919*." 1938. *Dos Passos: The Critical Heritage*, edited by Barry Maine, Routledge, 1988, pp. 167–74.

Schwartz, Delmore. "John Dos Passos and the Whole Truth." 1938. *Dos Passos: The Critical Heritage*, edited by Barry Maine, Routledge, 1988, pp. 175–90.

Sterne, Jonathan. "Sonic Imaginations." *The Sound Studies Reader*, edited by Jonathan Sterne, Routledge, 2012, pp. 1–17.

Stevens, Simon. "Review: Recovering Dos Passos?" *The Cambridge Quarterly*, vol. 18, no. 2, 1989, pp. 223–26.

Stuart, Henry Longan. "Review." 1925. *Dos Passos: The Critical Heritage*, edited by Barry Maine, Routledge, 1988, pp. 64–66.

Tercero, Sonia. Interview with Gema Castellano. "Entrevista a Sonia Tercero, Directora y Productora del Documental *Robles. Duelo al Sol*." *YouTube*, Informativos .net, 17 Nov. 2015, www.youtube.com/watch?v=47-5JtaoNcs.

6

AVATARS OF THE AMERICAN DREAM

Manhattan Transfer, King Vidor's *The Crowd*, and Modernity

Alberto Lena

Since its publication in 1925, John Dos Passos's *Manhattan Transfer* has been considered one of the most sophisticated literary representations of the emergence of the metropolis as a cultural and economic force that forever changed the relationship between individuals and their most immediate environment. Like Berlin, London, and Paris in the early 1920s, New York became a new and fascinating realm marked by the sudden increase of its population and the quick development of technology and new transport systems. New York became a thriving city, a symbol of modernity with the Brooklyn Bridge, the Grand Central Terminal, the Pennsylvania Station, and the Singer Building. A new language and a different narrative approach were needed to catch the speedy and multifaceted contours of this new city, which Dos Passos grasped by intercutting personal narratives written in a fairly experimental style and furnishing the reader with cinematic descriptions of New York in the early decades of the twentieth century.

In his depiction of the modern city, Dos Passos found inspiration in the Futurist paintings of Umberto Boccioni, the expressionist approach of Georg Grosz, and the machine painting style of Fernand Léger as well as avant-garde photographers such as Alfred Stieglitz and Paul Strand (Suarez 44). Early reviewers identified similarities between the novel's compositional strategies and the camera's ability to cross-cut different locales and actions in order to convey the abrupt jolts of modern life, merging multiple storylines into an overall design and featuring the city of New York as the novel's main character (Brogi 2). Like its Russian literary predecessor, Andrei Bely's *Petersburg* (1913), and through the use of montage and fragmented stories, *Manhattan Transfer* manages to express the color, beauty, and symmetry of the modern city as well as all of its chaos, horror, and loneliness (Fanger 471–73). Dos Passos's mosaic, semidocumentary approach has been compared often to that of Russian directors such as Sergei Eisenstein and Dziga Vertov (Foster 186–87; Suarez 50). Like these Russian cinematographers, Dos Passos employs a piecemeal and semirealistic style to feature the harsh realities of capitalist societies. The style shows with equal force the abrupt emergence of the modern metropolis as a symbol of a new era in American history in which there seemed to be no room for the preponderance of a single narrative. This issue produces new meanings and readings, for as Michael Wood comments on cinematic montage, "[It] is not only the organization of cinematic material, it is the implication of meaning—of a meaning that can be implied, since film, like dreams, have a syntax which functions chiefly by association and accumulation" (223).

Thus, by drawing upon cinematic fragmentation, contrast, and montage, Dos Passos managed to build drama. Employing cinematic technique, *Manhattan Transfer* replaces "all traditional narrative links with montage [. . . and] sets images, characters, and events side by side, leaving the reader to fill the spaces" (Foster 187). For instance, in its first two parts, *Manhattan Transfer* tracks the lives of Ellen Thatcher and Jimmy Herf in early twenty-century America. Part II ends when the World War I erupts, and Ellen and Jimmy are merely friends. Part III begins as Ellen and Jimmy come back to New York from the war. The reader discovers that they are married and have a son. Unlike the plot of a conventional novel, Dos Passos's work avoids not only any direct narration of their struggles and anxieties during the war, but also their prior love affair.

In *Manhattan Transfer*, Dos Passos uses a series of Griffith-like intercutting scenes in order to document a particular historical moment in New York. In many respects, the city—with its pyramid-like office buildings and its crowded streets—is the real character of the novel. Unlike the classic Hollywood narrative, which focuses on an individual or a small group of individuals, with its emphasis on the melodramatic potentialities of the plot, Dos Passos's novel features a polyphony of voices while inter-cutting realistic narratives together—a style that diverged significantly from the trends of American mass culture. A film such as Harold Lloyd's comedy *Speedy* (1928), shot in New York, is a case in point of Hollywood popular culture. *Speedy* shows how an average individual can face the complexity of the city. The plot rests upon the invasion of a villainous railroad company seeking to control the old New York tracks and therefore driving out of business an old horsecar line. Harold Lloyd embodies the Hollywood hero as well as a comic representation of the average man who successfully fights against the railroad company unscrupulously invading the city. Above all, as Phillip Lopate observes, "the film is about modes of transport, and its rhythm is largely distracted by many shots of people rushing via taxi, subway, streetcar, and motorcycle" (*Speedy*). Irrespective of the maelstrom of modern life, the average American as incarnated by Lloyd manages to control the threatening technological New York environment; as in many 1920s comedies, "the traditional social order was never breached" (Sklar 117).

Unlike Harold Lloyd's heroic and comic representation of individual will in *Speedy* (1928), *Manhattan Transfer* presents a brave new world, a city dominated by machines and speed that devour any insight into individual life. Dos Passos's New York is a polyphonic horizon of horror and impotence. By focusing on the concrete reality of everyday life in New York, the novel elucidates how humanity is at stake in the face of modernity. In many respects, the book cast doubts on the very core of the American Dream in the 1920s, as conveyed by both Hollywood productions and the commercial propaganda of the era celebrating the power of the individual to conquer the challenging urban environment.

In fact, in spite of its social realism, King Vidor's *The Crowd*, like Lloyd's *Speedy*, is very much the product of the melodramatic imagination and of a narrative model trained on the rise and fall of an individual. The melodramatic imagination dominated many 1920s films such as *The Four Horsemen of the Apocalypse* (1921), *The Sheik* (1921), and *The Divine Woman* (1928)—tales of passion built upon nineteenth-century plot narratives that appealed to an enormous mass audience (Sklar 97–103). Notwithstanding its very experimental nature, *The Crowd* could not escape the influence of melodrama on its narrative structure to the point of rendering it a box office success. In fact, as a Hollywood director, King Vidor was able to maintain his own ideals while remaining flexible enough to "serve the interests of his employers" (*An Evening's Entertainment* 234). No wonder that *The Crowd*'s traditional narrative structure is focused upon the melodramatic decline and fall of a single hero; it is therefore at odds with the complex, polyphonic narrative of *Manhattan Transfer*. Inspired by ballets such as Cole Porter and Gerald Murphy's *Within the Quota* (1923) and Sergei Diaghilev's *Les Noces*, Dos Passos's work conveys the frantic rhythms of the city and thus creates a sort of modernist literary choreography by speedily juxtaposing narratives, voices, and points of view (Ludington 228–29).

However, in spite of the differences between both works, I want to show that *Manhattan Transfer* and *The Crowd* represent a complex and sophisticated meditation on the relationship between average individuals and the emergence of the modern American metropolis embodied in early twentieth-century

New York. The pieces share a strong fascination with an urban environment dominated by technology, and each work tries to respond to the ideological challenges posed by modern capitalism. As Malcolm Bradbury points out, "[I]f Modernism is a particular urban art, that is because the modern artist, like his fellow-men, has been caught up in the spirit of the modern city, which is itself the spirit of a modern technological society" (97).

More to the point, both Dos Passos and Vidor confront, in their respective works, the challenges stemming from technology and mass culture at the very core of the American dream. As Phillip Lopate points out, the spirit of that dream—that is, the assumption that "any average individual with gumption could attain success"—was an "ideal that still seemed with reach in the twenties, before the Depression, Vietnam, and national disenchantment" ("*Speedy*"). It was in fact a powerful ideology perpetuated by Hollywood during two decades of extremely successful films such as *Boom Town* (1940), which celebrated individualism, the power of modern technology, and incessant geographical mobility (Schatz 466).

This essay seeks to show how both *Manhattan Transfer* and *The Crowd* bring a critical approach to the putative power and freedom of individuals in a modern urban environment. Moreover, their criticisms of standardization and mass culture anticipate the sociological studies of Robert and Helen Lynd as well as those of Frankfurt School philosophers Theodor W. Adorno and Max Horkheimer. Although produced before the gloomy days of the Great Depression, Dos Passos's novel and Vidor's film cast doubt on mass media optimism regarding economic progress during the twenties, in which America became, almost overnight, the economic master of the world. While Europe sank into an economic depression after World War I, America was "getting wealthier daily at a pace that was positively dizzying," and economic progress seemed to be available for everyone through hard work (Bryson 10). Thus, in this comparative study of *Manhattan Transfer* and *The Crowd*, I explore how both works challenge the postwar optimism, which was the ideological core of an era of abundance and prosperity.

KING VIDOR'S *THE CROWD*: A HOLLYWOOD'S EXPERIMENT

To begin, one must bear in mind that the project of producing and filming *The Crowd* was itself a modernist experiment that challenged the framework of the existing Hollywood production system in the early 1920s. After producing the major box-office hit *The Big Parade* (1925), King Vidor wanted to make an experimental film about everyday life. Vidor, a friend of F. Scott Fitzgerald, who immensely appreciated some of the director's films, was also an avid reader of modernist works and went to Paris to meet James Joyce (Fitzgerald 237; *A Tree is a Tree* 114). Vidor was too sophisticated to be just an ambitious Hollywood director. He wanted to show the complexity of modern life, the effect of publicity and machines in individual consciousness—very much in the fashion of writers such as Dos Passos and James Joyce. Vidor wanted to develop a film style that could integrate "the dramatic, the entertaining story line with the realism and credibility" of Robert J. Flaherty, whose documentaries *Nanook of the North* (1922) and *Moana* (1926) showed human beings struggling to overcome hostile environments (*On Film Making* 22).

With the help of modernist poet John V. A. Weaver—one of the first enthusiastic reviewers of e. e. cummings's *The Enormous Room*—Vidor started to produce a film narrative that challenged contemporary cinema. The script was completed by Harry Behn, another writer close to the modernist movement in the early 1920s. Thanks to the support of MGM's producer Irving Thalberg, Vidor and Weaver built up a narrative of a common man in 1920s Manhattan featuring a relatively unknown actor (James Murray) in the leading role as a kind of Everyman prototype embodied by a white-collar worker named John Sims, who struggles to survive in the metropolis. Like many of Dos Passos's characters in *Manhattan Transfer*, John has internalized the American Dream. Landing in New York ready to conquer the city, he is convinced that he is destined to be a man of importance. Twenty years later, he faces the harsh reality that he is just a character lost in the midst of the faceless masses. Married to a less-than-glamorous wife named Mary (Eleanor Boardman), John lives a rather average life. The couple struggles to raise two children in a small New York tenement with a balky toilet. In spite of the material limitations of his life, John does not give up his American dream. He struggles to become an important person and ascends the social ladder by writing slogans. He nearly achieves that dream when he wins $500 in a slogan contest. But all of his expectations suddenly collapse when he faces devastating setbacks, such as the death of his daughter (Alice Mildred Puter). Haunted by her memory, John is unable to keep on working at his job in the office and is soon fired. Driven by sheer despair, and unable to find a new job, he contemplates suicide. His son, John Jr. (Freddie Burke Frederick), thwarts the suicide attempt, declaring proudly that he wants to be like his father when he grows up. At the end of the film, the whole family is gathered in a theatre and looks happy being part of the crowd. The whole family appears engulfed by the power of the masses while watching a theatrical clown act. The end of the film shows that the American Dream was fading away. It was out of reach for many creative individuals, John Sims included, who were engulfed by the power of the masses that dominated urban America by the 1920s.

Like Dos Passos's *Manhattan Transfer*, Vidor's cinematic approach to urban America was realistic; although, as I have mentioned, the plot was anchored in the melodramatic tradition. This approach appears from the very beginning of the production of the film. Both John V. A. Weaver's first script treatment (called *The Clerk Story*) and Vidor's second treatment for the film (called *March of Life*) sought to recreate the cramped living conditions of thousands of New Yorkers dominated by anonymity and technology. No wonder that, in filming *The Crowd* on location, Vidor sought a realist approach to New York everyday life that was at odds with many contemporary Hollywood melodramas, which were conceived to enlarge the personality of stars such as Greta Garbo or Rudolph Valentino. As Vidor explains:

> I believe in filming *The Crowd* . . . I was one of the first directors to journey from California to New York to shoot scenes with actors working on city streets and to use the normal flow of pedestrians and traffic for atmosphere. Most of the scenes were photographed through a hole cut in the rear curtain of a delivery truck which we parked at an advantageous point at the curb. The brief rehearsals were all worked out by myself and two assistants, one of whom dressed in the costume favored by truck drivers and leaned against the tail gate of the truck in order to relay messages inconspicuously inside. Arm signals prevailed. In about ten days of shooting we employed no extras for the street scenes, nor do I recall that anyone detected what was happening.
>
> For some perambulatory walking shots we constructed what appeared to be three packing horses mounted on a rubber-tired push car but inside we hid a camera operator with a tripod-mounted camera. (*On Film Making* 22)

The Crowd is also less than a mythical representation of modern New York. For, as Raymond Durgnat and Scott Simmon point out, "what distinguishes Vidor's film from its genre is the way it captures everyday tensions of marriage and unemployment, the deadening habits in office routine, even the common place dreariness in romance" (79–80). Thus, in spite of the success of the film, the MGM studio head Louis B. Mayer expressed strong opposition to such cinematic experimentation, voting against Vidor's film at the First Academy Awards, arguing that he objected that the film showed a lavatory (Young 57).

PURSUITS OF HAPPINESS

Both Dos Passos's and Vidor's works, like Paul Fejos's *Loneliness*, confer enormous importance to a single date: the fourth of July. That date serves to trace the aspirations of both John Sims and Jimmy Herf. John was born on the fourth of July, and the very beginning of the narrative connects his aspirations to those of the main "protagonists" of American history: Thomas Jefferson, George Washington, and Abraham Lincoln. Jimmy, on the other hand, internalizes from the very beginning the motto of the Declaration of Independence: in the jungle of New York he seeks to pursue happiness. Both characters are anchored in the ideological ground of American history. Indeed, both Vidor and Dos Passos appear to be trying to show that, although New York could be seen as another modern city, one could not fully understand the ideological core of the city without bearing in mind its particular history.

To understand the very nature of such a date, the novel reminds the reader that modern New York and its inhabitants can only be appreciated if we realize that they are the very product of an enlightened dream: the pursuit of happiness. In other words, modern society is the product of a contract among individuals who no longer form part of a group seeking protection and security but, ideally, self-realization. In an article titled "America and the Pursuit of Happiness," published in the *Nation* (December 29, 1920), Dos Passos noticed that, when visiting Spain, many Spanish working people (a Malaga fisherman and a donkey boy) had the impression that "people didn't enjoy life in America" (*Major Nonfictional Prose* 54). The Spaniards believed that life in America was easy and marvelous with so "many policemen, elevators and automatic lunchrooms and electric lights" surpassing the material possibilities of average Spanish life. Thus, irrespective of its economic prosperity, there was something wrong with America; people were not really happy. These comments invited Dos Passos to meditate upon recent American history and the negative effects of the economic and political changes in American life that had deterred the country from developing its democratic potential in the twentieth century. America needed a democratic reinvention to once again be a nation of hope and happiness, a place where abstract ideals are compatible with material reality. Dos Passos concludes the essay, stating:

> Then, perhaps, after all this bitterness, we shall have replaced the lands where the streets are paved with gold of the immigrant's dream by a land to which the lacerated peoples of Europe can again aspire, where in a certain elemental freedom of thought and actions the foundations

> will have been for a life that people–in the sense the donkey boy on that blazing road in Spain intended–can enjoy, "the liberty and pursuit of happiness" of that too long forgotten declaration of our aims. (56–57)

These thoughts are mirrored in Dos Passos's exploration of Manhattan in the novel he would publish in 1925. From the beginning of *Manhattan Transfer*, Jimmy and Ellen are not merely survivors trying to adapt to an urban environment; rather, they are desperately pursuing happiness and struggling to make their dreams come true in a somewhat hostile modern realm. Their lives are full of great expectations that will be challenged by the urban environment. Thus, regarding Ellen, Alastair Beddow points out that "the city is a treacherous space . . . which traps her, flattens out difference and constantly threatens to engulf her into its mass identity (5). Jimmy Herf aspires to become an independent journalist in a democratic society, resisting his uncle's attempts to form his career; nor does he accept the values of other characters in the novel such as George Baldwin, Mr. Densch, and even Ellen (Wagner 61). But in the end, he is alone and abandons his job and the city. As Joseph Warren Beach remarks, he embodies "the protest of the self-determining individual against a world that would make of him a sensual automaton" (41). Like Dos Passos, Vidor in *The Crowd* confronts the lives of the characters who hold onto that American ideal. John, like Jimmy and Ellen, is an orphan struggling to create his own identity in the city; the only thing he needs is the right opportunity to help him achieve his dream. In many respects, in exploring how average individuals are caught up in American mass culture, these works could be considered precursors to the social criticism of Theodor Adorno and Max Horkheimer. In the early 1940s, these social thinkers stressed that mass culture and standardization had degraded American society by fostering conformity and resignation. Individuals become mere costumers. In capitalist America, the mechanisms that governed the schedule in the factory and the organization of office and workplace were the same as those in leisure time. As Horkheimer and Adorno point out, "Entertainment is the prolongation of capitalism. It is sought by those who want to escape the mechanized labor process so that they can cope with it again . . . the off-duty worker can experience nothing but after-images of the work process itself" (109). Thus, drinking, loving, and sleeping had become consumption. Modernization had turned human beings into mere machines. These realizations made the Frankfurt School theorists doubt American democracy and wonder if mass culture were the seedbed of political totalitarianism (Jay 212–16).

Moreover, the Jeffersonian pursuit of happiness, echoed by Dos Passos and Vidor, was an ideal linked to the origins of the American frontier and with the individualist and collective ideals of an agrarian world that was rapidly being challenged by the emergence of urban America in the twenties. As Richard Maltby points out:

> The American Revolution occurred at a moment in which a political doctrine of equality could be equated with a social doctrine of individualism. The institutionalization of that equation prevented the ready adoption of nineteenth-century Marxist theories to an American environment. Economic determinism and Marx's theories of class conflict ran counter to the traditions of a bourgeois individualism which was not only the legacy of the frontier experience but also the ideological inheritance bequeathed by the Founding Fathers. . . . Though not Arcadian, Jefferson's vision was nevertheless pastoral. Agrarian democracy represented an ideal to be valued above all for its social stability. (154)

Both *Manhattan Transfer* and *The Crowd* furnish the American audience with a new model of the individual inhabiting the modern metropolis, one who differs from generations past by challenging the foundations of individualism and equality defended by the Founding Fathers and western expansion. The myth of the self-sufficient farmer, virtuous and loyal to his community and enjoying the resources of the land, became impossible in the twentieth century in the face of the increasing rationalization of economy and space. In many respects, the new urban America embodied the high price to be paid by material progress as celebrated by industrialist tycoons such as Andrew Carnegie in his piece "The Gospel of Wealth" (1889):

> The poor enjoy what the rich could not before afford. What were the luxuries have become the necessaries of life. The laborer has now more comforts than the former had a few generations ago. . . .
>
> The price we pay for this salutary change is, no doubt, great. We assemble thousands of operatives in the factory, and in the mine, and to whom he is little better than a myth. All intercourse between them is at an end. . . .
>
> We accept and welcome, therefore, as conditions to which we must accommodate ourselves, great inequality of environment; the concentration of business, industrial and commercial in the hands of a few; and the law of competition between these, as being not only beneficial, but essential to the future progress of the race. (3–4)

Thus, the white-collar individual inhabiting the cities felt utterly alone and alienated, and the links among urban dwellers were extremely weak and casual within a fragmented realm. Unlike the migrant narrative appearing in works such as Abraham Cahan's *The Rise of David Levinsky* (1917) or Henry Roth's *Call It Sleep* (1934), some of the characters appearing in *Manhattan Transfer* and *The Crowd* seem completely alone. Figures such as Joe Harland or John Sims represent a middle-class America that no longer has the strong support of a wider social circle or of an ethnic group identity.

In *Manhattan Transfer*, Dos Passos depicts with detached realism the inability of modern individuals to cope with an alien environment. Some characters meet a tragic end. For instance, Bud Korpenning ends up jumping off Brooklyn Bridge. He is haunted by his past after having struggled for years to forge a new identity in New York and erase all traces of evidence leading to his father's murder. Joe Harland, a retired broker, becomes an impoverished drunkard unable to hold his status in the business world. Hard-working characters are also doomed, such as Dutch Robertson, who ends up in prison because he cannot make an honest living due to the immediate economic crash after the war. Like Dos Passos, Vidor shows how the indifferent industrial machine destroys the individual. Drawing upon the melodramatic tradition instead of on social realism, Vidor charts the decline and fall of John Sims, who, tired of struggling to sell vacuum cleaners door-to-door, is considered a bluff and a quitter by his wife. After leaving his middle-class job, John has become nothing but "a big bag of wind." Depressed and humiliated after knowing how formidable the opposition of the crowd is "when we get out of step with it," he contemplates committing suicide by throwing himself from a railroad bridge. Yet, unlike many of the characters in *Manhattan Transfer*, John does not face his destiny alone. John's son Junior encourages him to keep on fighting when he tells his father, "When I grow up I wanta be just like you." Buoyed by his son's words, John returns to the city and breaks into a line of unemployed workers who also want an opportunity. Regardless of its melodramatic mode, *The Crowd* forecasts the atmosphere of the 1930s: the job queues, the sense of human failure, and the power of anonymous economic forces to determine the lives of thousands of individuals.

Both works represent thousands of lonely individuals drifting along in a city permeated by capitalist seduction and a powerful press. In *The Crowd*, John proposes marriage to Mary after watching a subway advertisement for a furniture company, stating "YOU FURNISH THE GIRL—We'll—Furnish the Home!" In *Manhattan Transfer*, a bearded man comes across an advertisement on the window of a Canal Street drugstore. It shows an image of a prosperous and successful man, accompanied by the texts: "King C. Gillette" and "NO STROPPING NO HONING" (9). Immediately, the man enters the store and buys a Gillette razor. When he arrives home, he gives himself a shave. As Roland Marchand points out "advertisers frequently [promoted] products on the strength of their capacity to lift the individual out of the crowd" (269). However, both Dos Passos and Vidor show that this sort of individuality is a mere illusion. In *The Crowd*, John becomes beaten down by the crowd as much as John Harland, Bud Korpenning, or Dutch Robertson are in *Manhattan Transfer*. Eventually, average individuals succumb to the overwhelming power of New York. They turn into "obscure and dreary figures, wisps and straws on the churning surface of our industrial maelstrom" (Beach 36).

Like Ellen Thatcher, John dwells upon his expectations of becoming a prominent individual—that is, to become rich. Ellen and John do not seem to be living in the present; they are dreamers. They look forward to embracing an almost-impossible future that would redeem the futility, boredom, and inner frustration of their lives. They seem to be products of a late nineteenth-century version of the American dream born out of the Gilded Age, which placed emphasis upon self-determination and no longer considered the relationship between self and society in the full achievement of such an ideal. Dos Passos and Vidor's pessimistic approach to urban America anticipates the sociological investigations of Robert and Helen Lynd's *Middletown: A Study in American Culture* (1929). In their study of Muncie, Indiana, they conclude that, whereas small communities embody the values of American democracy—"the relatively stable ground of established institutional habits" (499)—the American city symbolizes the radical disorientation experienced by average individuals, much like "an escalator erratically moving in several directions at a bewildering variety of speeds (499). Moreover, the city embodies monetary and material acquisitiveness as well as an overwhelming racial and ethnic pluralism. In such a complex environment, individuals lose their bearings and direction, stamped out by the products of commercialized culture. In modern cities, community dissolves, neighbors became estranged, and the family unit gradually disintegrates (Poll 94–98).

INVISIBLE POWERS

The harsh reality of the city, however, reveals the impossibility of achieving that dream. The modern metropolis is itself another character that has trapped the lives of the main characters in the novel and the film. In *Manhattan Transfer*, James Merivale has returned to New York after World War I and feels completely dismayed. Opportunities in the job market remain scarce and the gap between rich and poor has been dramatically increased by the war. The old money of New York, depicted in novels such Edith Wharton's *The House of Mirth* (1905), has vanished away leaving few traces behind. New York has suddenly become a plutocracy, which fosters Wall Street speculation and ever-advancing technology. The post-feudal dimension of modern capitalism is highlighted especially in the way the main characters of *Manhattan Transfer* feel trapped by the city's urban architecture:

> Like sap at the first frost of five o'clock men and women begin to drain gradually out of the tall buildings downtown, grayfaced throngs flood subways and tubes, vanish underground.
>
> All night the great buildings stand quiet and empty, their million windows dark. (260)

New York, destined to become an enlightened city after the American Revolution, a city of progress and individual freedom, has become a new "Nineveh" (315). As Richard Dennis signals, "the specters of . . . ancient cities—Nineveh, Athens, Rome, Constantinople . . . continued to loom over New York in Dos Passos's *Manhattan Transfer,*" announcing a very bleak future for the metropolis (50). Almost two decades ahead of Horkheimer and Adorno's *Dialectic of Enlightenment* (1944), Dos Passos is one of the first American intellectuals who associated the expansion of technology under capitalism to a form of regression to an ancient era marked by slavery, social confinement, anonymity—and, eventually, doom.

The Crowd follows very closely Dos Passos's pessimistic depiction of the modern metropolis. In Weaver's original script, which was closely translated into images by Vidor, the film opens with a shot of a big city swarming with hurrying men and women going into office buildings. They represent "millions of America's youth—the white-collar army going to the daily grind" (qtd. in Young 17). In the original script, Weaver describes a series of dissolving shots in these terms:

> Finally a shot starting at the bottom of a skyscraper—with "The World Mutual Insurance Company" appearing over the door; slant the camera slowly upward, covering row after row of windows until finally it rests upon one particular window and PAN toward that window until the camera is looking through it into a large office. Sub-title something like: "Lets us pick out one cell at random in the honeycomb of business." (qtd. in Young 17)

In Vidor's film, the camera sweeps across seemingly infinite rows of toiling, anonymous, and faceless workers of the insurance office until it zooms in on its hero, whose desk is labelled "John Sims 137." It is an image that will be imitated by other Hollywood films. Alfred Green's *Baby Face* (1933), for instance, imagines the Office Tower as alienating and anonymous. In 1960, Billy Wilder, in his film *The Apartment*, pays homage to this image of anonymous faces stationed at a sea of desks in parallel rows. Both Vidor and Dos Passos stress that New York has become an uncaring environment that has engulfed the lives of millions of Americans—indeed, a vast city filled by beehives of workers. This new environment no longer fosters the realization of the American Dream. In its very origins, the notion of the American Dream stresses that individuals can change the world. As Benjamin Franklin says in his *Autobiography*, "I have always thought that one Man of tolerable Abilities may work great Changes, & accomplish great Affairs among Mankind, if he first forms a good Plan, and cutting off all Amusements or other Employments that would divert his Attention, makes the Execution of that same Plan his sole Study and Business" (93).

From the nineteenth century to the early twentieth century, American millionaires, politicians, and inventors such as Andrew Carnegie, Thomas Edison, and Theodore Roosevelt incarnated some of the values of the American Dream, claiming that their lives were empirical proof of that success. In *Manhattan Transfer* and *The Crowd,* the main characters soon discover that individuals can no longer assert control in their lives; nor can they manage to adapt to city's frenetic environment. Eventually, Jimmy Herf, Ellen Thatcher, and John Sims become mere survivors, trapped in claustrophobic apartments after a long day of work. For instance, Ellen "felt hungry and alone. The bed was a raft on which she was marooned alone, always alone, afloat on a growling ocean" (*Manhattan Transfer* 142). In Vidor's film, during a picnic on the beach with his two children and his wife, John starts playing a tune on his ukulele, expressing his unconscious alienation: "All alone / I'm so all alone."

Obstacles and competition in the modern metropolis make it difficult for the ordinary man to make a living or to become what he desires. The uncaring crowd surrounds John Sims, who is completely lost among the hordes of hardened, moving people going to and from work. In the new capitalist environment of the big companies, employees all look the same, lacking any hint of individuality. Vidor's camera explores the work environment, highlighting the worried faces of anonymous employees hurrying into a toilet. It is a new universe of revolving doors, gum-chewing stenographers, and mechanical elevators. The office is like an impenetrable forest inhabited by hundreds of rows of identical desks and faces. It is a cinematic view of the urban environment very much in the fashion of Dos Passos's description of the scurrying crowd in *Manhattan Transfer*: "Jimmy Herf stood in the City Hall Square with his hands in his pockets watching ragged men with caps and earsflaps pulled down over faces and necks of the color of raw steak shovel snow. Old and young their faces were the same color, their clothes were the same color" (292). The metropolis has become a strange forest where human beings have lost all sense of orientation, where every face seems to be the same.

The characters in *The Crowd* and *Manhattan Transfer* struggle to rebel against the dehumanizing environment of the modern world. In Vidor's film, John, emotionally broken after the death of his daughter (run over by a truck), sinks into a deep depression. He fights with numbers and figures in his office. He struggles to keep his job as an accountant in the face of the brute insensitivity of an enormous working environment, where John finally collapses. Vidor superimposes images of John's daughter running in front of a vehicle over those of figures scurrying through his head. When his superior exhorts him to accomplish his work with diligence, John loses his temper and begins yelling, "To hell with this job! I´m through!" Unlike John Sims, in *Manhattan Transfer*, Ellen Thatcher finds a sort of comfort in numbers, and reminds George Baldwin: "[Do] you realize that it's only because numbers are so cold and emotionless that we're not all crazy?" (317). Jimmy, however, is unable to find an impersonal shield against the invading powers of a threatening technological reality. When he dreams of engaging in an act of violence against Ellen, who is then his wife, he dreams up revenge not only against her, but also against the machines: "He was writing a letter on a linotype . . . The linotype was like a gulfing mouth with nickelbright rows of teeth, gulped, crunched" (280). As William Solomon comments, for Jimmy "writing as typing appears . . . as a weapon that helps him to defend against . . . orality, femininity, and technology. . . . The writer must strive to turn the functions of the machine to his advantage lest he be overwhelmed by its power" (329).

THE LOGIC OF CHANCE

In the 1920s, literary works such as *Manhattan Transfer* and Hollywood productions such *The Crowd* portray New York as an alien metropolis breaking down into inextricable chaos. Like Dziga Vertov's "Kino-Eye," Dos Passos documents every detail of reality, creating an immense body of snapshots of life. He presents a multiplicity of buildings, crowds, faces, colors, songs, shadows, sights, smells. Like Vertov, Dos Passos manages to give us an impression of reality. Yet, unlike Vertov's *A Man with a Movie Camera* (1929), which is shaped by a postrevolutionary reality quivering with new energies, a sense of chaos envelops *Manhattan Transfer*'s images (Kracauer 186–87). Like the cinema of Vsevolod Pudovkin, who stressed the notion of montage as a lineage of imagistic pieces intended to illustrate an idea, Dos Passos composed a series of provocative chapters as if they were movie subtitles. Indeed, the Pudovkin-like fragments of stories created by Dos Passos convey a strong sense of flux and the fleeting dimension of reality, placing emphasis upon the overwhelming chaos of everyday life. In part I, titles such as "Metropolis," "Tracks," or "Dollars" underscore the idea of the city as a symbol of power and energy. The titles appearing in part III, however, hold sinister connotations: "Rejoicing City that Dwelt Carelessly" and "The Burthen of Nineveh" stem from the Bible (Foster 18). New York symbolizes doom. Success seems illusory in such a tumultuous environment. Human beings are no longer able to control their own destinies regardless of technological progress. Like Dos Passos, Vidor stresses New York as a symbol of a chaotic and depersonalized metropolis, offering a panoramic view of its massive confusion and enormous size. Immediately after showing the first time that the ambitious John views the Statue of Liberty from a ferry, the film introduces the new environment by resorting to an elaborate montage that features a symphony of tall skyscrapers, bustling streets, and overwhelming traffic. From a high angle, the camera focuses upon a fleeting crowd crossing a city block. They look like ants. Henry Sharp's photography for Vidor's film illustrates how never-ending speed dominates the city, employing "the widest angel lens used in motion picture work" so far (qtd. in *Hollywood on the Hudson* 137). As in a Futurist painting such as Umberto Boccioni's *The City Rises* (La città che sale, 1910), depicting the city as fleeting lines of force that stamp out the representation of human beings, Sharp stresses how speed dominates people, cars, vehicles, and elevated trains. It is a chaotic environment clouded by white smoke from skyscraper tops. The sense of chaos increases when the camera starts to rotate in a dizzying clockwise turn after encompassing the top of a huge office building. Both works show the urban space invaded by a threatening crowd in similar terms to those put forward by Gustave Le Bon in his social study *The Crowd* (Psychologie des Foules, 1895). Le Bon describes the crowd as irrational, impulsive, irritable, instinctual, violent and ferocious. Le Bon's pessimistic view of the crowd as a symbol of mass culture would be admired by influential writers and psychologists such as Sigmund Freud (Carey 26–28).

In such a chaotic and crowed environment, Dos Passos and Vidor illustrate how human beings are unable to achieve the unalienable pursuit of happiness in a world dominated by images of endless success and failure stemming from the strange and whimsical logic of chance and sheer opportunism. In *Manhattan Transfer*, individuals are overwhelmed by a technological world that perpetually invites the invasion of the logic of chance in everyday life. As Linda W. Wagner points out, "the subway and its transfers represented the archetypical circumstances of meeting by chance at the crossroads"; moreover "the subway is an image for lives touching and diverging" (49). And, as Gretchen Foster explains, the very title of the novel, *Manhattan Transfer*, that of a railway station stop, "combines the city and its flux" (18).

In the novel, the logic of chance also affects the economic lives of some of the characters. The Jazz Age produces new sorts of millionaires who are no longer the product of creativity and effort but of adaptation to a series of favorable circumstances. One such example is Congo, a French officer who abandons the service and settles down in the States. After the war, he goes from rags to soaring wealth and luxury by means of his bootlegging activities. While hard-working men like Jimmy Herf and returning veterans like Dutch Robertson find nothing but failure and desperation after the war, Congo ends up living in a luxurious palace. By charting Congo's contrasting rise, Dos Passos challenges the ideological assumptions of a whole era defended by President Calvin Coolidge: "The success which is made in any walk of life is measured almost exactly by the amount of hard work that is put into it" (qtd. in Allen 138). Yet it looks as though both effort and work no longer count in the new urban environment dominated by the empire of crime, political corruption, and speculative stock market riches.

The Crowd also shows how hard working men such as John can only meet with failure and depression when he realizes that he is just a speck in a mob of people trying to climb the social ladder, unaware just how much he depends emotionally on his family. After his little daughter is killed by a truck, John reaches a breaking point. Driven by sheer despair, he tosses away his books and papers. He leaves the office after having thrown his desk. He quits his job at the insurance company and finds another, though he is unable to hold it for long.

In *The Crowd* other characters such as Bert (Bert Roach), John's co-worker and friend, fare better. Bert is less emotionally dependent than John, limiting his imagination to merely doing his duty in the office and rubbing shoulders with his superiors. Moreover, as Angela Dalle Vacche states, *The Crowd* demonstrates that "in order to belong to the mass, the individual must give up a certain degree of introspection to the point of simplifying one's own self-image" (219). Thus, both individualism and creativity should be severely trimmed in order to survive in the anonymous urban environment of the

1920s. No wonder that by the end of Vidor's film, it becomes evident that "Bert has moved up the ladder of his company much more effectively than John whose over-the-top fantasies doom him within the world of office politics" (Dalle Vacche 223).

Both Dos Passos and Vidor challenge the myth of the new industrial society as a type of natural environment for the fittest. At the end of the nineteenth century, Andrew Carnegie celebrated and defended this new caste of Americans in these terms:

> Having accepted [the new labor conditions], it follows that there must be great scope for the exercise of special ability in the merchant and in the manufacturer who has to conduct affairs upon a great scale. That this talent for organization and management is rare among men is provided by the fact that it invariably secures enormous rewards for its possessors, no matter where or under what laws and conditions. (4)

The Crowd and *Manhattan Transfer* lampoon Carnegie's romantic ideal that the capitalist world could foster a new race of creative individuals. The world emerging by urbanization, technology, and the gradual dehumanization of society is that of Bert in *The Crowd*, and Gus McNeil, James Merivale, and George Baldwin in *Manhattan Transfer*, "financially successful characters with some obvious moral taint" who no longer represent the creativity of the American entrepreneur proclaimed by Carnegie (Wagner 57).

THE LANGUAGE OF AUTHENTICITY

In *The Crowd* and *Manhattan Transfer*, men such as Bert and Congo manage to survive and succeed in the new material landscape of skyscrapers, steamrollers, trains, and mechanical doors. Yet, despite this pessimistic vision of the metropolis, neither Dos Passos nor Vidor gives up imagining other possibilities of happiness for their characters. Some characters manage to get through the horror of the urban jungle by learning the language of authenticity. Thus, in *Manhattan Transfer*, after many ups and downs along the bleak entrails of the urban landscape, Ellen Thatcher learns that love is more valuable than success or social position, and also rarer after "looking for gaiety and success yet aware of the unhappiness both surrounding her and inside her" (Wagner 10). Jimmy Herf grows in awareness when he begins to "learn a few of the things" he does not want (*Manhattan Transfer* 305). In *The Crowd*, after a failed suicide attempt by leaping to his death on a railroad bridge above the freight yards, John Sims discovers the staunch love of his son, Junior. Junior is ignorant of his father's wish for death, and he does not leave John's side. After this episode, John finds a sort of harmony and equilibrium with his inner self. He no longer wants to be a man above the crowd. Like Ellen, John comes to realize that there are things more important than social success, such as the love of his family, and he accepts a job as a clown who juggles balls as a sandwich-board man on the streets to advertise: "I am always happy because I eat at Schneider's grill." Years before, John had mocked the same menial job from the top of a double-decker bus. Now accepting this modest job, he has found not only a reason to survive but also a means of self-realization.

Finally, Dos Passos and Vidor's approaches to 1920s America take a pessimistic view of the democratic and social possibilities of the modern metropolis. The end of *Manhattan Transfer* shows Jimmy Herf as an endless drifter abandoning New York for good. The individualistic Jeffersonian dream seems no longer possible in the new realm. The last line of the novel is "Pretty Far," Jimmy's answer to a truck driver's question, "How fur ye goin?" (342). As a sort of negative dialectic, Jimmy has learned what he does not want to do; that is, he no longer belongs to the metropolitan environment. In *The Crowd*, the main male character cannot escape as Jimmy did; instead, John Sims is trapped within the walls of the city. John and his family find a sort of refuge in the theatre laughing at a vaudeville show featuring two clowns on the stage. The camera pulls away from their row in the center, until their faces disappear, suddenly engulfed by a sea of laughing faces in the audience. The end of the film shows that both city life and mass culture become tantamount of mediocrity (Brüstle 4–5). The uncanny harmony of their collective laugh presents a caricature of solidarity. It anticipates Horkheimer and Adorno's statement that "the occupants of city centers are uniformly summoned there for the purposes of work and leisure, as producers and consumers" (94–95).

In 1934, Vidor shot *Our Daily Bread*—a kind of sequel to *The Crowd*—defending, very much in the fashion that Dos Passos will do in the 1950s, the idea that the Jeffersonian individualistic dream is still possible in a rural America, but no longer in the metropolis. Like Dos Passos's and Vidor's works, German expressionist films, such as Fritz Lang's *Metropolis* (1927), faced the harsh realities of the modern world, the clash between the individual and a mechanized society. Unlike in the American artists' approach, in Lang's film, the dialectic between human beings and machines is worked out by demanding that the heart meditate between hand and brain, an idea that could well have been formulated by Goebbels, as Siegfried Kracauer points out (164).

Neither Dos Passos nor Vidor seems to find a solution to the clash between the individual and the modern metropolis. Nevertheless, both artists place emphasis on the importance of perpetuating the very basic elements of Jeffersonian individualism in the twentieth century, irrespective of the fact that the modern metropolis does not allow the possibility of developing this ideology. In *The Crowd* and *Manhattan Transfer*, the democratic spirit of America remains a symbol of a whole culture celebrating the average individual. This was one of the core elements of the American culture, as Fritz Lang especially noticed when he started to work in Hollywood:

> Everything [here] happens to Joe Doe—meaning to you and me–not to some upper-class man. And [the producer] explained to me that in an American picture one would have to have Joe Doe–a man of the people as a hero.
>
> And I thought, here is a kind of sign of a Democracy. In Germany, under the influence of military power—I'm not speaking of Hitler, but even before . . . the hero in Germany was always superman. Here in America, Al Capone was not a superman. In a totalitarian state, or in a state governed by a dictator, an emperor, a King, the leader himself is, in a way, a superman. (Bogdanovich 21–22)

Fritz Lang's opinions mirror the anxiety expressed by many European intellectuals during the 1920s, such as José Ortega y Gasset or H. G. Wells, both of whom cast doubt on the power of the average citizen to cope with the challenges of the modern world (Carey 3–4). Unlike many intellectuals, Dos Passos and Vidor believed that average individuals were able to regenerate society if they managed to step away from the oppressive urban environment. Dos Passos and Vidor's fear of the modern metropolis anticipates many of the tendencies of the film noir genre that emerged in the 1940s. For instance, Boris Ingster's *Stranger on the Third Floor* (1940) depicts a nightmarish urban landscape in which individuals are emotionally vulnerable and utterly alienated. In their search to preserve American values, Dos Passos's and Vidor's works can be considered precursors of cinematic and theatrical representations of small town America that appeared in the 1930s, such as in Thornton Wilder's *Our Town* (1938). This play, inspired by Robert and Helen Lynd's *Middletown*, lays emphasis on the notion of the small community as the core of American values. In a world dominated by speedy machines and skyscrapers, both Vidor and Dos Passos lay stress upon authenticity as an essential element of revolt against capitalism's dehumanizing use of technological and scientific resources. It was also a way forward into the future of American democracy in a world increasingly threatened by anonymous and mesmerizing forces. Above all, both works demonstrate that, unlike the nihilistic tendencies that would appear in Europe, especially in Italy and Germany by the 1920s, the American artist strongly sticks to the core of the republican and democratic ideals when facing the dark side of modernity. These ideals were based upon unflagging defense of social equality and of the dignity of the average American.

ACKNOWLEDGMENTS

I would especially like to thank Juan José Coy, Barbara Bandiera, Richard Bradbury, Mick Gidley, Tomás Herrero Domínguez, Robert Lawson-Peebles, Denise Mok, Richard Maltby, and Michael Wood for all their comments, encouragement, and generosity.

WORKS CITED

Allen, Frederick Lewis. *Only Yesterday: An Informal History of the 1920's.* John Wiley & Sons, 1997.

Beach, Joseph Warren. *American Fiction, 1920–1940.* Atheneum, 1972.

Beddow, Alastair. "Manhattan Nightmares: John Dos Passos, Charles Sheeler and the Distortion of Urban Space." *Moveable Type,* vol. 6, 2010. doi. 10.14324/111.1755-4527.051

Bogdanovich, Peter. *Fritz Lang in America.* Studio Vista, 1967.

Bradbury, Malcolm. "The Cities of Modernism." *Modernism,* edited by Malcolm Bradbury and James McFarlane, Penguin Books, 1991, pp. 96–104.

Brogi, Daniela. "Modernismo Antiborghese. Manhattan Transfer Di John Dos Passos." *Le Parole e Le Cose,* 28 Sept. 2012, www.leparoleelecose.it/?p=6791.

Brüstle, Peter. *Cinema of Mediocrity. The Representation of 1920s Mass Culture in King Vidor's The Crowd.* Grin Verlag, 2007.

Bryson, Bill. *One Summer: America, 1927.* Doubleday, 2013.

Carey, John. *The Intellectual and the Masses: Pride and Prejudice among the Literary Intelligentsia, 1880–1939.* Faber & Faber, 1992.

Carnegie, Andrew. *The Gospel of Wealth and Other Timely Essays.* The Century Co., 1901.

Dalle Vacche, Angela. "1928: Movies, Social Conformity and Imminent Traumas." *American Cinema of the 1920s: Themes and Variations,* edited by Lucy Fischer. Rutgers UP, 2009, pp. 211–33.

Denis, Richard. *Cities in Modernity: Representations and Productions of Metropolitan Space, 1840-1930*. Cambridge UP, 2008.

Dos Passos, John. *The Best Times; an Informal Memoir*. The New American Library, 1966.

———. *The Major Nonfictional Prose*, edited by Donald Pizer, Wayne State UP, 1988.

———. *Manhattan Transfer*, 1925. Mariner Books, 2000.

Durgnat, Raymond, and Scott Simmon. *King Vidor, American*. U of California P, 1988.

Fanger, Donald. "The City of Russian Modernist Fiction." *Modernism*. Penguin Books, 1991, pp. 467–80.

Fitzgerald, F. Scott. *The Letters of F. Scott Fitzgerald*, edited by Andrew Turnbull, Penguin Books, 1968.

Foster, Gretchen. "John Dos Passos' Use of Film Technique in 'Manhattan Transfer' & 'The 42nd Parallel.'" *Literature/Film Quarterly*, vol. 14, no. 3, 1986, pp. 186–94.

Franklin, Benjamin. *The Autobiography of Benjamin Franklin: A Genetic Text,* edited by J. A. Leo Lemay and P. M. Zall, U of Tennessee P, 1981.

Horkheimer, Max, and Theodor W. Adorno. *Dialectic of Enlightenment*, edited by Gunzelin Schmid Noerr. Translated by Edmund Jephcott, Stanford UP, 2002.

Jay, Martin. *The Dialectical Imagination. A History of the Frankfurt School and the Institute of Social Research, 1923-1950*. U of California P, 1996.

Koszarski, Richard. *An Evening's Entertainment: The Age of the Silent Feature Picture, 1915–1928*, vol. 3. U of California P, 1994.

———. *Hollywood on the Hudson: Film and Television in New York from Griffith to Sarnoff*. Rutgers UP, 2008.

Kracauer, Siegfried. *From Caligari to Hitler: A Psychological History of the German Film*. Edited by Leonardo Quaresima. Princeton UP, 2004.

Lopate, Phillip. "Speedy: The Comic Figure of the Average Man." *The Criterion Collection*, www.criterion.com/current/posts/3826-speedy-the-comic-figure-of-the-average-man.

———. "Lonesome: Great City, Great Solitude." *The Criterion Collection*, www.criterion.com/current/posts/2436-lonesome-great-city-great-solitude.

Lynd, Robert S., and Helen Merrell Lynd. *Middletown: A Study in Modern American Culture*. Harcourt Brace & Company, 1957.

Ludington, Townsend. *John Dos Passos: A Twentieth Century Odyssey*. Elsevier Dutton, 1980.

Maltby, Richard. *Harmless Entertainment: Hollywood and the Ideology of Consensus*. The Scarecrow Press, 1983.

Marchand, Roland. *Advertising the American Dream: Making Way for Modernity, 1920–1940*. U of California P, 1986.

Nanney, Lisa. *John Dos Passos and Cinema*. Clemson UP, 2019.

Pavese, Cesare. *La letteratura americana e altri saggi*. Einaudi, 1962.

Petrie, Graham. "The Travels of Paul Fejos." *The Criterion Collection*, www.criterion.com/current/posts/2437-the-travels-of-paul-fejos.

Poll, Ryan. *Main Street and Empire: The Fictional Small Town in the Age of Globalization*. Rutgers UP, 2012.

Reed, Jeremy. "Another Essay on *The Great Gatsby* and the American Dream: Passing, Criminality and the Self-Made Man." *American Dreams: Dialogues in US Studies*, edited by Ricardo Miguez, Cambridge Scholars Publishing, 2007, pp. 165–93.

Schatz, Thomas. *Boom and Bust: American Cinema in the 1940s*. U of California P, 1999.

Seed, David. *Cinematic Fictions: The Impact of the Cinema on the American Novel up to World War II*. Liverpool UP, 2013.

Sklar, Robert. *Movie-Made America: A Cultural History of American Movies*. Vintage Books, 1994.

Solomon, William. *Literature, Amusement, and Technology in the Great Depression*. Cambridge UP 2009.

Suárez, Juan A. "John Dos Passos's *USA* and Left Documentary Film in the 1930s: The Cultural Politics of 'Newsreel' and 'The Camera Eye.'" *American Studies in Scandinavia*, vol. 31, no. 1, 1999, pp. 43–67.

Vidor, King, prod. and dir. *The Crowd*. Perf. James Murray and Eleanor Boardman. MGM. 1928. Film.

———. *On Film Making*. W. H. Allen, 1973.

———. *A Tree Is a Tree*. Longmans, Green and Co, 1954.

Wagner, Linda W. *Dos Passos: Artist as American*. U of Texas P, 1980.

Wood, Michael. "Modernism and Film." *The Cambridge Companion to Modernism*, edited by Michael Levenson, Cambridge UP, 2011, pp. 217–232.

Young, Jordan R. *King Vidor's The Crowd: The Making of a Silent Classic*. Past Times Publishing Co., 2014.

PART 3

CHRONICLING POLITICAL AMBIVALENCE IN THE AGE OF TOTALITARIANISM

7

JOHN DOS PASSOS AND THE RUSSIAN THEATRE, 1928

Jessica E. Teague

In his 1934 preface to *Three Plays*, John Dos Passos asks: Why write for the theatre anyway? The question, which is also the title of the introduction, sounds half-hearted, even resigned. Dos Passos had left the little theatre scene in New York five years earlier, and the publication of his *Three Plays*, which includes *The Garbage Man* (1926), *Airways, Inc.* (1928), and *Fortune Heights* (1934), marked the end of his brief theatrical career.[1] And yet, the question might also be read as a hopeful call to action and assertion of why one *should* write for the theatre. In the introduction, Dos Passos dedicates his plays to a vision of an American national theatre that "certainly does not exist now" but perhaps might one day (xxii). Because of the fame of Dos Passos's novels, we do not tend to read his plays today, or indeed to think of him as a playwright. However, Dos Passos was intimately involved in theatrical productions in both Europe and New York, and was a founding director of the New Playwrights Theatre (1927–1929), for which he not only wrote plays but painted scenery and took part as a producer. During the 1920s and 1930s, he also wrote a number of essays and reviews about theater for publications ranging from the *New Masses* to *Vanity Fair*.

Scholars like Alix Beeston and Thomas Fahy have drawn attention to the links between Dos Passos's plays and his early novels;[2] but Dos Passos's interest in the international theatre scene and the role of theatre in American life were more than just inspiration for the novels. In his plays and his critical writings about the theatre in both Russia and America, Dos Passos articulates an uncomfortable tension between collectivity and individuality. As a chronicler, Dos Passos wrote plays that reflect the individual social and economic realities of Americans living under capitalism while his critiques of the American theatre at large reflect his observations of the economic realities of producing a mass art like the theatre. As I aim to show, Dos Passos's dream of an American national theatre was not only a response to the kinds of Broadway theatre of the 1920s, or to the kinds of theatrical performances he encountered in the avant-garde scene in Paris; his dream of a national theatre was greatly influenced by his travels to Russia in 1928. In addition to experiencing socialism up-close, he took the opportunity of going to the theater nearly every night in Moscow. These encounters with Russian performance practices and traditions shaped Dos Passos's theatrical vision on stage and page, and solidified his belief that the United States needed a publicly funded national theatre of its own—one rooted in real American communities.

EARLY ADVENTURES IN THEATRE

As early as 1917, the year of his father's death and the year he sailed to Europe to join the ambulance corps on the Italian front, John Dos Passos was contemplating a theatrical career. In his memoir, *The Best Times*, he recalls his accidental meeting with playwright and director John Howard Lawson on the ship to Europe: "I'd had a certain introduction to the theater through my friend Ed Massey, who took a Baker course at Harvard and who was already involved in directing. It wasn't long before Jack [John Howard Lawson] and I were telling each other how, when we got home from the wars, we would turn the New York theater inside out" (*Best Times* 47). Although Dos Passos points to his college days for his interest in theatre, archival evidence reveals that he had been involved in the theatre during his high school years at Choate, and photographs depict him playing a young woman in a production of *The Secretary* ca. 1909.[3] In the years following World War I, Dos Passos spent much of the 1920s living between Europe and New York City's bohemian center, Greenwich Village. Unsurprisingly, he became steeped in the theatre and cabaret life on both sides of the Atlantic, not only Broadway and the Little Theatre scene in New York, but also the avant-garde cabarets of Berlin and Diaghilev's Ballet Russes in Paris, and later the national theatre in Moscow. He even helped build sets for Stravinsky's *Les Noces* for its Paris debut in 1923 (Fahy 16). While living in Paris, he and Don Stewart also met the "zanies" of Tristan Tzara's *Manifestation Dada* (*The Best Times* 159–60). Back in the United States, Dos Passos was especially taken by the plays of Eugene O'Neill. Partly inspired by O'Neill and partly by his friends Ed Massey and John Howard Lawson, Dos Passos began writing his own piece for the theatre in 1923, which was first produced as *The Moon Is a Gong* (later published as *The Garbage Man*). As he describes in the production note to *Three Plays*, the play was "an attempt to bridge the horrible chasm between the 'serious' play that takes itself seriously and the regular Broadway show that everybody is ashamed of, but that manages to keep a houseful of people sitting straight up in their seats from eight-thirty to eleven-thirty six nights a week" (*Three Plays* 75). For Dos Passos, the distinction between art and entertainment in the theatre was an artificial one. Ed Massey produced *The Moon is a Gong* with the Harvard Dramatic Club in the spring of 1925, followed by a production at the Cherry Lane Playhouse in New York in 1926.[4]

In many ways, *The Garbage Man* was an early attempt to translate his vision of an American theatrical that could blend entertainment, American rhythms, and social consciousness. On the surface, the play is a musical comedy with a "boy and girl" love story between Tom and Jane at its center. However, running beneath the standard plot—boy loves girl, boy loses girl, boy and girl reunite—is a critique of industrial capital and a more existential storyline about the nature of time and the inevitable march toward death, which is portrayed, at times, as a garbage man. By blending the themes and strategies of the more serious modernist Little Theatre with the entertaining antics of Broadway, the play reads as a satire, both making fun of Broadway clichés and engaging in them.[5] Though the play features a jazz band and several big musical numbers, musicality is often thwarted by the noises of the modern age, including machines, power plants, trains as well as phonographs and the radio. At the climax, Tom yells: "Voice of the machine, voice of the machine, I defy you" (151).[6] But of course, part of the irony of Tom's line is that his individual voice would have been barely audible above the collective cacophony. Throughout the play, Jane and Tom seem to find themselves at odds with capitalist machinery, the sounds and images of factories often looming behind them. It is a play that reflects Dos Passos's ideological position regarding urban life and factory work, which Amy Koritz has argued parallels that of Lewis Mumford, who strongly disliked the Taylorist model of the city as a machine (Koritz 143). Elevated poetic diction, music, and the melodrama of the love story work in tension with the mechanical movements of many of the other characters, foreshadowing Dos Passos's affinities with actor/director Vsevolod Meyerhold's theories of biomechanics, which he would encounter two years later during his travels in Russia. Although the play faced mixed reviews when it transferred to New York, the experience nevertheless confirmed Dos Passos's interest in the explosive possibilities of theatre.

The year following the New York premier of *The Garbage Man*, Dos Passos was invited to become a founding director of The New Playwrights Theatre (NPT), along with Mike Gold (editor of the *New Masses*), Em Jo Basshe, John Howard Lawson, and Francis Faragoh, with funding from Otto Kahn—the benefactor who also supported the Provincetown Playhouse. "The aim," Dos Passos later reflected, "was to set up a repertory theater dedicated to revolutionary expressionism in New York" along the lines of the Vieux Colombier in Paris and the Piscator in Berlin (*Best Times* 164). The theatre company offered only two full seasons between 1927 and 1929, but Dos Passos's participation in it became a catalyst for his experimental approaches to writing. During its brief existence, the New Playwrights Theatre brought together some of the preeminent writers of the day to produce plays such as *Loud Speaker* (1927) by John Howard Lawson, *The Belt* (1927) by Paul Sifton, and *Singing Jailbirds* (1929) by Upton Sinclair, among others.

In his manifesto, "Toward a Revolutionary Theatre," published in the *New Masses* in December 1927, Dos Passos articulates a vision for a theatrical community that would focus on the concerns of the working class in order to shape a left-leaning populist politics:

> *Definition*: By theatre I don't mean a building or an idea, I mean a group of people, preferably a huge group of people; part of the group puts on plays and the rest forms the audience, an active working audience.
>
> By American I don't mean that the group's interests must necessarily be limited to America, but that they should be as deeply rooted here as possible.
>
> By revolutionary I mean that such a theatre must break with the present day theatrical tradition, not with the general traditions of the theatre, and that it must draw its life and ideas from the conscious sections of the industrial and white collar working classes which are out to get control of the great flabby mass of capitalist society and mould it to their own purpose. In an ideal state it might be possible for a group to be alive and have no subversive political tendency. At present it is not possible. (101)

By imagining a theatre as collaboration between audience and performers, Dos Passos hoped the revolutionary theatre might be more grounded in real, lived experiences. In an earlier article for *Vanity Fair* in May 1925, "Is the 'Realistic' Theatre Obsolete," Dos Passos had outlined in greater detail his desire for a break with the present-day theatrical tradition by praising the kind of theatre that broke the "fourth wall," including the works of O'Neill and Lawson's *Processional: A Jazz Symphony of American Life* (1925). In such productions, "the actors are actors, you feel the boards of the stage in every line" because the audience is fully aware that "they are in a theatre seeing a show" (77). Dos Passos's descriptions sound very similar to ones Bertolt

Brecht would write in his own manifesto for the epic theatre but, in fact, the writings of Dos Passos and Lawson about the new revolutionary theatre predate Brecht and appear to have been developed independently.[7] Although Dos Passos recognized that what he was proposing was "big talk," he felt such talk was necessary: "A play or book or a picture has got to have bulk, toughness and violence to survive in the dense clanging traffic of twentieth century life" ("Toward a Revolutionary Theatre" 101).

Although Dos Passos's writings about the revolutionary theatre anticipated his 1928 trip to Russia, the sentiments expressed have much in common with the kinds of theatre to which he would later be exposed, and he had very likely already been exposed to Russian theatrical traditions indirectly through his friend and colleague Mike Gold.[8] An ardent communist, Gold had travelled to Russia in 1925 and praised the Russian theater in his 1921 manifesto, "Toward Proletarian Art," in the *Liberator*. Critical of capitalist art that was too far removed from regular people, Gold calls for a return to a Whitmanian ethic in American arts, but with a revolutionary edge. As Gold puts it, "the Revolution, in its secular manifestations of strike, boycott, mass-meeting, imprisonment, sacrifice, agitation, martyrdom, organization, is thereby worthy of the religious devotion of the artist" (22). In particular, Gold advocates for an art born from the soil. In contrast to American artists, "The Russians are creating all from the depths upward. Their *Prolet-Kult* is not an artificial theory evolved in the brains of a few phase-intoxicated intellectuals, and foisted by them on the masses" (23). Although the theatrical productions were themselves born of grass-roots initiatives, the Proletkult, which was formed after the Revolution of 1917, was essentially a state-funded arts initiative that supported hundreds of local affiliate arts organizations and thousands of individual artists making experimental art, including theater. Despite the fact that Dos Passos's writings in 1925 and 1927 do not specifically mention the Proletkult by name, his interest in a populist, publicly funded theater has much in common with such models.

As the manifestos of Gold and Dos Passos evidence, the ideals of the New Playwrights were high but the productions met mostly with small audiences and lackluster reviews, even outright scorn. As Dos Passos explains in "They Want Ritzy Art" (*New Masses,* June 1928), the plays received "a tremendous shower of brickbats from all sides" of the "capitalist press" (112). Lamenting the current desire for "the Ritzy finish that Americans are getting accustomed to," he asserts that, "this sort of finish is incompatible with growth and experiment" (114). However, Dos Passos would find the kind of stripped-down theater he was dreaming of just a few months later during his trip to Moscow.

RUSSIA, 1928

Dos Passos's journals indicate that he had been thinking about making his own trip to Russia since at least 1920 and, like many in the *New Masses* set, he was interested in seeing postrevolution socialism up close.[9] Writing to Ernest Hemingway, e.e. cummings, and others during his Russian travels, he reported that it was an incredibly "invigorating trip"—he called it "magnificient country" and thought his trip "pretty darn swell."[10] Later in life, he would stress his delight in seeing the Moscow theatre, treating his interest in socialism as secondary. Realistically, it was a trip with multiple motivations. For instance, most scholars who have addressed Dos Passos's Russian travels tend to focus on his famous meeting with film director and pioneer of montage, Sergei Eisenstein. In her entry on Dos Passos for *A New Literary History of America*, Phoebe Kosman stresses how Dos Passos's meeting with Eisenstein coincided with his work on the first book of the *U. S. A.* trilogy, *The 42nd Parallel*. But as even Kosman recognizes, while many have tried to assert that Dos Passos imitated Eisenstein's montage in his novels, "it's more accurate to say . . . that the two men's ideas were congruent" (624). After all, Dos Passos had been including montage-like effects in his novels since *Manhattan Transfer* in 1925, which predates his encounter with Eisenstein and his films. But Eisenstein was just one of Dos Passos's many encounters. In his collection of travel essays, *In All Countries* (1934), much of Dos Passos's account of his Russian travels details his struggles with the language as he attempted to interview workers and average people—he had expected revolutionary fervor, but for the most part he was met with indifference. However, in the letters and essays he wrote during his travels and immediately after, the real revelation for Dos Passos was the Moscow theater, which he attended nearly every night during the months he was there. In the Moscow theatre, the revolutionary possibilities of a collectivist society were made concrete, rather than abstract. This was true not only of the artistic subject matter, but of the economic structures of the theatre. He was especially impressed by Vsevolod Meyerhold's production of *Roar China!* and Mussorgsky's opera, *Boris Godunov*.[11] He noted too that although Konstantin Stanislavski was no longer living in Russia, they were still performing his productions of Chekov's plays. Even his meeting with Eisenstein included a debate about the proper roles of theatre and film, and in a letter to his friend e.e. cummings, Dos Passos wrote that "Eisenstein is worried over the talking movies, because he says he fears they may become an art, and bring all the worst features of the stage back on the silver screen" (*Fourteenth Chronicle* 386). One can speculate about what exactly Eisenstein meant, but most likely he feared a return to dialogue-heavy realism.

About a year after his trip Dos Passos wrote an article for *The New Republic* titled "The New Theater in Russia," which contrasts theater in New York and Moscow, arguing that the former could stand to learn from the latter, in terms not only of its style and artistry, but also its economic structures. He is bitterly critical of the New York theatre: "Everybody except the technical staff and the audience is there on speculation, hoping against hope to cash in on the various forms of exhibitionism involved, to see their names in electric lights, to make a million dollars" (236). What is more, the aesthetic values of the New York theatre were, in Dos Passos's opinion, crass:

> In New York they want to feel part of the imperial American procession towards more money, more varnish, more ritz, that obsesses all our lives; in Moscow they want to feel part of the victorious march through history of the world proletariat.
>
> The end is different, but the mechanism isn't so different. The Moscow theater gives them their money's worth and the New York theatre doesn't. (236–37)

Dos Passos's defense of the Moscow theater responds to American critics who had reported that the Moscow theater was mere propaganda, and not very good at that. However, Dos Passos felt that the problem that most Americans had with Russian theater was that it was "raw and crude" and informal (237). The theaters are more like "barns" and lacked decoration, he notes; the crowds of proletariats decidedly lack "ritz." In contrast, Dos Passos finds the American theater (by which he more nearly means Broadway) is too commercial. He writes:

> If you tell them they can learn from Moscow they'll think you're crazy. But it's so. The stage in America as a purely business proposition tends to become a mere subsidiary of Hollywood. Any theater that's to continue alive has got to appeal to other than money motives and to other feelings than the dominant dollar religion. Perhaps to the revolt against them. (237)

The problem, as Dos Passos saw it, was not merely a commercial one, but rather the lack of a true repertory theatrical tradition in America. In Russia, he writes, "each theater organism has a permanent tradition behind it. Every Russian theater has a corporate existence, like a college" (237). The benefits of this system are a sense of continuity from season to season, not just among the players and producers, but also among the audiences. Dos Passos notes that, far from being too traditional or stodgy, the Russian theater insures its vitality with "the opportunity to experiment offered by the subsidiary studios that shoot up around the roots of the big theaters. These studios are the germs of new theaters and at the same time the try-out grounds for new methods and ideas" (238). Part of the reason that Russian theater was able to flourish, explains Dos Passos, is that they are subsidized by a division of the Department of Education. As someone who had watched a little theatre company struggle to survive, Dos Passos had become keenly aware that theatre was not a business, at least not a good one; most lost money. To prove his point that theatre does not require commercialism to thrive, he names at least twenty shows being performed on a Tuesday in November in Moscow and offers a special profile of the works of Vsevolod Meyerhold.

Meyerhold was an actor, director, and producer first for the Moscow Art Theater and then for his own Meyerhold Theater. Following the revolution of 1917, he became an activist for the Soviet theater and would develop a very influential approach to acting called "biomechanics." Early in his career in 1898, Meyerhold had starred in Chekhov's *The Seagull*—at the time the cutting edge of realistic theater. But in the wake of the revolution, he rejected realism in favor of an approach to theater that emphasized carefully choreographed gesture and the laboring body. In his manifesto, "The Actor and the Future and Biomechanics" (1922), Meyerhold argues: "Art should be based on scientific principles; the entire creative act should be a conscious process. . . . Since the art of the actor is the art of plastic forms in space, he must study the mechanics of his body. This is essential because any manifestation of a force (including the living organism) is subject to the constant laws of mechanics" (qtd. in Roach 195). With this in mind, Meyerhold saw each movement of the body as "a hieroglyph which has its own meaning. On the stage there must be only those movements which can be deciphered instantly, otherwise they are superfluous" (143). This approach to the actor's body was heavily influenced by Meyerhold's belief that there must be a strong connection between actors and workers; by casting laborer-actors, he hoped to blur the line between acting and labor (142). He argued that "the actor of the future will be even more dependent on the general principles of a working society" (141), and that "the actor of the future must first of all be *well-formed, rhythmical,* able to organize his body in space (142). Biomechanics drew upon a number of different influences ranging from psychophysiological research to theories of industrialized management and, along with Stanislavsky's famous "method," biomechanics was one of the foremost theories of theatre of its time. In particular, Meyerhold was influenced by the science of reflex action pioneered by

Ivan Pavlov (best known for his experiments with dogs)—whose labs Dos Passos visited during his Russian visit (Roach 198–99). Of course, one of the ironies of the affinities between Dos Passos's and Meyerhold's productions is that Meyerhold was also interested in Frederick Winslow Taylor's *Principles of Scientific Management* (1911), which offers theories of how to make workflows (like assembly lines) more efficient and how to improve the productivity of laborers (Roach 203). While Dos Passos was skeptical of Taylorism as a model of the city, its applications to the theatre via Meyerhold's techniques struck Dos Passos in a different way. Coupled with Constructivist scenic design, Meyerhold's theater was raw, emotional, and anti-realist. Dos Passos called it "muscularly exciting" ("New Theater in Russia" 239).

Writing about two of Meyerhold's productions, Nikolai Gogol's "The Inspector General" and an *agit-spectacl* production titled "D.E., *or* Pay Up Europe," Dos Passos marvels at how Meyerhold had entirely broken with the "'fourth-wall' convention of the realistic theater" (239). Even the sets are moved by stage hands in full view of the audience, and "every effort is made to break up the tense boundary between the audience and the play, so that the audience feels the action going on in itself like a circus act or a prize fight" (239). Part of what impressed Dos Passos about the production of "The Inspector General" was the extent to which Meyerhold had plumbed the archive to create an entirely new production by drawing on letters and documents from the time. In doing so, the play offered an elaborate satire of the old Russian bureaucracy. With "D.E." Meyerhold turned his satirical eye to an American corporate empire ultimately squashed by a Red Army liberating revolution. Although Dos Passos notes the flimsiness of this plot, he is mesmerized by the technical ambition of the play's staging with a jazz band playing the music, and "the only scenery big flat wooden screens on rollers that moved almost continually, so that scenes could be shown alone, simultaneously, or alternately, with a fluidity equal to that of the movies" (239). This combination of theatrical styles—drawing on a range of traditions from Kabuki to vaudeville—was almost certainly the future of the theatre, in Dos Passos's estimation.

In reading Dos Passos's praise for Meyerhold's production, I was struck by how much his language mirrored the praise he once gave Lawson's *Processional* and productions of Eugene O'Neill's *The Emperor Jones* and *The Hairy Ape*, not to mention the vision he articulated for *The Garbage Man*.[12] There are perhaps also resonances between the Constructivist set designs of Meyerhold's productions and the backdrops Dos Passos had painted for his own plays, and especially those for Paul Sifton's *The Belt*.[13]

"Assembly Line" for *The Belt*. Image courtesy of the John Dos Passos Estate.

While Meyerhold's plays were smash hits in Russia, the same techniques did not seem to excite American audiences. And yet, the incredible popularity of these experimental plays in Russia seemed to confirm the value of the work Dos Passos and others had attempted, even if companies like the New Playwrights Theater struggled to survive in New York. As a case in point, Dos Passos's play *Fortune Heights* (1934)—about real estate speculation and the Great Depression—had multiple successful productions in Russia; stateside, however, it was a flop.

FORTUNE HEIGHTS

> "Why not look over our lots now? FORTUNE HEIGHTS We help U along the road to ownership and independence" (163)

Fortune Heights follows the lives of a complex array of characters as they intersect in a small-town filling station along a national highway near the Four Corners in the years leading up to and following the crash of 1929. Not unlike his novels, the play attempts to balance the intricacies of individual lives against their larger social contexts. The play depicts the boom and bust of real estate speculation—in particular, a housing development called Fortune Heights—and characters' attempts to stay afloat in an economic system that does not value workers and small business owners. One might claim that the story centers on Owen and his wife Florence, the owners of the filling station, and yet its decentralized narrative seems equally invested in Morry, the restless filling station attendant; Rena, the waitress whose destitute family has fled Youngstown for the west; Ike, the Jewish crime writer and would-be private investigator; and Ellery, the overly optimistic real-estate speculator who goes belly-up after the crash but later runs as a New Deal independent candidate for the state legislature. These are not mere types, but complex, rounded characters. Each of the three acts chronicles a different moment in America's transition from the Jazz Age to the New Deal Era: act one takes place two years before the stock market crash, act two charts the economic downturn as foreclosures on properties seem imminent and the stock market crashes, and act three portrays the "present," a year after the election of Franklin D. Roosevelt and the start of the New Deal. In the play's final scenes, the town is on the verge of riot as farmhands and itinerant laborers, led by Morry and joined by New Deal politician Ellery, join forces against the sheriff, who has been enforcing evictions and foreclosures. But rather than end the play with the triumph of the working class against the sheriff and the banks, the foreclosures take place anyway, and even Owen and Florence are forced to leave the filling station. Following the slow shuffling march of workers and farmers out of Fortune Heights, the play concludes ambivalently, foreshadowing a return to boom and bust real estate speculation with a kind of grim irony.[14]

The play is almost certainly too long, and the first two acts move rather slowly until a climactic moment of violence near the end of the second act. As a chronicle, however, the lengthy exposition of the first two acts is critical to establishing the context for the complex political commentary of the third act. By 1933, when Dos Passos wrote *Fortune Heights*, his commitment to revolutionary socialist politics was already starting to waver; FDR, who had campaigned on a New Deal for America, had recently been elected, and fascism in Europe was on the rise. In the play, one can see Dos Passos's attempt to grapple with how the politics and interests of formerly "red" rabble-rousers on the left were being folded into New Deal–era politics of populist democracy. Speeches made by Morry and Joe in act three, for example, invoke the Declaration of Independence, the Constitution, and American democratic values, all while stressing the need for resistance, rebellion, and organization. Alluding to the opening lines of the Constitution, Morry asks, "Well who the hell's the people if it ain't us?" (283); by Morry's account, "Resistin' oppression was how this country was started" (284). A workingman named Joe repeatedly insists: "we'll find the United States" (285). It is an uprising that looks very much like a worker's uprising, but one that is also very committed to American democratic ideals. A character like Ellery, for example, the real estate broker turned New Deal candidate offers a biting critique of Wall Street capitalism and its failure to protect the working classes while optimistically endorsing the New Deal–era programs—even as he recognizes them as too late to save the finances of many Americans (287–90). For a brief moment, it seems like the workers and the New Dealers are united, heading toward collective action; but after a mistaken shot kills Morry, things fall into disarray once again. While not exactly hopeless, the play's politics are ambivalent at best. A writer like Dos Passos, who prized individual freedom, could never comfortably sacrifice the individual to the collective cause.

Of Dos Passos's theatrical endeavors, *Fortune Heights* reached the fewest American audiences, with only a couple of small productions stateside, including one by the Chicago Workers Theater.[15] Reviews of the published version of the play that appeared in *Three Plays* were mixed. Was the play revolutionary? Was it leftist propaganda, or was it a sign that Dos Passos's political leanings had shifted? Responding to critiques against the propagandistic elements of the play, John Chamberlain of the *New York Times* wrote that "If this play is 'propaganda,' then so are the news stories about job and food riots in Minneapolis, so are the news stories about organization to resist evictions, so is the panhandler you meet on the street." Instead, Chamberlain finds Dos Passos "a novelist and playwright who knows how to listen to the Americans we all know" (17). In *Fortune Heights*, Dos Passos—ever the chronicler—attempted to capture the world as it exists. But Chamberlain may have been responding to a straw man, and critics from the left-leaning American press did not find much revolutionary material in the play to speak of. Writing for the *New Masses*, Michael Blankfort was initially intrigued by the revolutionary potential of *Fortune Heights* but felt that ultimately it "failed" in part because of Dos Passos's tendency to focus on the middle class, toward whom he can only muster a "slightly humorous and despondent attitude" (26). Isidor Schneider of *Partisan Review*, meanwhile preferred to call Dos Passos an "observer" rather than a revolutionary (54). While *Fortune Heights* presents "the American social dilemma," Schneider writes, there is no clear villain. "The villain is an abstraction which we may call Chance, although the victimized heroes are very concrete, human and suffering people. Like many squeamish writers, Dos Passos is moved by deep pity for the victims of our system but avoiding hatred, he avoids any clear representation of the men on the other side" (55). However,

Dos Passos's so-called villains are hardly abstract—they too are human; even the banker who commits suicide in *Fortune Heights* is presented as sympathetic. Were *Fortune Heights* to live up to its revolutionary ideals, it seems, a clearer villain and a more decisive victory of labor over capitalism would need to prevail. But even while Dos Passos remained convinced of the revolutionary potential of theatre as a form, by the early 1930s he was losing his taste for an abstract revolutionary socialism.

Despite these perceived deficiencies in the play's revolutionary stance by the American left, *Fortune Heights* sustained multiple successful runs in the revolutionary theaters of Russia and was even published as an excerpt in the April 1933 issue of Russia's preeminent literary journal *International Literature* (Internatsionalnaya Literatura).[16] The play made a popular debut at the Kamerny Theatre in Moscow directed by the well-known Alexander Taïrov (a collaborator of Meyerhold), with several other prominent stagings across Russia. As Dos Passos notes in a letter dated April 27, 1934, to Bernice Baumgarten at the literary agency Brandt & Brandt, "I got a word from Taïrov that the first night of his production of Fortune Heights was very successful—whatever that means, that was at the Kamermy Theatre, Moscow. It's also being done at the Trade Union Theatre in Moscow and at the Alexandrinski Theatre in Leningrad."[17] As further evidence of the play's interest to Russian audiences and readers, it was published in translation in 1934 as *Vershina schast'ia: P'esa v 3 deistvii.* [Fortune Heights: A Play in Three Acts] by Valentin Smetanich. Dos Passos was arguably the best known author of his generation in Russia; according to Lynn Purkey, only Langston Hughes and Upton Sinclair had a similar reception.[18] It is difficult to say exactly how Russian producers and audiences interpreted a play like *Fortune Heights*, but one possibility is that they viewed it as an uncomplicated satirical critique of the failures of American capitalism. The optimism and hope that many Americans felt with the election of FDR and the inauguration of the New Deal was a context that might not have fully registered with Russian readers and audiences, but it is certainly one that Dos Passos approaches ambivalently in the final scenes of *Fortune Heights*.

IMAGINING A NATIONAL THEATER

Despite the demise of the New Playwrights Theatre, the failure of *Fortune Heights* in America, and Sergei Eisenstein's prediction that talking pictures would kill theatre, Dos Passos remained cautiously hopeful about theater in America, in part because of its social function.[19] In his 1934 essay "Why Write for the Theatre Anyway?," which serves as an introduction to his collection

Three Plays, Dos Passos tries to encapsulate something of the trajectory of theatre in America in the early twentieth century, and offer a blueprint for a populist national theatre that would reinvigorate "Main Street's" interest in itself.[20] It was a vision for the theater decidedly influenced by his travels to Russia. Writing in 1934 in the midst of the Depression—a time when there was very little money for theatre and the WPA Federal Theatre Project had not yet been formed—Dos Passos wanted to recast The New Playwrights Theatre and the plays he worked on there as a kind of precursor to what could be a national theatre. Issuing a call to action, he asserts: "The musical comedies are the theater of prosperity. Let's have a theatre of depression, a theater that perhaps will be able to mould the audience a little instead of everlastingly flattering it" (xx). By Dos Passos's estimation, only a handful of theatres were making work of substance as of 1934. Those included the newly formed Group Theatre, which was highly influenced by Stanislavsky, the Theatre Union, and the Theatre Collective—but given the fate of so many little theaters, he feared such groups would not survive (xiii–xiv). Recounting the previous twenty years in American theatre, Dos Passos acknowledged that the nationwide little theatre movement (which included groups like The Provincetown Players) had revolted against Broadway but failed to unseat it (xv). But as ever, Dos Passos remained undecided about Broadway genres and unwilling to discount the reasons for its popularity: "The real American theatre art lies in musical comedy, revues, vaudeville, night club entertainment. Here there's outlet for the technical skill, the feeling for machinery, expression for the milliondollar fantasies that jazz and pretty girls and dancing liberate in the blood of office workers and business men" (xix). On the one hand, he called it "cheap art and tinselly," but on the other hand, "it tends to mirror very directly every whim and change in the popular mind. This makes it socially more valuable than the legitimate stage, as well as infinitely less shallow" (xix). This contradictory assessment at once praises American theatre's populism and denigrates its cheapness. Much to his own consternation, Dos Passos could not disentangle the popular from the populist in American culture. He might not love the tinsel of Broadway, but he recognized its real appeal to average Americans.

In the Russian theatre, however, these two things—the popular and the populist—did not appear at odds, but this partly had to do with the differences in what Dos Passos referred to as each country's national myth. For Russia, this myth was inherently political, but in America it was personal and individualistic:

> Every theatre has at any given moment a basic myth that lives in the subconscious fantasies of the audience. In Russia it's the myth of the

> leader killed and the revolutionary mass sweeping on. In America it's a boy and girl love song under the cheese cloth apple blossoms, and the boy's just made a million dollars, and they achieve Success, that mystic tabloid crown that hovers over the bright lights and skysigns of Manhattan. (xix)

But even were the American myth to change to account for a more populist, collective narrative, Dos Passos thought it more likely to manifest itself in a popular musical comedy than in the art theatre. Only after such a change could the theatre in America support "a cohesive social force, something like the Abbey Theatre or the Theatre of the Revolution in Moscow, a permanent non-speculative organization to put on plays which will express the side of the American mass myth that the musical comedies leave out," but without sacrificing entertainment value (xix–xx). In other words, a national theatre requires plays that attempt to express a national or collective identity and experience. One can sense in Dos Passos's own plays (and even in novels like *U.S.A.* and *Manhattan Transfer*) a commitment to a more decentralized and therefore more populist narrative. With *The Garbage Man*, he uses the musical-comedy form to critique the noise of industrialization, but still includes a boy-girl love story. *Airways, Inc.* turns the myth of the American aviator-as-hero on its head.[21] However, *Fortune Heights*, with its ensemble cast of characters and historical sweep, is a more conscious attempt to capture a collective narrative of America in the midst of the Great Depression. But in each of these cases, there is always a tension between the lives of the individual characters and their collective circumstances.

Writing from the vantage point of the 1930s, Dos Passos understood that American industrial life was experiencing a transition and felt that the role of art would be to chronicle and explain the "new order" that emerges. Theatre, Dos Passos felt, was the medium for such art because it had always been a mass art. The theatre, he argued, "is one of the most simple and obvious organs of contact between the mass and the individual member of the crowd. It's proving that in Russia. Granting all the differences of race and education, it could hold the same position in America." (xx). Imagining a non-commercial theatre, he writes:

> Such a theatre will have to be subsidized by some group for its own purposes. A theatre oughtn't to be expected to pay any more than an artgallery or a library. A really national or municipal theatre will be a social service, not a business. Such a theatre can play an important

> part in creating the new myth that has got to replace the imperialist prosperity myth if the machinery of American life is ever to be gotten under social control. If the theatre doesn't become a transformer for the deep high tension currents of history, it's deader than cockfighting. To such a theatre, that certainly does not exist now, and that perhaps never will exist, I respectfully dedicate these plays. (xxi–xxii)

But while Dos Passos's dream of a national theatre on the Russian model seems to staunchly reinforce his belief in the power of the collective, his larger political beliefs—and in particular, his attitudes toward Soviet Russia—had started to shift away from radical socialism, as was increasingly evident in writing he published around the same time as *Three Plays*.

RETHINKING RUSSIA

As John Trombold points out, between roughly 1935 and 1938, a series of events would change Dos Passos's ideas about the relationship between politics and art, and especially his feelings about Russia. These events included the murder of his friend Jose Robles during the Spanish Civil War, and realizations about Stalin's ongoing execution of political enemies. His attitude toward Russia following his 1928 trip was decidedly ambiguous. In the impressionistic introduction to his collection of travel reportage, *In All Countries* (1934), he recalls making his good-byes at the Sanitary Propaganda Theatre and meeting the young actors. "They were all factoryworkers in the daytime and actors at night," Dos Passos noted, but mostly "'They want to know,'" the theatre director told him, "'where you stand politically. Are you with us?'" (*Travel Books* 274). Dos Passos shakes their hands, but fails to give them an answer, fumbling in elliptical fashion as he rushes to make the train: "'But let me see . . . But maybe I can explain . . . But in so short a time . . . there's no time'" (275). This subtle evasion of the question is reflective more generally of the ambivalence he expresses throughout his essay "Russian Visa." Revising reportage and recollections from his 1928 trip in 1934, he shows in his interviews with various Soviet workers across the vast country a clear dissatisfaction. Travelling from Leningrad down the Volga to the Caspian, to the Caucasus, and through Georgia before arriving in Moscow, he spoke with various people who seemed to have their own mixed feelings about the Soviet order—eleven years after the revolution of 1917. Some were ardent communists; others were simply people trying to make a life. Of Leningrad, Dos Passos remarks darkly, "I have all the time the feeling that I'm walking around the burntout crater of a volcano.

Things I've read about it, Dostoyevski's St. Petersburg, and the Petrograd of Jack Reed's and Ransome's despatches still are more vivid in my mind that this huge empty city" (292). The spirit of the revolution eludes Dos Passos at every turn. The only place it really seemed to live was the Moscow Theatre. "In Moscow people go to the theatre to feel part of the victorious march through history of the world proletariat"—that is, they went to the theatre to feel their connection to their fellow man (306). While Dos Passos may have turned away from the politics that would make Soviet terror possible, he could never fully reject the dream of a common spirit alive in the theatre.

NOTES

1. When *Three Plays* appeared in 1934, *The New York Times*, like many publications, gave it a lackluster review, suggesting that the plays "are better as reading than they could be on stage," but even as reading found them "blurred, confused, haphazard" (P.H. BR2).
2. Alix Beeston argues that while most scholars look to the cinematic as the inspiration for the form of *Manhattan Transfer*, more attention should be paid to Dos Passos's interest in the theatre, and specifically the Follies-style revue, especially since the central character (Ellen Thatcher) is a chorine. While Beeston focuses less on Dos Passos's own theatrical endeavors, Thomas Fahy writes somewhat extensively about Dos Passos's plays, claiming that they "focus on the myths surrounding suburbanization in America" in order to critique the technologies that enable suburban growth (86). Fahy sees the plays as a seedbed for the kinds of themes that later appear in the *U.S.A.* trilogy.
3. See, Box 130 – Photos – Folder – Childhood and Youth 1896–ca.1906 (2 of 2) – Choate 1907 –1909 (Papers of John Dos Passos, Accession #5950, Special Collections, University of Virginia Library, Charlottesville, Va.)
4. The 1926 edition of *The Garbage Man* includes helpful cast lists for both productions in its appendix.
5. In one of the most recent works of scholarship to address Dos Passos's plays, *Staging Modern American Life: Popular Culture in the Experimental Theatre of Millay, Cummings, and Dos Passos* (2011), Thomas Fahy suggests that these three authors "wanted to transcend the highbrow/lowbrow divide for similar reasons," and points out that "Dos Passos's sympathies for the working class shaped his belief that art could resonate with the masses and bring about social change" (15).
6. For the purposes of this paper, I am citing the 1926 Harper & Brothers edition of *The Garbage Man*; however, it is worth noting that Dos Passos made quite a few changes to the play when it was re-published in *Three Plays* in 1934.

7. Bertolt Brecht's theoretical essay "The Modern Theatre is the Epic Theatre" was published in 1930.
8. According to Philip Gyde Poulsen, interest in Russian theatre was common to the members of the New Playwrights Theatre, and both Mike Gold and Em Jo Basshe were also pro-machine aesthetics and sympathetic to Futurism ("Drama On and Off-Stage").
9. See Box 126, Notebooks 1919–1927, n.d. 4 folders (Papers of John Dos Passos, Accession #5950, Special Collections, University of Virginia Library, Charlottesville, Va.)
10. See letters to e.e. cummings and Ernest Hemingway from September 1928 in Dos Passos and Ludington, *The Fourteenth Chronicle*, 386–87.
11. In his memoir, Dos Passos reflects, "I always felt that anybody who wanted to discover what life was like in the Soviet Union could learn more by listening to Moussorgsky's opera than by five years reading of *The New York Times*" (*Best Times* 179). For more about Meyerhold's production of *Roar China!*, see Meserve and Meserve, "The Stage History of Roar China!"
12. In "Is the 'Realistic' Theatre Obsolete?" Dos Passos remarks on the "throb of the drum" and "chesty roar" of O'Neill's expressionist plays (76). Of *Processional*, he notes the play's spectacular elements and how "you feel the boards of the stage in every line" because "There is no attempt to convince the audience that, by some extraordinary series of coincidences, they have strayed into a West Virginia mining town in the middle of an industrial war. They are in a theatre seeing a show" (77).
13. Special thanks to Lisa Nanney and Lucy Coggin for providing the image.
14. The final scene features an agent showing a foreclosed piece of a real estate to a couple "*who look as much as possible like owen and florence without being mistaken for them*" (297). "One man's misfortune is the next man's opportunity," the agent proclaims (298).
15. The Chicago Workers Theater (1933–1934) was a precursor to the Chicago Repertory Group (CRG), which would be an important venue for plays written under the WPA Federal Theater Project. The advisory board for the CRG included Langston Hughes, Clifford Odets, Morris Carnovsky, and Lee Strasberg, and the company maintained close ties to New York's Group Theatre. For more about the theater, see Chicago Repertory Group.
16. This publication is listed in the Chronology of John Wrenn's biography of Dos Passos.
17. See Box 18, Folder (1 of 11) Brandt and Brandt "Dos Passos File" (Papers of John Dos Passos, Accession #5950, Special Collections, University of Virginia Library, Charlottesville, Va.) The letter also alludes to a production in Chicago by The Workers Theatre that was "greatly panned by what critics saw it."

18. See Purkey, "Famously (not) Forgotten."
19. In response to Eisenstein, Dos Passos asserted:

    > I don't think the talkies are ever going to give an audience the sense of personal participation they can get out of a circus performance, vaudeville show or ballet, and as industrial life becomes increasingly social, with the individual unit more and more penned into its own unicellular life like a coral insect, the need for group excitements that the individual can really (not only through the radio) participate in, like theater and sport, is obvious. ("The New Theater in Russia" 239)

20. On the one hand, he acknowledged that performance practices in post–World War I America had been influenced by an influx of theatre, opera, and ballet from Germany and Russia. On the other hand, American performance also had also begun to have an international influence: "Cosmopolitan ritz became everybody's idea. American jazz, the Ziegfeld show, the New York type of revue, became the dominant expression in the world of the millionaire fantasy" (*Three Plays* xvi). The only problem with this American cosmopolitanism, as far as Dos Passos was concerned, was that "Main Street" took to "looking arty and the Dôme and lost interest in their home towns" (xvi).
21. Writing about *Airways, Inc.*, Edmund Wilson observes, "The aviator is one of the authentic heroes that our American civilization now produces. But for Lawson or Dos Passos, an aviator cannot be an authentic hero, or even apparently, a genius, because he is not on the side of revolution" (33).

WORKS CITED

Beeston, Alix. "A 'Leg Show Dance' in a Skyscraper: The Sequenced Mechanics of John Dos Passos's *Manhattan Transfer*." *PMLA*, vol. 131, no. 3, May 2016, pp. 636–51. doi:10.1632/pmla.2016.131.3.636.

Belkind, Allen, editor. *Dos Passos, the Critics, and the Writer's Intention*. Southern Illinois UP, 1971.

Blankfort, Michael. "A Novelist in the Theatre (Three Plays, Review)." *New Masses*, vol. XII, no. 4, July 1934, p. 26.

Carr, Virginia. S., and Donald. Pizer. *Dos Passos: A Life*. Northwestern UP, 2004.

Chamberlain, John. "Books of the Times." *New York Times*, 23 May 1934, p. 17. https://www.proquest.com/docview/101249463

Chicago Repertory Group Collection of Scripts and Scrapbooks 1933–1947, Finding Aid, Special Collections Research Center, University of Chicago Library. https://www.lib.uchicago.edu/e/scrc/findingaids/view.php?eadid=ICU.SPCL.CRG.

Dos Passos, John. *Airways, Inc.* The Macaulay Company, 1928.

———. *The Best Times: An Informal Memoir*. New American Library, 1968.

———. *The Garbage Man: A Parade with Shouting*. Harper Brothers, 1926.

———. "Is the 'Realistic' Theatre Obsolete?" *John Dos Passos: The Major Nonfictional Prose*, edited by Donald Pizer, Wayne State UP, 1988, pp. 75–78.

———. *John Dos Passos: Travel Books & Other Writings 1916–1941*. Library of America, 2003.

———. "The New Theater in Russia." *The New Republic*, Apr. 1930, pp. 236–40.

———. "They Want Ritzy Art." *John Dos Passos: The Major Nonfictional Prose*, edited by Donald Pizer, Wayne State UP, 1988, pp. 112–14.

———. *Three Plays: The Garbage Man, Airways, Inc., Fortune Heights*. Harcourt, Brace, 1934.

———. "Toward a Revolutionary Theatre." *John Dos Passos: The Major Nonfictional Prose*, edited by Donald Pizer, Wayne State UP, 1988, pp. 101–03.

Dos Passos, John, and Townsend Ludington. *The Fourteenth Chronicle: Letters and Diaries of John Dos Passos*. Gambit, 1973.

Fahy, Thomas. *Staging Modern American Life: Popular Culture in the Experimental Theatre of Millay, Cummings, and Dos Passos*. Palgrave Macmillan US, 2011.

Hook, Andrew, editor. *Dos Passos: A Collection of Critical Essays*. Prentice-Hall, Inc., 1974.

Koritz, Amy. *Culture Makers: Urban Performance and Literature in the 1920s*. U of Illinois P, 2009.

Kosman, Phoebe. "1928, Summer: A Radical Writer Visits the Soviet Union and Meets Sergei Eisenstein." *A New Literary History of America*, edited by Greil Marcus and Werner Sollors, Belknap Press of Harvard UP, 2009, pp. 623–25.

Landsberg, Melvin. *Dos Passos' Path to U.S.A.: A Political Biography*. 1972. Associated UP, 1984

Law, Alma, and Mel Gordon, editors. *Meyerhold, Eisenstein and Biomechanics: Actor Training in Revolutionary Russia*. McFarland, 1996.

Ludington, Townsend. *John Dos Passos: A Twentieth Century Odyssey*. Dutton, 1980.

Maine, Barry. *John Dos Passos*. Routledge, 1997.

Meserve, Walter J., and Ruth I. Meserve. "The Stage History of Roar China! Documentary Drama as Propaganda." *Theatre Survey*, vol. 21, no. 1, May 1980, pp. 1–13. *Cambridge Core*, doi:10.1017/S004055740000764X.

Papers of John Dos Passos, Accession #5950, Special Collections, University of Virginia Library, Charlottesville, Va.

P. H. "The Combative Plays of John Dos Passos: THREE PLAYS." *New York Times*, 20 May 1934, p. BR2. *ProQuest*, https://www.proquest.com/docview/101246309.

Pizer, Donald. *Dos Passos' U.S.A.: A Critical Study*. UP of Virginia, 1988.

———. *Toward a Modernist Style: John Dos Passos*. Bloomsbury Publishing, 2013.

Pizer, Donald, Lisa Nanney, and Richard Layman. *The Paintings and Drawings of John Dos Passos: A Collection and Study*. Clemson UP, 2016.

Poulsen, Philip Gyde. "Drama On and Off-Stage – The New Playwrights Theatre." Third Biennial John Dos Passos Society Conference, 20–22 June 2018, The Geographical Society of Lisbon, Lisbon, Portugal. Conference Presentation.

Purkey, Lynn. "Famously (not) Forgotten: The Russian Reception of John Dos Passos." Third Biennial John Dos Passos Society Conference, 20–22 June 2018, The Geographical Society of Lisbon, Lisbon, Portugal. Conference Presentation.

Roach, Joseph R. *The Player's Passion: Studies in the Science of Acting*. U of Michigan P, 1993.

Schneider, Isador. "Dos Passos: Sympathetic Spectator (Three Plays Review)." *Partisan Review*, vol. 1, no. 3, July 1934, pp. 54–55.

Trombold, John. "From the Future to the Past: The Disillusionment of John Dos Passos." *Studies in American Fiction*, vol. 26, no. 2, 1998, pp. 237–56. *Crossref*, doi:10.1353/saf.1998.0000.

Wagner, Linda W. *Dos Passos: Artist as American*. U of Texas P, 2014.

Wilson, Edmund. "Dos Passos and the Social Revolution." *Dos Passos: A Collection of Critical Essays*, edited by Andrew Hook, Prentice-Hall, Inc., 1974, pp. 31–35.

Wrenn, John H. *John Dos Passos*. Twayne Publishers, 1962.

8

DOS PASSOS AND THE PROMISE AND FAILURES OF THE SECOND SPANISH REPUBLIC, 1933

David Murad

Readings of John Dos Passos's life and writings have often explored his ties and interests in Spain through the Spanish Civil War (1936–1939), citing especially his falling out with Ernest Hemingway and supposed "disillusionment" with the left over the disappearance of his long-time Spanish friend José Robles.[1] However, it is telling that Dos Passos's informal memoir *The Best Times* ends not with his trip to Spain in 1937 but rather in 1933, a six-week journey across several regions during the Second Republic. Scholars have given scant attention to this trip, typically only noting brief run-ins with Hemingway at the restaurant Botín, which Dos Passos remembers as "the last time Hem and I were able to talk about things Spanish without losing our tempers" (*Best Times* 220). From such comments comes a narrative in the period's literary scholarship that, until 1937, Dos Passos and Hemingway were generally aligned regarding Spain or politics. Soon after 1937, critics suggest, Hemingway embraced the left with his homage to the Spanish Republican fighters in *For Whom the Bell Tolls,* while Dos Passos, wallowing in disillusionment, gradually swerved right, starting with his anti-communist sentiments in "Farewell to Europe" (1937), and then *Adventures of a Young Man* (1939).

While these readings have merit, they often ignore Dos Passos's entire oeuvre, including "The Republic of Honest Men," the chapter title of his Spanish excursions and interviews in the summer of 1933 and published in *In All Countries* (1934).[2] The lack of critical attention to this chapter—which contains over a dozen short essays covering a wide swath of Spanish life and politics, from the Golden Age through 1933—may partly stem from Dos Passos's own original assessments. Upon returning to the United States that fall, in a letter to his editor, Cap Pearce, Dos Passos commented that "things in Spain politically are not as interesting as I'd thought. . . . As I was laid up a good deal of the time I was not able to do half the traveling I'd intended" (qtd. in Ludington, *John Dos Passos* 317). Townsend Ludington concludes that "Because of this and because Spain was less interesting politically than he had expected, he would have to change the character of the book" (*John Dos Passos* 317). Ludington later highlights an October letter in which Dos Passos tells Hemingway the "Summer was pretty much a fracaso," or a "failure," a quote featured as the epigraph to Virginia Spencer Carr's chapter covering these years.[3] Is it any wonder critics typically ignore this stretch of Dos Passos's writing—given that the author and his biographies have so foregrounded the disappointments of this period?

"Failure," of course, was partly having had to alter the trip's itinerary. That spring, Dos Passos had been hospitalized with rheumatic fever, which waned into the summer, hampering his travels. Years later, he also revealed how car troubles had interfered (*Best Times* 228–29). One sympathizes with his disappointment: how many lost opportunities to write, report, assess? Meanwhile, he had big expectations and was planning—even financially counting—on publishing a full volume (not just one chapter) on Spain.[4] In the spring, he had signed a contract with Harcourt-Brace and mused about how a resulting book might "be burned by Hitler, pissed on in the Kremlin, used for toilet paper by the anarchist syndicalists, deplored by the Nation, branded by the New York Times, derided by the Daily Worker and left unread by the Great American Public" (*Fourteenth Chronicle* 431). A book receiving that kind of vitriolic (and so noted) reaction would need to make a significant, even jarring, critical statement. And Dos Passos was hoping to deliver by traveling a country on fire with progressive change. Yet, despite the promise of a "Second Republic," there were deep divisions and mounting challenges. As I argue below, his remark that "things in Spain politically are not. . . interesting" does not suggest his ensuing chapter was itself uninteresting or lacking political insights. Rather, Dos Passos's phrase is a lamentation that the country's changes in government (after years of monarchical and, more recently, dictatorial rule) had not meaningfully reformed the political power structures. Thus, given his original expectations, his own limitations, and the less promising political landscape, the summer of 1933 was, admittedly, a partial "fracaso."

With these factors in mind, we can approach "The Republic of Honest Men" more soberly against the realities of the day and with the advantage of hindsight. History shows today that 1933 is deeply embedded within the larger context of the coming Civil War. But in 1933, such a conflict was not a given. In a series of thought-provoking sections, Dos Passos speaks to the political hostilities and complexities that would ultimately result in war. Despite its smaller stature, "The Republic of Honest Men" is a prescient chronicling of the emotions, attitudes, upsides, and defeats of 1930s Spanish life and politics. A close reading also indicates that Dos Passos was not a blind cheerleader of idyllic leftist causes or a once-doe-eyed liberal whose naïve worldview was later shattered by tragic events. Rather than serving as some partisan disciple's lament, "The Republic of Honest Men" scripts, even warns of, the structural problems and intense divisions despite the promise of the new Republic. Thus, Dos Passos emerges as a critical, and ultimately impartial and consistent "chronicler" of world affairs, in Spain or beyond.

Dos Passos was not a Spaniard, and we should accept that his critical approach, or "chronicling," was as someone who spent only so much time in the country and learned only so much of language and custom. However, his intellectual and personal background should not be undervalued. Harvard-educated, he was also somewhat of a linguist, having grown up fluent in both French and English, and his life and writing up to 1933 were well in-touch with international (specifically European) affairs. Although long categorized as an American writer, his upbringing was transnational in nature. Born in America in 1896, he was quickly moved to Europe, where residences included Belgium, Germany, France, and England. Much of his schooling was in the United States, but over the years he moved back and forth between the continents (travel destinations included Italy, Egypt, Greece, Turkey, and Mediterranean islands), so that by the time he was sixteen, he had spent much of his life abroad. This transnational journey continued the following two decades, as he spent time in Europe during World War I, with stints in Spain before and afterward. Reading Dos Passos's works through a lens of transnationalism—which acknowledges that individuals or communities are not necessarily divided into strict, distinct national units or identities—provides a useful construct for understanding this unique, thoughtful, and well-traveled writer. He was well-suited to address national issues that might both extend beyond and span his burgeoning American identity.

Dos Passos was also particularly well-read and well-acquainted with Spain. When he first arrived, in 1916, he secured various contacts, many of them, Dos Passos recalled later, "couldn't have been better chosen": "They were the journalists and literary people of what was then known as the generation of 1898." He befriended numerous Spaniards, including "José Giner, a nephew of Giner de los Rios, the great educator who was the apostle of the Spanish liberals" (*Best Times* 30), and a relation to Francisco de los Ríos Urruti, who plays an indirect and rather inauspicious role in "The Republic of Honest Men." By 1933, he had travelled often to Spain, totaling to more than a year's experience, and had published over twenty articles, poems, stories, and translations, among other materials, pertaining to the country. While some appraisals had a tourist's eye—a romantic sheen attributable to his age and early writing style—he maintained a student-like and then scholarly approach, aiming to learn as much as he could. Learning developed into sincere social criticism and pragmatism: his artistry can be both "fascinated by Spain" (as he wrote to friend Rumsey Marvin [*The Fourteenth Chronicle* 66]) and instructive. For, if on the one hand we recognize, as Donald Pizer argues, that "the basis for his fascination with Spain" rested on "its difference from other Western societies" (6), we should also understand that *difference* was ultimately the impetus for further learning. These Spanish lessons impressed upon his entire oeuvre. As Ludington argues, "From the moment in October 1916 when he first arrived in Madrid until he departed Barcelona in early May 1937, he was a kind of student of the Spanish and their culture . . . Spain was the most important factor among many in shaping Dos Passos's ideas and forming the way he saw the world" ("I Am" 313). Spain impressed him, and his writings about the country were, in turn, an amalgamation of personal reflections, critical observations, and poignant commentary.

The strength of "The Republic of Honest Men" derives from this blended approach as well as its scholarly, journalistic analysis of events and ideas at both the micro and macro levels. One section leads the reader down to the streets of Madrid, Santander, or Casas Viejas, as if reporting to non-Spaniards abroad; another looks out broadly to the Golden Age, Restoration, or Generation of '98, as if weighing national or global implications to a history class. Previous works on Spain, notably *Rosinante to the Road Again* (written and revised through the early 1920s), incorporated a shifting perspective of time and content but primarily as an artistic mode. "The Republic of Honest Men," on the other hand, does so to further characterize the push and pull of right-left politics and Spanish reform movements—political shifts that too often squeeze working class folks against the weight of a larger historical trajectory. For centuries, Dos Passos writes, Spain had "been acting out a very old and very beautifully arranged play" toward liberal reforms. The story was of a "redeemer coming to life in the spring" to overtake an old system. But an oscillating "older and newer" Spain was ever-present and difficult to overcome (*In All* 137). Ultimately, while various Spanish governments promised to be the savior of the people, none succeeded in fully bringing those reforms to reality.

Observing a "new" Spain constrained by its past, Dos Passos examines the back-and-forth between ideals and reality, hopefulness and cynicism during a political transformation. Consider the very title, picked up from the "cries of *Vivan los hombres honrados*, Hurray for honest men" chanted so earnestly at a Socialist rally in Santander (*In All* 121). At one level, Dos Passos accepts the word *honest* sincerely, as rightfully attesting to the good, honest men and women represented by the new Republic. Yet his chapter also accosts *honest* as an irony, a sarcastic if not tragic undertone to the surrounding realities. In the first section, "Doves in the Bullring," rally-goers and laborers (and their idealism) are put into contrast with dishonest political forces (the stark reality) through images of white birds, sheep, and wolves (respectively emblematic of peace, innocence, and violence). Along with their wives and children, Virginia Spencer Carr observes, "Miners, mechanics, and farmers had come in mule carts, buses, on bicycles, and on foot from all over northern Spain. . . . [They] sang the 'Internationale' and proclaimed the Second Republic to be 'the Republic of Honest Men.'" The parade opens peacefully and with promise. But when two white pigeons are let go in the hopes of symbolizing "the reign of peace and goodwill that was to come," they only "dropped to the ground because they had probably been cooped up in the heat too long." That was "a portent that the Second Republic was destined for trouble" (317).[5] The pigeons signify hope threatened by the reality of circumstance or environment, which aligns with the predicament of the rally-goers. After the rally, the workers and families parade back through town, "mild, straggling, wellmannered and," Dos Passos adds, "a little embarrassed" given the "silent hatred of the people at the café tables"—"people with gimlet eyes and greedy predatory lines on their faces." A silent yet obvious "hatred" signals palpable tensions between "predators" and prey. These onlookers "knew how to make two duros grow where one had grown before," and the rally-goers must "[file] on by as innocent as a flock of sheep in the wolf country" (*In All* 122–23). Rather than a triumphant symbol of optimism and prosperity, the rally only exposes deep divisions between economic or political classes. A sharp schism between those who own the country's wealth and those who labor for that prosperity will be a recurring theme in the chapter.

The Santander rally is just one demonstration that this period of Spanish history is far from "politically uninteresting." A constitutional monarchy in the decades preceding, Spain had recently been ruled by the king-supported, nationalistic military dictatorship of Miguel Primo de Rivera during the 1920s. In January 1930 (after falling support from the right, including the military and the king), Primo de Rivera resigned, creating an abrupt chasm of power. King Alfonso XIII attempted to stabilize the government with Dámaso Berenguer, then viewed as a more liberal alternative; but as Javier Tusell and Genoveva Queipo de Llano point out, Berenguer's approach was also anachronistic: he aimed to revert to a pre–Primo de Rivera era of government that relied on an outdated constitution and system of order. Moreover, at the outset of a worldwide great depression, the country needed a far more proactive government (218). Within a year, coalitions from radicals to centrists would successfully draw out Alfonso's own "abdication" (not officially but ultimately so), following the first wave of "Republic" elections in April 1931. As Dos Passos quips in the subsection "The Royal Palace," Alfonso fled for France "as stealthily as a defaulting bank cashier," leaving behind "The crown of Spain . . . found poked into a green baize bag, in a wardrobe in the palace" (*In All* 126). The crown's discovery in an actual closet bag is partially humorous and an odd, sober ending to a dynastic monarchy that lasted over two centuries in Spain. But in analogizing Alfonso's fleeing in economic terms, Dos Passos effectively links the monarchy to wealth and banks. Given the class tensions outlined in the previous section, the passage further suggests that even if Alfonso had left Spain, the repercussions and consequences of that old system had not: the monarchy and wealthy classes still owned Spain's riches while a potent symbol of the monarchy still lurked in the shadows.[6]

In the immediate wake of Alfonso's leaving, the country's schisms might have appeared less pronounced, less threatening. As widespread excitement, anticipation, and hope followed the 1931 elections, Tusell and Queipo de Llano find an "awakened," "impassioned" populace: "Spain had never known elections in which all citizens, across all classes, were so interested," and "Spanish society gave the impression that it was dispensing with monarchist institutions because these were an impediment to its modernization" (219). Comparing it to Weimar Germany, they observe a "strong reformist character" (220). Nigel Townson affirms that this early spirited wave gave rise to a Republican-Socialist coalition that later "won a landslide victory in the general election of June 1931" (224). "The Republic of Honest Men" captures this initial jubilation with Dos Passos keying in on themes of celebration and unity:

> You could shout "Viva la Republica" into the moustaches and mausers of the Civil Guard without being arrested. Trucks paraded the main thoroughfares crowded with armyofficers and sailors and workingmen in blue denim singing the *Marseillaise* together. In the Puerta del Sol an army officer appeared on the balcony of the Gubernacion (the ministry that traditionally has charge of breaking the heads of dissenting citizens) and hoisted the new tricolor, red yellow and purple, to the flagpole. (*In All* 126–27)

Like the Santander rally, the atmosphere is a "parade," but here shouts of joy and song are woven harmoniously among the various representatives of Spanish life: "armyofficers" and workingmen cheer in unison—or at least on equal terms (an everyman "you" who could look eye-to-eye with a Civil Guard). In this passage, there is not yet the glimmer of a silent hatred, as distinct Spanish classes appear able to co-exist.

Had Dos Passos's chapter only emphasized this immediate jubilation—or had it only focused on the brighter side of the Republican or reformist causes—it might have been like any other political propaganda. And it would have been disingenuously incomplete. Historians have since argued that the initial waves of Republican gains were not a symptom of a completely progressive, converted, or likeminded population. The parade was real; but it was also a façade. Townson observes that the election results were a "misleading snapshot of the balance of forces within the Republic. First, the right, still disorientated and disorganized, was underrepresented." Moreover, monarchists had joined Republicans under the impression monarchy was a lost cause (an impression that reversed course soon after). "The failure of 1931–1933," Townson adds, "to take such recent converts realistically into account would frustrate and even prevent the application of reform," ultimately undermining "relations between the left republicans and their socialist allies" (224). Francisco J. Romero Salvadó concurs that, while "unprecedented festivities erupted in Spain" in the first days and months of the Second Republic, "there existed latent and profound social conflicts barely concealed by the national celebrations. They were only momentarily submerged but would reappear in full once the initial euphoria was over" (27).

In Dos Passos's text, these latent conflicts are purposefully "unsubmerged." He will take the "recent converts realistically into account," without falling into the trap of misplaced optimism or unsubstantiated outcomes. Amid the "Viva la Republica" celebrations, where "unpopular" "generals and politicos" were leaving the country, there remained behind powerful and far less enthusiastic community members, who did not support a Republic from the same perspective, if at all. "Wealthy businessmen stayed at home with shutters closed and doors barred till they found out how a liberated Spain was going to behave. Even the dyedinthewood republicans," Dos Passos adds, "were uneasy when they stepped out of doors that morning and found themselves in the middle of the glorious republic of honest men . . . (*In All* 127). In one respect, the passage may allude to the threat of sporadic violence in 1930s Spain, especially between antagonistic groups: workers and owners or various political groups and the Spanish state. Although the transition out of the monarchy was "rapid and bloodless," Romero Salvadó writes, "[t]hroughout 1931, strikes and riots [were] induced by" various anarchist or communist groups (28, 38–39). Meanwhile, although labor conflicts during the Republic were "greatest in the countryside," relations between workers and employers worsened in both "urban and rural areas" given economic crises at-home and abroad (Townson 225–27). Perhaps businessmen and politicians had sufficient cause to "bar" the doors and tread "uneasily" outward.

Ultimately, though, much like the predatory café dwellers of Santander, these powerful classes serve primarily as a *threatening* presence (not a *threatened* one). The wealthy businessmen are quite like the defaulting bank cashiers or the Spanish crown: they clearly still own the wealth; though shuttered away, for now, their power and presence remain only behind closed doors. In calling out Republican politicians, moreover, Dos Passos appears far less naïve about the political transformation. Criticizing outgoing parties is easy; warning of the incoming—and one you might generally agree with—takes steady judgment, critical awareness, and foresight. While Dos Passos sympathized with a reformist spirit and progressive cause, he was not going to be convinced simply by rhetoric or platform. During the Santander rally, for instance, Socialist leaders spoke "simply and definitely," but by incorporating their own "vague" political slogans, they too mirrored their conservative forebears (*In All* 120–21). Looking for a "kind of order the workers and producers wanted," the Socialists claimed they "had no choice but to go ahead and install socialism right away (cheers) . . . through a dictatorship if need be (more cheers)" (120, ellipses in text). Any optimism generated by the first phrase is undermined by the cynicism of the next. Ultimately, the rally—almost a microcosm of the whole reform movement—reflects a political battle for power (order and control) and not a people's revolution. Furthermore, that the main speaker was Ríos Urruti, cousin to an early Spanish friend, shows Dos Passos's criticism stretched across party and friendly lines.[7]

The chapter's criticism lands on two primary culprits: an old guard, represented by aristocratic lineages and attitudes, an established upper class, and entrenched wealth; and a new Republican leadership, whose initial aims were to represent the people and open wealth and prosperity to all, but who Dos Passos ultimately classifies as a new version of the old story. With Alcalá Zamora, whom Dos Passos calls the "silvertongued head of the new government," "It was the turn of the intellectuals to spring to the defense of order, progress, and the rights of private property" (*In All* 128). Given the concentration of wealth and land in the hands of so few, the last point upends the first two, and order and progress become a farce. *Order* means protecting the wealthy and those already entrenched; *progress* means business as usual. Partly cynicism—and one that at first glance ignores significant, even radical reforms by the Zamora government in the coming months—the passage is rather cautionary. Despite the Republic's best intentions, overturning centuries of worker and peasant exploitation is not just about changing governments, whatever the slogans promise or portend.

That a Spanish working class might not benefit from this changing of the guard is further emphasized in two sections about Madrid, one on the Ateneo—an academic parlor, lecture-forum, library of sorts—and another on cafés. "It's no accident," Dos Passos writes, "that Manuel Azaña, the dominant political leader of the liberal republicans, was president of the Ateneo before he was president of the council of ministers," nor was it an accident that writers of the recent constitution were "Ateneistas" (*In All* 129). While Dos Passos can praise the Ateneo as "the finest flower of free thought of the rising middle classes in the nineteenth century and Madrid is the very special soil in which it grew" (*In All* 130), these spaces of influence (Ateneo, cafés, Madrid itself) are representative of a greater problem: stale intellectualism that comprises or endorses an out-of-touch elite. First, Madrid is a city "invented by Philip II" (notably, a man of "order") to move Spain out of its medieval past and into the sixteenth century and beyond. Yet in also being a "lay capital" full of clerks recording and holding down "scattered empires," Madrid becomes "the first great bureaucracy in the modern world" (*In All* 132). The pejorative is *bureaucracy*: when the Spanish empire died, "[o]nly the bureaucracy went on giving out reflex motions like the legs of a dead frog . . . the bureaucracy was admittedly nothing but a jobholders' paradise," void of any "concrete thought of service to the commonwealth" (*In All* 132–33). While they might be "the brains and spinal column of Madrid," the cafés and Ateneo symbolize the faults of bureaucratic malaise and the disconnect between the "commonwealth" (the average citizen, worker) and the "jobholders" (not productive laborers but an entitled class, whose "jobs come from family pull, money comes from a salary or a stipend, or from the lottery or roulette" [*In All* 134]). Zamora, Azaña, and the Ateneistas were intellectual proponents of the Republican cause, but they were also remnants and propagators of a decadent middle- to upper-class ethos. Would this entitled intelligentsia be able to overturn centuries of bureaucratic indolence and worker exploitation? Under ideal settings, perhaps in time, but not if merely appropriating past systems of order. Dos Passos continues, wryly, that in this decadent atmosphere, everyone "was very wellbehaved indeed. Property and persons were respected. Everybody was for law and order in the shape of the now republican Civil Guard led by the now republican General Sanjurjo" (*In All* 127). At best, "wellbehaved" and "respected" speak to a "law and order" that either maintains the status quo or else offers change of little or no consequence. At worst, the passage is dark humor, given Dos Passos's coming commentary on abuses carried out under the Republic.

Perhaps the most significant phrase is "now republican," which suggests many of these individuals or institutions are converts in name only—they have come off the sidelines not out of duty to the people or ethic but for personal gain or survival. The case of General José Sanjurjo is especially telling. In one respect, Sanjurjo exemplifies the double-faced nature of Spanish politics in these transition years. A well-known leader from the Moroccan Rif wars, Sanjurjo represented the older, traditionalist, militarist, conservative Spain. Despite this, he originally offered assurances to Republican leaders that the Civil Guard, which he oversaw, would not interfere with the 1931 election results (i.e., would not defend the monarchy in the event of their loss). This "defection" (which might also be viewed as allegiance or opportunism, depending on perspective), Gerald J. Blaney writes, helped instill the "neutrality of the Civil Guard" and was "fundamental for the peaceful, and perhaps successful, installation of the Republic" (33). However, just a year later, Sanjurjo's public support for the new government (whether façade or not) ended abruptly when he led a failed uprising. He had been reassigned from his Civil Guard post following a deadly response to a protest in Arnedo, a small town in La Rioja.[8] "After Arnedo," Paul Preston writes, "Sanjurjo declared that the Civil Guard stood between Spain and the imposition of Soviet communism and that the victims [of the Civil Guard's deadly response] were part of an uncultured rabble that had been deceived by malicious agitators" (*Spanish Holocaust* 23). Socialists were also a threat to the Spanish government "because their presence encourages those who favour excess" (qtd. in Casanova 54).

It could be argued that Sanjurjo was merely defending the Spanish people against a corrupted government, but his stock characterizations of the socialist left, and of whom to blame for Spanish woes, align well with the coming rhetoric employed by the anti-Republican right in the Civil War. With this malcontent and perspective—and just nine months after Arnedo—Sanjurjo declared a "state of emergency" from Seville, using "the classic tradition of the military *pronunciamento*" to announce a military dictatorship (Casanova 75). The insurrection—to be called the *Sanjurjada*—was short-lived, as other Civil Guard corps and military garrisons failed to join, and Sanjurjo was promptly arrested.

In the "Port of Seville" subsection, Dos Passos alludes to this uprising as a "typical" clash between right and left, but it is noteworthy that his harshest criticism is for the disorganization, ineffectiveness, and ultimate failure on the left's part especially. Despite Seville having "suffered the worst slump of any Spanish town," its strong working-class organizations had helped "[nip] General Sanjurjo's uprising in the bud." And how did various leaders on the left (including "the government rightwing socialists," a sharp three-word description) respond? They jailed the very groups who had defended against the monarchists, and "[w]hat resulted was the crushing of the Longshoremen's Union, the buildingup of a small weak Socialista Tammany, a bitter triangular fight between socialists, communists and anarchists, all equally threatened with unemployment and starvation, shooting, gangsterism and bleak discouragement." In effect, the left's response was no better than chaotic governance or harsh autocratic rule. Reflecting on the repercussions of this mess—and with a nod to the fall 1933 elections in particular—Dos Passos observes that "[i]t's not surprising that propertyowners, backed up by the unsleeping everunited organization of the church, carried the day" (*In All* 149–50). Again arrives an image of a rightist coalition on the sidelines ("unsleeping," as if silent but alert), and the whole passage reaffirms that forces capable of undermining the Republic were not addressed in the 1931 elections and that the political left's own disunity or corruption need only stir such forces out of slumber. Writing in the fall of 1933, Dos Passos obviously has the benefit of knowing that this "everunited" right coalition (in Seville and beyond) gained seats in later elections. But his critique of the reasons why—especially that "triangular fight" within the left—makes the chapter precise, diagnostic, and ultimately prescient to what transpired in the years leading up to and during the Civil War.

In a way, Sanjurjo is emblematic of the "unsleeping" coalition right: he is a figure who, much like other characters in "The Republic of Honest Men," may be originally removed from power only to return time and time again, and this even well beyond what Dos Passos could have known or imagined in 1933. Following the revolt, Azaña's government originally sentenced Sanjurjo to death, but Azaña, aiming to quell a "long tradition of uprisings and firing squads," commuted that penalty to life in prison, a sentence pardoned by a later government in 1934, which allowed Sanjurjo the freedom to participate against the Republic in the more impactful rebellion of July 1936 (Casanova 75–76). Sanjurjo's core motivations and allegiances would perhaps come full circle, but in the text Dos Passos is not suggesting a complete obliteration or purge of the political right to preemptively guard against such possibilities. Instead, his chapter outlines why the Republic at-large failed to secure a true people's/worker's movement that might successfully defend itself from such anti-Republican threats. The recipe for failure is a mixture of ineptitude and betrayal by various parties.

Sentiments of ineptitude and betrayal arrive in sections recounting the 1931 constitutional reforms, as well as the Republican government's response to civil strife. As Townson argues, the 1931 elections emboldened the left, and Azaña's government initiated legislative reforms, but its

> new lease on life came to an abrupt end in January 1933 with the repression of a CNT insurrection that had stretched from Catalonia to Cádiz. In the southern village of Casas Viejas, the Republic's own security force, the recently created Assault Guards, killed 22 peasants, most of them in cold blood. Although the Azaña administration was not directly implicated in the massacre, its image was badly tarnished. (228)

In "The Republic of Honest Men," Dos Passos carefully addresses these 1931–1933 actors and events, depicting various political parties vying for power and various local events taking on nationwide import. Before addressing Casas Viejas directly, "Las Constituyentes" covers the Republic's legislative efforts as idealistic, yet impractical at best and harmful at worst. While he admits that the intellectuals and their "tertulias" (more informal academic conversations or debates that might occur in the cafés) were "the republic's strength," they were also its "weakness": "The trouble was that the life of a professor, of the holder of a sinecure in a government office, or an entertaining talker in a café, offers little training in dealing with the grim coarse hardtoclassify and often deadly realities of the life of a country day by day. They never could span the distance between word and deed" (*In All* 135). Like other passages in the chapter, idealism runs heavy into reality. The intellectuals were good at rhetoric—and had articulated lofty ideals—but they fell short on putting those ideas into practice. Despite all "their various ideas about liberty, education, transportation, and farming," these "wellintentioned gentlemen" "helped create a Spain they did not intend" (*In All* 135–36).

In a lengthy paragraph that follows, Dos Passos lays out the various liberal reforms, many with possibly fine intentions but that are ultimately unable to "span the distance between word and deed." Among the more disputed reforms, the Republic

> established a new corps of strongarm men, the Assault Guards, whose business it is to break up demonstrations hostile to the Republic of Workers and to private property . . . and passed a Law of Public Order and a Law against Vagrancy that would have made old

> Fernando VII, the Bourbon who got most pleasure out of shooting down his subjects, stand aghast. They sanctioned casual arrests of batches of citizens, mass deportations of working men and shootings of the rebellious. . . . (*In All* 136)

The Republic had created its own "strongarm men"—in a sense, its own "business" of maintaining order and private property. The allusions to a past Bourbon king further cement the current political movement as just another "old act" in that "arranged play" of Spanish reforms. This play, or act, is on the one hand almost a satire. "Don Alfonso," Dos Passos continues, must be bitter about the trickery of history: "He'd been put on the skids for carrying out the death penalty against two mutinous army officers, and here were the honest men of the republic, in the name of progress and socialism, shooting down their fellowcitizens by the hundreds" (*In All* 136). That final statement, however, invokes a tragedy: in the name of *law* and *order*, *progress* and *socialism*, well-intentioned folks were responsible for hypocritical and appalling outcomes.

No single incident more sharply reflects the climax of tragedy—or Dos Passos's bitterness—as Casas Viejas. Directly or indirectly, it encompasses roughly a third of the text. In one long question laced with frustration and incredulity, Dos Passos asks, "How was it that these honest men, lawyers, doctors, socialist professors and lecturers, that finer element of the population that it is the dream of reformers the world over to get into positions of power, found themselves so situated that it was easy for them to vote approval of the deportations on the *Buenos Aires* or the shootings at Casas Viejas . . ." (*In All* 137). Most all comprehensive histories covering this decade include some mention of Casas Viejas, given its lasting, negative impact on the new Republican leadership. In his *Coming of the Spanish Civil War*, Preston argues that it was the "greatest blow" to the unity and momentum of the Republican administration. Anarchists had organized a nationwide uprising for January 1933, which was generally held in check everywhere except "in the village of Casas Viejas (Cádiz), [where] the most violent events of the rising and its repression took place." When violence erupted between the local residents and the Civil Guard, many villagers "fled to the fields and some took refuge in the hut of the septuagenarian Curro Cruz, known as Seisdedos . . . after a night-long siege, the Civil Guard and the Assault Guard . . . set fire to Seisdedos's house" (*Coming* 108–09). Those who did not die there, in the words of Romero Salvadó, "together with other arrested villagers, were put against a wall and shot, leaving a final toll of 19 peasants and 3 policeman dead" (42). The tragedy was immense, and it was amplified by the participation of not only Civil Guards but the Republic's newly created Assault Guards. Blaney argues that the Assault Guards' original intent was "to avoid bloodshed when restoring order" (41), and in his opus on the Civil War (which devotes two pages to the incident), Hugh Thomas states, "This corps, more efficient than the older civil guard, had been founded after the May riots in 1931 as a new special constabulary for the defence of the Republic" (99). Again, though, whether well-intentioned or not, the Assault Guards became emblematic of the Republic's reform failures, not its success.

The Casas Viejas tragedy reverberated across the nation, ultimately gaining strength within propaganda campaigns against the Republican-Socialist coalition. The central government, Thomas writes, "had plainly never given such" specifically deadly orders to the Assault or Civil Guards, but "they never recovered from the consequences of this outrage" (100). For Townson, Casas Viejas was "symbolic of the reformist government's inability to tackle the structural problems of rural society such as the inequitable distribution of land, unemployment, and *caciquismo*" (228). Historians like Raymond Carr press this point even further: The "long-term effects of Casas Viejas . . . destroyed Azaña's government in September 1933. The cycle of disorder and repression not merely alienated the proletarian forces but put a weapon into the hands of malcontents on the right: the Republic was presented as other governments of the past—corrupt, incapable of preserving public order, yet violent" (625). Perhaps no sentiments can better introduce readers to why "The Republic of Honest Men" is so cynical yet so validated in its criticism. Dos Passos lays before the reader various reasons why the Spanish government in 1933 was viewed as not that much different than "other governments of the past—corrupt, incapable of preserving public order, yet violent."

To further emphasize this long, drawn-out staging of both promising and yet failing Spanish reforms, the final section of the text weaves together various subsections—on "History," "Geography," "The Caciques," "Casas del Pueblo," among others—all of which lead to a final warning from "The Ghost of Casas Viejas," the final section. Dos Passos traces Spanish revolts and conflicts back through Napoleon to the Roman era. Early Valencians "held out for months against the enormous army of Hannibal" just as "Zaragoza and Gerona are famous for the heartbreaking sieges they stood from the French." For centuries, small groups and villages had been relentless in fighting off invaders, even in the face of insurmountable forces or lack of resources: "the history of the workers' struggle," he argues, "is full of strikes carried on and on by small groups to the point of starvation" (*In All* 140). As an example, he briefly covers Lope de

Vega's *Fuente Ovejuna*, "the story of the revolt of a small town . . . ," which, in 1873, had revolted in the Federalist Revolution, and whose "daylaborers were involved in revolutionary anarchist strikes in the first decade of this century." From Rome to Fuente Ovejuna, Dos Passos argues, "you can run a straight line through recorded history to the shootings at Casas Viejas . . ." (*In All* 141). One silver lining this chapter presents, then, is that despite the structural failures, the perseverance and—at times—triumphs of the Spanish people and working class remained.

The barrier to progress was, then, the disconnect between the central government and these individual Spanish workers and communities that comprised the nation. As in past appraisals, Dos Passos observes there are "many Spains" in order to acknowledge the difficulty of centralizing power and governance under one national model. "Spain remains a country of independent towns . . . [and] seen from Madrid is a very different country." To each respective province or city, "They are Gallegos or Catalans or Valencians. . . . Few of them seem to know the many and diverse Spains that exist under the surface." As such, the independent towns have little relationship to or faith in any centralizing forces or goings on in Madrid: "The monarchy has long since ceased to mean anything," even "the republic that has replaced it means very little" (*In All* 142–43). Added to this challenge of political representation was the "cacique," "a Tammany wardboss Iberian style with some traces left of a feudal commendador" (*In All* 143). His description of this ever-exploitative system of voter corruption, regional control, and pseudo-landed gentry supports the Spanish "play" thesis, of an antiquated system that continually resurfaces in contemporary politics. Perhaps subtly recalling the case of Sanjurjo, Dos Passos observes that the politics of caciques "were liberal or conservative according" to the governing powers in Madrid. If Madrid is a dictatorship, they join that party; whence it became a Republic, "it was only natural . . . [they] should undergo an overnight change of spots into a republican or into a socialist . . ." (*In All* 144). The more ominous parallel of this cacique system is to the "wellintentioned gentlemen," the "jobholders" and intellectuals currently running the Republic who gained money by position or by lottery: "The old type of cacique was not very active outside of his home town, tended to sit in the casino receiving friends and retainers and settling business . . ." (*In All* 144). Spain's fragmentation on various fronts—regionally but also politically and by wealth—speaks to the trials of the Republic, one that Dos Passos warns as potentially incongruous, if not destructive, to national unity.

Fragmentation was not necessarily a problem in itself, for Dos Passos had a history of admiring Spain's regionalism, of autonomous control among various geographic and political entities. In the subsection "The Casas del Pueblo," Dos Passos turns from the negativity of fragmentation—represented by caciques—to the potential successes, represented by workers' movements that aimed for reforms apart from state governments. He describes the Casas del Pueblo as "political and cultural centers for the workingclass," but while these had originally good intentions, they, too, had been converted into "small Tammanies" under Azaña and Largo Caballero, then Ministry of Labor and vocal leader of the Socialist Party (*In All* 147). The Republican government was centralizing political power: Why would this be any better or different than if under king or dictatorship? His prefatory words on "Libertarian Communism" and the Socialist Party in Spain suggest missed opportunities from this perspective: "The Spanish working class awoke to the modern world under the spell of Bakunin," the nineteenth-century Russian intellectual, generally referred to as a father of modern anarchism. In other words, anarchist philosophies that promoted individual or regional autonomy developed in Spain as a rising response to the older order, as a way for Spain to enter modern governance. No government could hope to progress without addressing, perhaps appeasing, that anarchist spirit.

To understand Casas Viejas, one must understand Bakunin, anarchism, libertarianism, and a long stretch of workers' movements. This, then, was a failure of the Republic, but not one solely directed to the Ateneistas in Madrid but also leadership within the workers' collectives themselves. Organized anarchists, Dos Passos writes, are more like "agitators" seeking "immediate action and any kind of action," including violence, and are rather unlike the socialists, "cooling the ardor of their adherents" and seeking more moderate, legislative, or state-bound solutions (*In All* 151–52). What results is a disorganized January 1933 uprising, but one that the small town of Casas Viejas (or "Benalup") still believes in: "The landless peasants who live like serfs on the great Andalusian estates, and millhands in Catalonia ground down between rising prices and lowering wages, had been excited by the ease with which the bourgeoisie of the big towns had run out the king and at least temporarily paralyzed the power of the church." Becoming ever more economically "desperate," they watch as "the landlords and millowners were quietly sabotaging the new deal social legislation of the liberals in Madrid" (*In All* 152–53). Again, Dos Passos was sympathetic (at least hopeful if not laudatory) of the "new deal social legislation" by the Madrid intellectuals. If only the Republican government could have implemented it successfully . . . if only the entrenched moneyed or political classes would not have "sabotaged" the reforms . . . if only union agitators would not have instigated violence.

In each case, Dos Passos remains sympathetic and committed to the people over the leadership. Years later, in a 1962 interview with *The Paris Review*, Dos Passos remarked that throughout his writing, "I have tried to look at it from the point of view of the ordinary man, the ordinary woman, struggling to retain some dignity and to make a decent life in these vast organizations" ("Interview with David Sanders" 246).[9] He was always for the "ordinary man," the "common laborer," the "workingclass." In 1933, the "vast organization" was not just a monarchical, conservative legacy that exploited "the ordinary man"; it was, in part, the very Republican, Socialist, or union leadership whose professed goal was to overturn that legacy. Perhaps this leadership had better intentions; but their actions could not rise to the occasion. Thus, even as Dos Passos acknowledges the problems inherent in the Casas Viejas uprising—that Seisdedos was always a "village rebel," that the local syndicate had their guns "oiled and ready" for an uprising, that Seisdedos confronted the local authorities to surrender, and that when violence broke out two guards were shot in the head—amid all this, the chapter is unabashedly for the workingclass and ordinary folks, the "[h]ungry men who had been shivering in their thin denims," living as "the landless live from hand to mouth as daylaborers" in "complete poverty" (*In All* 154–57). Dos Passos hated war, violence, and conflict. But he understood what years and decades of starvation, oppression, and exploitation would do to a person, to a village. And the villagers needed more than a few scattered reforms and empty promises to overturn that.

Undoubtedly, the timing of Dos Passos's stay in Spain is important to the tone and scope of the chapter, which signs off with "Madrid, August, 1933." But while that date probably reflects an early draft, he had most likely kept revising it that fall, for the text alludes to the November elections, which brought in further power to conservative coalitions.[10] Thus, when his final pages relate the "Ghost of Casas Viejas," readers also have the benefit of hindsight to see how the chapter's ominous tone and implications stretch out across Spain: "Whether it was the shooting of the daylaborers of Casas Viejas, or the repudiating of it afterwards that turned out most unluckily will be a matter for historians to decide. Anyway the hour has struck for the liberals and the day of reactionaries has come" (*In All* 168). "Reactionaries" perhaps aptly characterizes the whole of 1931–1936, the days and politics leading up to the Spanish Civil War, but it specifically refers to radical interests that gained power in 1933. Within this context, we see what "failure"—or "fracaso"—meant to Dos Passos after all. The most judgmental passage in the chapter berates and blames those

> [s]teeped in that academic ignorance . . . the intellectual and professional classes . . . [who] called for jails and Mausers and machineguns to protect the bureaucracy that was the source of the easy life and the hot milk and the coffee and the Americanmade cars, and order, property, investments. . . . Maybe the new Spain wasn't the Spain of the Madrid bureaucracy, or the Spain of those who weren't holding jobs yet; the honest men. So the Republic of Manual and Intellectual Workers turned out to be the Republic of those who work others so that they shan't have to work themselves. (*In All* 138–39)

In the fall of 1933, there was no way of knowing exactly how the Spanish Republic would turn out. It was still a Republic at that point, regardless of conservative wins. No one could know the extent to which progressive reforms would be undermined by incoming conservatives, how a 1936 election would return a leftist "Popular Front," and how these pendulum swings would precipitate to war in the summer of 1936. But that "The Republic of Honest Men" ends with a question—and not a firm sense of the country's direction—provides yet more evidence that Spain and its future were certainly in crisis, even if Dos Passos's political attitudes were not. There had been a disillusionment of the left—and Dos Passos could see it clearly even in 1933.

ACKNOWLEDGMENTS

This chapter is dedicated to Dr. Kevin Floyd, whose friendly mentorship and critical insights were invaluable during my graduate school days. I would also like to thank Aaron Shaheen and Rosa María Bautista-Cordero for their leadership in undertaking this edition and their (Rosa's, especially) strong, encouraging feedback on my draft. In 2013, a generous Taylor Fellowship provided me two amazing months working with Dos Passos papers at the University of Virginia, a summer of reading that greatly influenced my thinking and writing about the author.

NOTES

1. The "disillusionment" depiction is almost ubiquitous in literary scholarship. "Disillusionment in Spain, 1937," is the title of biographer Virginia Spencer Carr's chapter covering this epoch. Though fellow biographer Townsend Ludington opts for "Crisis in Spain, 1937," the last sentence of the biography puts Dos Passos as a "disillusioned moralist" (*John Dos Passos* 507). The characteriza-

tion manifested almost immediately in literary criticism, including 1939 reviews of Dos Passos's *Adventures of a Young Man*. John Chamberlain asserts that "Dos Passos has been disillusioned about Spain and Europe" (193); Malcolm Cowley criticizes Dos Passos for having "come down from the high mountains of idealism," and his review was entitled simply "Disillusionment" (163). Later academic and popular appraisals echo this idea, with only scattered exceptions. For instance, Eugenio Suárez-Galbán rightly observes that one need only read Dos Passos's "Republic of Honest Men" or other 1930s writings to see that 1937 and "the Robles incident was simply the straw that broke the camel's back" (170). My essay aims to temper this "disillusionment" thesis, as if one or two catastrophic events created an abrupt crisis or about-face for the author.

2. Throughout the essay, I refer to "The Republic of Honest Men" as a *chapter* in the larger volume of *In All Countries*, which is the cited text. That chapter contains three *sections*, "Doves in the Bullring," "Topdog Politics," and "Underdog Politics," the latter two containing *subsections*. On some occasions, *sections* can refer to sections and/or subsections.
3. See Ludington (*John Dos Passos* 319–20) and Carr (315), of which the latter's translation reads, "Summer was pretty much of a fiasco."
4. Letters from Dos Passos in May 1933 suggest that, while he was not necessarily broke, his financial situation had attracted the attention (and money) of friends, including Hemingway (who offered a thousand dollars) and Gerald and Sara Murphy (who offered to support passage abroad). As he wrote to his wife Katy from Johns Hopkins Hospital, "What this is turning into is a gigantic panhandling operation in which all our friends are being victimized. Now that our debts are funded we must try to pull ourselves together and extract some jade from our natural enemies" (Letter to Katy Dos Passos). In other words, with a feeling of indebtedness to friends, Dos Passos had further motivation to "extract some jade," or royalties, from the book publishers.
5. Ludington (*John Dos Passos* 318) and Carr land on this idea of *portent* given Dos Passos's own recollection in *The Best Times* ("That summer I kept seeing signs and portents" [227]), and it remains a just characterization given events after 1933.
6. Romero Salvadó offers a similar appraisal of these lurking and ultimately antagonistic institutional forces, observing that the "rapid and bloodless" transition out of the monarchy in April 1931 was perhaps a reason why the "principal pillars of the old regime (the army, the Church and the land-owning oligarchy) not only managed to preserve their social and institutional might, but were also able to act as a constraint upon change" (28)—all of which reflects Dos Passos's idea that a reformed Spain was unable to fully outlive its "old" past.
7. Dos Passos had much respect for the family and man, but, as his criticism of this

rally shows, he also held Ríos Urruti and other leaders responsible for many of the ill-actions, including that of Casas Viejas (further explained below). According to Preston, Ríos Urruti had told Azaña, "that what had happened at Casas Viejas was necessary . . ." (*The Coming* 109).

8. Julián Casanova aptly describes the Civil Guard's response to this Arnedo shoe factory strike as a "bloodbath": Among workers, families, and townsfolk, eleven were killed and over thirty wounded (Preston puts the wounded to over fifty [*The Spanish Holocaust* 22]): "All ages were represented: among the dead were a seventy-year-old woman and a child of four, whose mother was also killed; the wounded included men and women of over sixty and a five-year-old child whose leg had to be amputated" (Casanova 53). I also provide this Arnedo discussion as a primer for my discussion on Casas Viejas.
9. In his footnote covering the interview (from the *Major Nonfictional Prose* edition of Dos Passos works), Donald Pizer says that the *Paris Review*'s 1969 publication erroneously noted the interview had occurred in 1966.
10. The elections drew a "hung parliament," Townson observes, but given the "pendulum effect of the electoral law . . . the only majority possible was a coalition between the centre and the right" (229), and the right generally, if also insecurely, held power through January 1936. Moreover, the party with the most seats was the Confederación Española de Derechas Autónomas (CEDA), a conservative and Catholic-based party that, Townson notes, "although not a fascist party itself admired the Nazis and their legalistic tactic for the conquest of power" (230); in the words of Thomas, although not its platform or focus, CEDA "included those who wanted to restore a monarchy" (4).

WORKS CITED

Blaney, Jr., Gerald. "Keeping Order in Republican Spain, 1931–1936." *Policing Interwar Europe: Continuity, Change, and Crisis, 1918–1940*, edited by Gerald Blaney, Jr., Springer, 2006, pp. 31–68.

Carr, Raymond. *Spain, 1808–1975*. 2nd ed. Clarendon, 1982.

Carr, Virginia Spencer. *Dos Passos: A Life*. 1984. Northwestern UP, 2004.

Casanova, Julián. *The Spanish Republic and Civil War*. Cambridge UP, 2010.

Chamberlain, John. Rev. of *Adventures of a Young* Man, by John Dos Passos. *Saturday Review*, 3 Jun. 1939, vol. xx, pp. 3–4, 14–15. Rpt. in *John Dos Passos: The Critical Heritage*, edited by Barry Maine, Routledge, 1997, pp. 189–196. EBSCOhost, search.ebscohost.com/login.aspx?direct=true&db=lfh&AN=17447557&site=eds-live.

Cowley, Malcolm. "Disillusionment." Rev. of *Adventures of a Young Man*, by John

Dos Passos. *New Republic*, vol. 99, no. 1280, June 1939, p. 163. EBSCOhost, search.ebscohost.com/login.aspx?direct=true&db=pwh&AN=15033064&site=eds-live.

Dos Passos, John. *The Best Times*. The New American Library, 1966.

———. *The Fourteenth Chronicle: Letters and Diaries of John Dos Passos*, edited by Townsend Ludington, Gambit, 1973.

———. *In All Countries*. Harcourt, Brace and Co., 1934.

———. "Interview with David Sanders." *Writers at Work: The "Paris Review" Interviews*, edited by George Plimpton, 4th ser., Viking, 1976, 68–89. Rpt. in *John Dos Passos: The Major Nonfictional Prose*, edited by Donald Pizer, Wayne State UP, 1998, pp. 241–52.

———. Letter to Katy Dos Passos, 14 May 1933, Box 13, John Dos Passos Papers, 1865–1999, Accession #5950, etc., Albert and Shirley Small Special Collections Library, University of Virginia.

Ludington, Townsend. "'I Am So Fascinated by Spain:' John Dos Passos, January 1917." *Nor Shall Diamond Die: American Studies in Honor of Javier Coy*, edited by Carme Manuel and Paul Scott Derrick, Universitat de València, 2003, pp. 313–320.

———. *John Dos Passos: A Twentieth Century Odyssey*. 1980. Carroll & Graf, 1998.

Pizer, Donald. *Dos Passos' U.S.A.: A Critical Study*. UP of Virginia, 1988.

Preston, Paul. *The Coming of the Spanish Civil War: Reform, Reaction, and Revolution in the Second Republic*. 2nd ed., Routledge, 1994.

———. *The Spanish Holocaust: Inquisition and Extermination in Twentieth-Century Spain*. Norton, 2012.

Romero Salvadó, Francisco J. *The Spanish Civil War: Origins, Course and Outcomes*. Palgrave, 2005.

Suárez-Galbán, Eugenio. *The Last Good Land: Spain in American Literature*. Rodopi, 2011.

Thomas, Hugh. *The Spanish Civil War*. Modern Library, 2001.

Townson, Nigel. "The Second Republic, 1931–1936: Sectarianism, Schisms, and Strife." *Spanish History since 1808*, edited by José Alvarez Junco and Adrian Shubert, Arnold Publishers and Oxford UP, 2000, pp. 221–35.

Tusell, Javier, and Genoveva Queipo de Llano. "The Dictatorship of Primo de Rivera, 1923–1931." *Spanish History since 1808*, edited by José Alvarez Junco and Adrian Shubert, Arnold Publishers and Oxford UP, 2000, pp. 207–20.

9

REPRESENTING AUTHORS AS PRODUCERS

Labor and the New Deal Intellectual in John Dos Passos's *U.S.A.* Trilogy

Addison T. Palacios

In his well-known 1934 lecture "The Author as Producer," Walter Benjamin succinctly articulated one of the key ideological contradictions and struggles that persists within Marxist studies today. Benjamin emphasized that the central task of any revolution is "to win over the intellectuals to the working class by making them aware . . . of their conditions as producers" (79). That is, authors must see themselves as producers in order to both authentically align themselves with revolutionary causes as well as ensure the success of any revolutionary endeavor. In theory, this is not particularly difficult to understand or accept. On the level of artistic praxis, however, this revolutionary step is much more complicated than it may seem. This revolutionary tension is represented throughout Dos Passos's *U.S.A.* trilogy, and Dos Passos utilizes the camera eye as a means of remedying the impasse Benjamin's argument sets forth.

To more fully understand the intellectual's quandary, Benjamin's initial lecture is useful for understanding the stakes and nuances of this predicament. Speaking of the German left-wing intelligentsia, Benjamin argued that activism, "however revolutionary it may seem, has a counter-revolutionary function so long as the writer feels his solidarity with the proletariat only in his attitudes" (84). Writers and artists might feel a solidarity with the working class but that hardly goes beyond the affective domain. If they only feel an affective connection and not one in which they conceptualize their own position in production, then no enduring class consciousness could be realized though it might momentary be felt. Benjamin suggested as much when he claims that authors who align themselves with activist causes are "at best a social group" whose "very principle . . . is reaction. No wonder its effect could never be revolutionary" (84). Having common attitudes toward capitalism is therefore an insufficient means of class solidarity. Instead, what is needed is a different conception of artistic production wherein the labor process is emphasized rather than products. As I will show, Dos Passos's *U.S.A.* enacts this emphasis by turning a cinematic eye toward the labor process to reposition intellectuals within the sphere of production. To do so removes the separation between the producer and his product as well as the alienation of that separation, as the work of art is no longer detached from the author but is itself a representation of his labors. The trilogy can be read as a process-oriented work that imagines authors as producers through the camera eye.

To better understand Dos Passos's goal to reintroduce the author into the world of production, an historical account of the shifting concept of the intellectual in American culture is instructive. By looking at how that very term took on myriad meanings and connotations within the span of a few decades, we begin to better understand how pivotal the New Deal era was for intellectual history as well as Dos Passos's contribution to its theorization. While the Dreyfus Affair, which spanned from 1894 to 1906, is well known for its transnational response, less apparent is the degree to which this high-profile case propelled prominent artists, writers, and leading critics into a political spotlight. No longer could the realm of culture remain isolated from the sociopolitical, and a certain political commitment moved to the forefront of artistic production. Such was made clear Emile Zola himself in a follow-up publication to the infamous "J'Accuse . . . !" that was succinctly titled "Manifesto of the Intellectuals." In this second publication of 1898, Zola petitions for a reopening of the case with the support of the leading intellectuals of the day, including Émile Durkheim, Marcel Proust, and Stéphane Mallarmé. This second publication is noteworthy for a few reasons. For one, it grouped together scholars, authors, and artists under the common banner of "intellectual," which imparted a sense of unity among hitherto distinct groups. With these various mental laborers assembled, Zola's publication added a decidedly political bent to all those who would fit under the amorphous term in a way that would add a socially committed tint to the products of their labor—shifting away from previous notions of social detachment and aloofness (Whyte 151). Lastly, this shift in conceptualizing intellectual work was done in a public way at the height of a global event with the effect of ushering in the concept of the public intellectual. The public intellectual imagined by the manifesto was not only politically committed, but unabashedly so. No longer would the products of intellect be separated from their creators who would publicly, and at times nationally, commit themselves to the political sphere.

It is within this shifting context that the very term "intellectual" found its way into the American lexicon. Shortly after Zola's publication, American philosopher William James argued in an 1899 letter, just months after Zola's pivotal publications, that "We 'intellectuals' in America must all work to keep our previous birthright of individualism, and freedom from these institutions [church, army, aristocracy, royalty]," as he argued for the author's ability to freely critique political institutions as Zola had done (qtd. in Hofstadter 39). It is important to note, however, that when James conceptualized the intellectual in the American context, he added the concept of individualism, in contradiction to the original manifesto. While Zola's publication demonstrates a coming together of the educated classes into a body politic, James re-introduces a liberal value of the individual that prizes autonomy over collectivity. This seemingly small contradiction informs a much larger inconsistency behind theorizations of the intellectual wherein individual creative freedoms are, at times, forced to contend with collective aims and institutions. Yet, as I will show, it was through the documenting camera eye that Dos Passos saw the possibility of coupling artistic autonomy and individualism with a collective, participatory vision.

This contradictory nature of the American intellectual continued to develop from the turn of the century up to the New Deal era. For instance, the first decades of the American intellectual after James's proclamation are largely recounted as periods of exile and solitude. While there were certainly writers who sought to use realism as a means of achieving heightened class consciousness by mutually identifying the crises inherent in capitalism—*A Hazard of New Fortunes* was published in 1890, for instance—the public perception of the intellectual class was less one of unity and more of separation. Whether self-imposed or not, turn-of-the-century public thinkers were characterized by their obscurity and exile to the point that these qualities seemed to be inherent in mental labor in general. According to an expatriate friend of Dos Passos, Harold E. Sterns, whose *America and the Young Intellectual* was originally published in 1921, the "problem of America and . . . the young intellectual" was of "first-rate importance" (9). For Stearns, the main issue at stake was the fact that American society largely rejected the political importance of authors and artists, which, in turn, did not provide the atmosphere needed to create a lasting tradition of American cultural thought. This belief was reiterated by Floyd Dell, literary critic and editor of *The Masses,* who wrote that exile and alienation in the 1920s was "forced upon sensitive minds by the conditions of a culture hostile to creative dreaming" (101). Because of the hostile American culture, the "habituation to, and finally the temperamental preference for, such alienation" took hold and contributed to the social exile of the American literati. Thus, the early cultural imagination regarding the newly public thinking class was largely marked by a seemingly myopic preference for solitude, which is not to say, however, that all authors of the time lacked social commitment. One can turn to the work of writers like Theodore Dreiser, Jack London, and Upton Sinclair to point out political artistic production that forecasts the overtly socialist leanings of later periods. However, these figures were unable to adequately see themselves and their work within the sphere of production in a way that the 1930s would usher in or to the degree to which Benjamin would later call for. As others have argued, work like London's *Martin Eden* and Howell's "The Man of Letters as Man of Business" articulates the alienation and solitude of artistic practice in contrast to the marginalized, collective communities that that work so often represented.

Yet by the 1930s, this temperament for individualism and obscurity seems to have changed. In place of the disinterested thinkers of previous decades, artists and authors of this period are remembered for their social engagement and political import. In large contrast to the previous conceptualization of the exilic and elitist artist of the turn-of-the-century, many accounts of the so-called New Deal era argue that a "uniquely long and intimate alliance of . . . intellectuals with the labor movement" was almost palpable, which adds a Leftist slant to public perception of intellectuals that has arguably extended throughout the twentieth century (Neufeld 117). An American iteration of Zola's manifesto is even found in the form of the 1932 publication "Culture and the Crisis : an open letter to the writers, artists, teachers, physicians, engineers, scientists and other professional workers of America" with prominent Western Marxist Lewis Corey taking Zola's position as the lead writer, though others like Malcolm Cowley co-authored the publication (Denning 99–102). Interestingly, a November 1932 issue of *New Masses* quotes from the pamphlet and titles it "An Open Letter to the Intellectual Workers of America," suggesting an expanded notion of intellectualism akin to Zola's original expansion of the term ("Every Vote a Blow!" 4). Signed by writers like Sherwood Anderson, Malcolm Cowley, Langston Hughes, Edmund Wilson as well as Dos Passos, the pamphlet encourages "intellectual workers" to distance themselves from the "ruling class that frustrates them, stultifies them" and "patronizes them" (League of Professional Groups 28). This New Deal intellectual manifesto demanded that such "intellectual workers" realize that they "are of the oppressed" and to "renew the pact of comradeship with the struggling masses," which largely echoes Benjamin's call for authors to view themselves as producers. Much like Zola's manifesto, the pamphlet is often looked at as a turning point in American intellectual history, with Michael Denning claiming that the "origins of US Western Marxism lie in the 1932 pamphlet" and the work of those who crafted it "shaped the cultural theory of the Popular Front social movement" (98, 104). Indeed, the pamphlet may be viewed as a high point in a decade-long "attempt to bridge the gap between intellectuals and workers" (Fitzpatrick 427). In the time from William James's 1899 adoption of the individual intellectual to the 1932 "Culture and the Crisis" pamphlet's "brain worker" who would act as a "true comrade" to the "muscle worker," the American thinker occupied varied and often conflicting positions both in public perception and literary representation. As I will show, it is this very progression that Dos Passos chronicles yet not without putting forth his own reading of mental labor that might join these competing perceptions.

This shift would only grow more apparent as the New Deal programs expanded. Particularly through the Works Progress Administration and the Federal One Project, the funding provided by these programs would reframe, in Dos Passos's words, the "whole question of what writing is" and in doing so further the shift away from authors as isolated elites to the more collectivized group of laborers imagined by Benjamin ("The Writer as Technician" 545). With an initial attempt to restructure agrarian economies with the Agricultural Adjustment Act of 1933, Roosevelt's New Deal quickly developed into a proliferation of "new federal programs, including regulations and federal mandates, social insurance programs, and an unprecedented amount of new federal spending" that more than tripled the federal expenditures of 1929 (Fishback, et al. 36). By the mid-thirties, the New Deal was an "amalgam of numerous multifaceted programs" that included splinter initiatives like the Public Works Administration (PWA), the Federal Emergency Relief Administration (FERA), the Civil Works Administration (CWA), the Works Progress Administration (WPA), and the Federal Housing Administration (FHA), which were all geared toward reviving economic activity and work relief (37). This wide-reach of federal aid made many Americans more receptive to the socialist ideals espoused by those who signed the "Culture and Crisis" publication, which helped soften public acceptance of more left-leaning and radical writers and artists. That is, their political radicalism seemed more palatable when Americans were receiving the very forms of sociopolitical benefits for which such writers were arguing.

In addition to the economic side of softening the public's reception to the politically engaged literati, the number of cultural initiatives FDR's New Deal encapsulated also prompted the union between writers and the public. For instance, Federal Project Number One, a designation for the cultural projects of the New Deal, "employed some 40,000 writers, musicians, artists, and actors," while the Federal Writers' Project (FWP) alone enlisted, at its peak, more than 6,500 writers (Mutnick 126). Among these were writers like Richard Wright, Ralph Ellison, Anzia Yezierska, Zora Neale Hurston, John Steinbeck, and Claude McKay. Though Dos Passos was never officially employed by the FWP, his ability to "represent the intractable social forces that squelch human agency" made his work vital for enlisted writers who similarly sought to return that agency to the downtrodden through the arts (Rutkoswki 11). FDR realized that not only did the economy need a revitalization but so did the sentiments of the working Americans who were most affected by the Depression. The mental labor of writers, artists, and critics could therefore be used to increase morale and faith in the American future, which positively reshaped the intelligentsia's relationship with the public on a national scale.

Soon, the driving labor force behind the New Deal became colloquially referred to as Roosevelt's "brain trust," stemming from a 1932 article on the New Deal by *New York Times* journalist James Kiernan (Lecklider 119). Perhaps unintentionally, Kiernan's use of the word "trust" aptly addresses both the economic importance of mental labor as well as the faith placed in their ability to reimagine a more humane and democratic future. According to Eric Lecklider, FDR's employment of artists and authors "forced Americans to rethink their occasional dismissal of intellectuals" while "depicting [them] in a decidedly favorable light" (121). Far from the disinterest of earlier decades, the New Deal brain worker was politically engaged and a champion of class reform. Just as the authors of the "Culture and the Crisis" pamphlet would hope, historians have characterized the latter half of the 1930s as a period wherein the "rapprochement between intellectuals and the public" took place in an unprecedented way, leading to a "complete harmony between the popular cause in politics and the dominant mood of the intellectuals" (Hofstadter 214). It therefore bears restating that the era in which Dos Passos composed the *U.S.A.* trilogy was one in which the author, artist, and public thinker was being reimagined as a member of the working class—as a producer— in incredibly optimistic ways.

Some, however, were more critical of this radical revision of the literary class. Marxist theorist George Novak noted that, for "the first time in American history the doors of the government bureaucracy were thrown open" to the American literati, and that they "plunged into political activity with great zeal" (23). This did not, however, result in the political reform or harmony imagined by Hofstadter and others. Rather, some saw the so-called brain trust as little more than a capitulation to capitalism as "the advent of the New Deal deflected the leftward movement of the liberals into governmental channels," which took away from the radical fervor rising at the height of the Depression (24). Instead of viewing the New Deal as a viable method of lasting class reform, a more critical view posited that "the entrance of the intellectuals into the administration" was little more than "the rush of the liberals to secure places in the apparatus when the Roosevelt administration required agents with a liberal coloration to carry out the operations necessary to restore a sick American capitalism to health" (24). Instead of acting as revolutionary agents, those thinkers employed by the government became precisely the means by which it was able to recover. On the one hand, enlisted writers with proletarian sympathies are remembered as the voice of the downtrodden who seamlessly integrated into the working public. On the other hand, these writers can be viewed opportunists who diverted radical potential away from the public and channeled their own energies into the very government structures that maintained existing class relations.

The cultural zeitgeist regarding artists in the 1930s was not as harmonious as some accounts might make it seem. Rather, this was a time of transition and contradiction wherein the working-class sympathies of authors and artists were most closely aligned with the public reception of them though that does not mean that there was any complete harmony. Many in the intellectual camp, as indicated by Novack's criticisms, were keen to note that the new forms of government and public support added a commitment to the very systems and ideologies that artistic production often sought to revise, thereby pacifying any counter-cultural response by making it part of the system rather than apart. Such is clear in Michael Szalay's *New Deal Modernism: American Literature and the Invention of the Welfare State, which draws a* corollary between Roosevelt's New Deal desire to "wipe out the line that divides the practical from the ideal" and the artistic desire to practically place the author within production (9). For Benjamin, such a process-driven view of artistic practice would allow authors to view themselves, and be viewed by others, as producers. Szalay makes this connection clear by claiming that the answer to Benjamin's imperative as well as Dos Passos's question of what writing is lay in the belief that "radical writing was a form of labor not primarily or necessarily productive of an artifact" (46). The re-imagined New Deal intellectual practice could best be defined by "embracing performative aesthetics" while writing itself is viewed "not as a commodity to be consumed but as a form of collective labor" (266). Whether the artists of the time achieved this goal, Szalay's argument persuasively shows how the interplay between aesthetic practice and revolutionary politics was mediated by an attention to labor that insisted that authors be viewed as producers.

The driving organ of this change for Szalay is the liberal government of 1930s, as mentioned with the Works Progress Administration. Szalay points to the "regulative function of a wage" that turned authors into "salaried writers" who "struggled to negotiate" artistic autonomy with collectivity (55, 5). In my view, however, Dos Passos's work takes a more ideological and institutional approach to expand beyond the regulative wage. In showing the various institutions in which mental labor is performed, the trilogy articulates Dos Passos's answer to his own question of what writing is in a way that focuses on the labor process, as Szalay contends, while reintroducing the author as producer in multiple institutions and spaces not limited to government programs. By viewing writers as little more than "word-slinging organisms" caught within the web of capital as well as the cultural imagination of what the writer was to be, the *U.S.A.* trilogy provides an instructive theorizing of mental labor more broadly conceived (Denning 103). Sites like the university or the advertising firm, sites outside the scope of what New Deal policy targeted as vital mental labor, therefore become important tools seeing the author as a producer in a way that was more substantial than the effect of temporary government programming. Dos Passos sought to represent the lasting, structural ways that authors were deeply embedded within capitalistic production, that they were vital for its functioning, and that New Deal attempts to align authors with the public would also need to contend with the spheres of production that *U.S.A.* explores. In doing so, the trilogy paints a new critical history that works through the theoretical difficulties described by Benjamin and other Marxists while adding a historical revision to a period of unprecedented government restructuring. If the "contradiction between the notion of bringing consciousness to the working class from without," and "the ideal of proletarian self-emancipation" remains a theoretical impasse today, as it is for Jerome Kabal, then it is "the paradoxical authority of the intellectuals in workers' movements," that Dos Passos sought to resolve through his own production (140). Dos Passos admits as much when he claims that the "middle class . . . [was] untrustworthy," yet that it was up to the "workers and producers" of the world, both "manual and intellectual," to institute a truly revolutionary class reform (Kallich 183). To do this, the trilogy neither paints intellectuals as petty opportunists or class saviors but, rather, as the conduits, via the camera eye, through which the speech of the people becomes organized.

One of the figures that Dos Passos introduces to the reader is the alienated thinker, whose solipsistic take on the world recalls the effete high-mindedness described by Stearns and Dell. In the brief patch of prose titled "U. S. A." before *The 42nd Parallel*'s table of contents, Dos Passos immediately creates the image of the author in exile who is disconnected not only from the political debates of his time but also those around him. In fact, the section's formal separation from the rest of the narrative speaks to the divide between the exilic thinker and the people who fill the pages the come. The young man is shown to be walking alone, though in a crowd, while his "mind is a beehive" that is "buzzing and stinging," though that frantic energy is never communicated through his comportment (xiii). While it is likely that the man's destitution reflects Depression-era poverty, and the fact that his "muscles ache" for work supports that reading, the emphasis Dos Passos places on the man's mental state should not be discounted. Indeed, he continues to place focus on the mental labor taking place, as Dos Passos notes that the man's head is "swimming with wants," which are not limited to the bare necessities of life. Rather, the mind swims with a desire for words that the mental technician can work with. It is the "words telling about longago" and the "speech that clung to the ears, the link that tingled in the blood" that are the brain worker's tools. With these tools, the "speech of the people" can be constructed, both by the figure shown in this introduction and by Dos Passos himself.

Despite this desire to connect and assemble, Dos Passos emphasizes that the man is alone, suggesting that isolation is an inherent quality of the life of the mind. Within the short section, Dos Passos notes a total of five times that the young man "walks by himself" and is "alone." While the man appears to be alone due to his separation from the working world, as the people have "packed into subways, climbed into streetcars and buses" while he walks alone, his alienation is also mental. Even the "jostling crowds at night" could not make the man "less alone," nor could the "training camp at Allentown, or in the day on the docks at Seattle," or a host of other workplaces where one would find some sense of community (xiv). Nevertheless, the man watches with "greedy eyes" and listens with "greedy ears" in a way that foretells the social function of the author that the following narrative will portray (xiii). The early portrait of a young man as an author is therefore one of alienation, loneliness, and desire. Much like the turn-of-the-century figure whose propensity for free thought places him outside the realm of capital, which is to say the realm of American culture, the alienated thinker's inability to connect with the world around him renders him out of work.

This imagery of isolation bookends the trilogy. After opening the series with the image of the young thinker, Dos Passos ends *The Big Money* with a similar image. Within the final "Vag" section, presumably short for vagrant or vagabond, there is another young man, perhaps the same from the trilogy's foreword, whose "head swims" (446). The anonymity of the figure depersonalizes the character, portraying them as simply another word-slinger manipulated and used by capital in a way the removes the type of artistic privilege and elitism that pre–New Deal conceptions of the intellectual portrayed. Moreover, the character and the name recall Floyd Dell's widely read *Intellectual Vagabondage* (1926), which articulates the hostility the public had toward authors and artists of his time. Thus, Dos Passos creates a literary representation of the very figure that Dell's previous work had lamented. Unlike the opening of *The 42nd Parallel*, however, Dos Passos emphasizes the eyes in this closing section instead of the ears. The vagrant's eyes "black with want" that "seek out the eyes" of the drivers passing by, as if something has changed that has disrupted the audible speech of the people and has made sight the only mode of perception fast enough to distill the passing of the modern world (*Big Money* 447). Yet even this sight fails as the young man is unsuccessful in making any connection to the "transcontinental passenger" who passes by (448). And rather than having a mind swimming with the constructive wants imagined by the speech of the people, the passenger's mind is buzzing with the thought of "contracts, profits," and "vacationtrips." (448). In this case, the forces of capital have taken over the humanistic wants of the vagrant thinkers, have literally passed over him, as the "speeding traffic" of the scene contrasts the empty streets of the foreword, which demonstrates the hasty development of capitalism throughout the course of the trilogy's narrative. Like the brain trust that slowly dissolved after economic recovery, leaving the mental laborers that powered it to return to their old stations of obscurity, Dos Passos similarly returns the thinker to the state of vagrancy once capitalism, embodied by the transcontinental passenger, has gotten its use out of him.

The trilogy is therefore introduced and concluded with the image of the author in isolation, though the historical circumstances surrounding him have changed from one point to the other. One would imagine that through the course of the 1930s, given the increasing social prominence of mental laborers, that Dos Passos would end the series with a different image. Particularly given the New Deal's repositioning of authors and artists from the sociocultural margins to its center, it seems reasonable to assume that these figures in Dos Passos's fiction would fare better than they do. However, the closing image suggests that once capital had gotten what it needed from its brain trust, it quickly laid off its workers with no demonstration of either loyalty or gratitude. While the Depression had cleared the way for authors to revise their social position and class alliances, their success within the New Deal resulted in their undoing, making them redundant. *U.S.A.* therefore shows that, like any other worker, the writer can be made disposable. Perhaps ironically, Dos Passos makes it clear that if the literati truly wished to align themselves with the working classes, then they, too, would have to reckon with the possibility of destitution.

While it is true that "in the thirties Dos Passos made the worker his primary concern," as John P. Diggins argues, he did so by considering how writers like himself can be viewed as workers (487). Between the bookends of vagrancy and vagabondage, Dos Passos shows the myriad ways in which mental labor was being utilized throughout the New Deal era, both for and against capitalist production, in a way that moves away from the alienation fetishized at the turn-of-the-century and toward the structures and institutions where mental work gets done. Whether it be on the shop floor or in the university, Dos Passos saw labor—mental labor—as the means to understand the author's role in the working world. With this view, the sections that discuss Charlie Anderson's inventiveness become just as much about brain workers as the Camera Eye sections that document university life do. Dos Passos's renewed understanding allows traditional categories of intellect—the kind that the Harvard man Richard Savage would occupy—to be viewed alongside more organic and pragmatic form, like Mary French, the journalist and activist.

The various intellectual types that the trilogy works to portray, expanding from simply the arts to more broadly conceive of mental labor and its various spheres of production, can be further understood within the theoretical context laid out by Italian Marxist Antonio Gramsci. Like Dos Passos, Gramsci saw authors, artists, and critics as less as "an autonomous and independent group" and more as a "specialized category" of worker that belongs to a larger social group (5). In this way, these figures are not apart from the productive forces of the world but are elaborated by them, despite "that social utopia by which the intellectuals think of themselves as independent" (Gramsci 8). Yet like the young man who drifts along in isolation, the traditional intellectuals described by Gramsci are viewed as autonomous, without class interests, and serving an independent pursuit of truth rather than working for class interests. This would include the clergy, men of letters, or university professors who are not readily identified with their role in production or class belonging. However, Gramsci shows that this alienation is a ruse that allows for a covert class function. While they may not appear to be part of the productive base, they exert an ideological influence that preserves hegemony, the glue which binds the ideological apparatuses of a society with its economic base.

Dos Passos, too, saw the class interests lurking beneath the sociopolitically disinterested surface of traditional intellectuals. More specifically, he targets the most prominent site of these figures of the early twentieth century—the university. The university also happens to be the site from which FDR drew much of his brain trust, and Dos Passos's representation of academia as the site in which revolutionary fire dies speaks to his lack of faith in the New Deal's ability to institute lasting class reform. Rather than encouraging social progress and equity, the university becomes another opiate of the masses. For instance, in Camera Eye (25) of *The 42nd Parallel,* Dos Passos mentions Harvard, his own alma mater, by name. Rather than portray the university as an institution where knowledge could be channeled into action, the young man seen in the section "hasn't got the nerve to break out of the bellglass" (236). Within this same section, Dos Passos notes again that the young man lacks the "nerve" to take any pragmatic action (236). Instead of cultivating critical awareness, Harvard is portrayed as an "ethercone," wherein the dictum to "get A's" replaces the slow countdown to anesthetic slumber (236). The effect that this has on the would-be radical is that he grows "cold with culture" like a "cup of tea . . . not strong like a claret lemonade." This stultifying effect of academia is also present in Camera Eye (28) of *1919,* where students are drawn to "Copey's beautiful reading voice" and the "artificial parmaviolet scene under the ethercone" (7). Copey, the friendly moniker given to the Harvard professor and poet Charles Townsend Copeland, represents academia while the use of the ethercone once again signifies the loss of critical vitality. Unless one escapes the "dim voices in lecturehalls," "Copey's voice," the "thin voices" of instructors, and the "dying fall," as Jack Reed does in "Playboy," the potential vanguard of the revolutionary class is doomed to mediocrity (8). Despite the New Deal's attention to the professoriate, Dos Passos resists the belief that it has the nerve necessary to spearhead a lasting class reform. Instead, his work portrays academics as a pacifying force that work in the service of capital rather than against it, replacing the drive for action with what Donald Pizer has called an "effete aestheticism" (139).

However, Dos Passos includes some exceptions to this rule as he shows that academic life might still harbor dissent, which demonstrates his nuanced view of the New Deal intelligentsia. In contrast to the ethercone of Harvard, Dos Passos includes a news reel of Professor Francisco Ferrer in *The 42nd Parallel.* The reel informs the reader of the "former director of the Modern School in Barcelona" who was "sentenced to death" for being an alleged "instigator of the recent revolutionary movement" and anarchist (85). The real Ferrer founded the Modern School in Barcelona, which relied upon a noncompulsory educational model focused toward working-class education akin to the work popularized by Paolo Freire. The hope was that the noncompulsory model of teaching resisted the ideological mapping that compulsory education placed upon students, which would allow the lower classes to gain a heightened class consciousness through education. However, by noting Ferrer's death rather than his life's work, Dos Passos shows the coercive measures that control such revolutionary minds while also delineating the dangers of university affiliation despite the anesthetic effects it might have. Dos Passos returns to this point in the American context in *1919*'s "A Hoosier Quixote," which fictionally recounts the mock execution of Paxton Hibben performed at the "twentieth reunion of his college class," with Princeton forming the American counterpart to the Modern School. Though Hibben is not literally killed, the phrase "lynch the goddam red" is chanted and a real noose was placed on his neck as a "collegeboy prank" (142). In this case, the termination of the revolutionary is more ideological than physical, yet similarly shows the ways the university acts against class reform while retaining an air of social disinterest. Perhaps most emphatically, Newsreel XLII includes the detail that Harvard President Lowell "has urged the students to serve as strikebreakers" and encouraged them to act in accordance with its "tradition of public service" to "maintain order" (365). In this case, the university becomes the ideological state apparatus preserving class hegemony *par excellence*. Yet even when one does not align with the ideological values of the university, its affects are no less potent. For instance, the fictional representations of Thorstein Veblen, though filled with veneration, portray the "stuffiness of classrooms, the dust of libraries" and the "trustees, collegepresidents" and all the other jobs "kept for yesmen" as the titular "bitter drink" that slowly eroded him (*Big Money* 75). Though the fictional Veblen retains his critical acumen while at Yale, as evident in his inability to "get his mouth round the essential yes," positioning him in clear contrast to the other university "yesmen," Dos Passos reiterates the narcotic qualities of academia that his personal letters suggest (78). Through his various university appointments, the "sharp clear prism" of Veblen's mind becomes whittled down. and we are left not with an image of intellectual vigor but of a "greyfaced shambling man lolling resentful at his desk" (83; 74). Even the most acutely critical minds are susceptible to the institutions that condition mental labor.

The academy therefore is shown to be either a force of pacification or covert class preservation, despite the New Deal's attempts to revise the cultural perception of the egghead to include a revolutionary bent. Yet even prior to FDR's brain trust, Dos Passos took a critical stance toward formal education. In a 1916 personal letter to Rumsey Martin, Dos Passos wrote that nothing is lower than the "stupidity of the educated whose education is nothing but a wall," reiterating the bell jar notion of isolation in Camera Eye (25) (*Travel Books* 643). In Dos Passos's view, American "schools and colleges [did] that merely," drawing a firm distinction between the educational models abroad and those he observed while on American soil. Such a position is more drastically illustrated in Dos Passos's 1917 letter to Arthur McComb, which shows the budding author wishing to "annihilate these stupid colleges of ours" and eradicate the "middle class snobbism" of the thinkers they churn out (659). Here, Dos Passos emphasizes the class dimensions of formal education, which limits the degree to which its students can identify with the working class. Instead of promoting the types of thinking needed for class reformation, Dos Passos saw education as a means of preserving class relations. In a diary entry on January 24, 1918, Dos Passos wrote that the Ivy League was built on little more than a "merry mountain of lies," lies that may have enabled the educated classes to believe they were champions of the lower classes despite their actual class position and function (705). Through the inclusion of the Francisco Ferrer vignette, Dos Passos shows the coercive forces that would restrict any attempt to break that class alliance.

Despite being "rather cynical about American colleges," Dos Passos notes that schools like Yale and Harvard have "many faults and, I suppose, virtues" (*Travel Books* 655). He writes that though the "intellectual life in any of them [universities] is slim enough," it is possible to "emerge without having one's intellect utterly mossed over," which suggests that there are advantages to formal education that might otherwise not be had. In fact, Dos Passos hoped that education might be re-conceptualized so that it could create and foster the types of working-class consciousness that his own artistic production worked toward. In his letters, Dos Passos lauds the possibilities of alternative educational models that depart from the stultifying and highbrow education at places like Harvard. In another letter to Rumsey Marvin, Dos Passos makes it clear that there "are so many *other* sorts of education" such as that of a "farmer's boy who has never been to school but may be beautifully deeply educated" (643). While being a farmer does not automatically make one educated, Dos Passos does note that a "stupid farmer is no lower on the scale than a stupid Harvard graduate," which signals a broadened understanding of aptitude that is not dependent on class signifiers or even institutions. In keeping with the working-class ethos around mental labor espoused throughout the trilogy, the type of education that the farmer's boy would receive would be through an organic tradition, deriving from the observable world and community, wherein labor and the speech of the people become the basis.

This alternative model of education is also in keeping with Antonio Gramsci's work, which also considers the role of what he terms organic intellectuals. These figures maintain direct ties to their class of origin and continually work to improve the conditions of those that belong to it. And beyond simply serving an economic function, these figures have an "awareness of [their] own function not only in the economic but also in the social and political fields" (Gramsci 5). These latter fields are particularly important in that these organic thinkers can perform the ideological functions that can give rise to and organize a critical class consciousness. No longer is mental labor tied to specific institutions like the university or the clergy before it, but it is expanded to include all levels of production and social classes. Thus, for Gramsci "all men are intellectuals . . . but not all men have in society the function of intellectuals" (9). Dos Passos made a similar point when writing to the First American Writers Congress in his piece "The Writer as Technician," a title that is not unlike Benjamin's "Author as Producer." Indeed, just as Benjamin makes the claim that all humans are intellectuals though they do not all occupy that station in society, Dos Passos similarly argues that "anybody who can put down words on paper is a writer in one sense . . . the difficulty begins when you try to work out what really distinguishes professional writing from the average man's letters . . ." (545). The breadth of characters and occupations dealing with mental labor discussed below speak to the proliferation of intellectual types, moving from a strictly traditional model to more organic types.

What Gramsci hoped for was that such homegrown thinkers could, through their mental labor, organize and homogenize the disenfranchised, despite the attempts of the ruling classes to further divide and isolate them. He writes that such a figure must "be an organizer of masses of men; he must be an organizer of the 'confidence' of investors in his business, or the customers for his product, etc.," which emphasizes the point that these thinkers could be found in any sphere of production (Gramsci 5). In other words, these figures are "specialists who fulfill technical, directive, organizational needs" (Sassoon 139). Because they have these mutually constitutive qualities, they act as interlocutors between productive forces, skilled with a technical knowledge as well as an inclination for praxis, making one a "constructor, organizer," and "permanent persuader" (Gramsci 10). If this type of organizer was not only an advocate for a particular class but also belonged to it, they could "engage in all aspects of the struggle" through an awareness of "the complexities of production" (Sassoon 149). If such a permanent persuader was to come about, Gramsci believed, then the working classes could "wage the cultural struggle for hegemony" while preparing for "the political struggle which will culminate in the seizure of power" (149). Clearly, this type of mental labor had the type of political ends that one would be hard-pressed to find at the Harvard that Dos Passos so critically describes.

Between his fictional representations of the politically anemic academicism of Harvard, Dos Passos also works toward a more organic tradition that can provide the very organizational capacity described by Gramsci. For instance, the "The Boy Orator of the Platte," who appears in "Newsreel XII," represents such a figure. The real boy orator, William Jennings Bryan, was also known as the "Great Commoner" due to his populist sensibilities and is shown to assemble rural communities for political ends. Dos Passos emphasizes Bryan's rural roots, noting his upbringing as a minister's son as the boy speaks to a small town of farmers. He notes that the boy's "silver voice . . . filled the ears of the plain people" and the "mortgageridden farmers of the great plains" gather to hear him speak, allowing him to fulfill the organizational quality outlaid by Gramsci (*42nd Parallel* 135). His speech certainly does ignite the revolutionary fervor that both Gramsci and Dos Passos would hope for, as the farmers' "roared their lungs out" at the boy's claim that the government shall not "press down upon the brow of labor this crown of thorns." The reference to Bryan's silver tongue is akin to the permanent persuader role while also being an historical reference to debates around the gold standard, which many saw as ultimately serving wealthy, global businessmen at the expense of local labor. Dos Passos, however, was unwilling to let the rural autodidact completely fulfill the class function envisioned by Gramsci. Instead, the novel demonstrates a more global understanding of capitalism's resilience. After a stroke kills Bryan, Dos Passos also includes the detail that "South Africa flooded the gold market" thanks to a "cyanide process for extracting gold from ore" taking place in "the Rand" shortly after (136). What these details suggest is that even organic intellectuals, despite the mythic status they may have accrued during the 1930s, are still susceptible to sudden mortality while the mention of South African gold shows a macro-scale of capitalist enterprise in stark contrast to the local efforts of the boy orator.

Not only was Dos Passos skeptical of the capacity for organic orators to initiate substantial change in the face of global exploitation, he was also aware that some of them would simply act in their own favor rather than maintain a class loyalty. Just as George Novack saw the New Deal programs as being largely composed of opportunists who simply wanted more power rather than its overhaul, Dos Passos shows the self-serving aspects of the so-called brain workers. Gramsci similarly recognized this and argued that organic figures could still function as the dominant class's "deputies" who "exercise functions of social hegemony and political government" that ideologically influence the lower classes in order to elicit their "spontaneous" consent (12). Within the context of the brain trust, this critical side of the working-class thinker paints a rather different picture of the New Deal thinker than accounts like Hofstadter's give. Rather than being the champions of the oppressed, they may have been the very forces that maintained order through ideological pacification while putting on a progressive face.

Dos Passos was keenly aware of this ideological function that serves class hegemony, and he turned to advertising as a medium through which it can be enacted. For instance, J. Ward Moorehouse embodies this, given his rise in fortune through his specialization in an emergent market—public relations. According to Harry Levin, this new industry came down to nothing more than "opinion-moulding for the postwar American public" (409). In modeling Moorehouse's character after Ivy Lee, who is considered to be a founder of public relations and known for his work with the Rockefellers, Dos Passos demonstrates how the so-called permanent persuader can become a necessary adjunct of capitalist enterprise, even when they come from classes outside that realm (Casey 250).

Once Moorehouse achieves some measure of financial success through his work in information management, another emergent industry that Dos Passos presciently saw as an aggregate of mental labor, he resolves to promote a new educational system for the public. Moorehouse recognizes the ideological function of sites like the Ivy Leagues and claims that it is the "business of the industry to educate the public" through an "information bureau" as well as his own "advertising agency" (*42nd Parallel* 200). In a sense, Moorehouse strives to create a system that will perpetuate the ideologies most congruent with capitalist production while also allowing for the reproduction of thinkers like himself. In arguing that the "education of the public and of employers and employees" is a primary tool for avoiding the terrors of "socialism and demagoguery and worse," Morehouse acts as the Gramscian, ideological deputy, whose creation of an "educational campaign" ultimately works to regulate the public and preserve the state (214). At the end of his speech arguing for a capitalist educational campaign, Moorehouse seeks out Judge Planet, who "looked impressed" with the speech, with his "blue-eyed smile" (214). In this quick exchange, Dos Passos is showing the very relationship between ideological and coercive forces that Gramsci also outlines. Moorehouse provides the ideological basis for hegemonic consent while Judge Planet represents the legal, coercive force that supplements it. Dos Passos therefore chronicles the many facets of the American thinker as he shows that without them the working class cannot effectively organize and revolutionize *while at the same time* noting how intellectuals are themselves tools through which the status quo is maintained.

Fortunately, the trilogy moves toward another possibility that can achieve something close to the revolutionary potential imagined by Benjamin and the sponsors of the "Culture and the Crisis" manifesto. According to Janet Galligani Casey, the Camera Eye sections of *U.S.A.* collectively form an "acutely sensitive observer" and a "writer whose mission will be the championing of the disenfranchised" (252). While I agree with the argument that the Camera Eye persona is the "guiding spirit of the trilogy" and a "socially responsible ego" that "eventually comes to believe in the power of art," I also view this guiding spirit as a representation of the Dos Passos-envisioned intellectual and word slinger, who catalogs and organizes the speech of the people for political means without succumbing to the coercive powers of capital (252). Indeed, much like the young man shown at the start of the trilogy, the Camera Eye persona is eager to capture and record the sights and words that make up America. While all other characters succumb to the "inimical corporate structure of America," creating what John P. Diggins has described as Dos Passos's "criticism of what he considers the Roosevelt reign of regimentation," the Camera Eye recorder lies outside the bounds of such regimentation (492). In this sense, this figure is more an organizer of disparate voices rather than a representative, which offers a corrective to the impulses surrounding the literati of the 1930s.

This role of the author as chronicler becomes most pronounced at the end of the trilogy, wherein their function as productive word slinger becomes paramount. In Camera Eye (49), the implied narrator wonders how he can "make them feel how our fathers our uncles haters of oppression" lived, seeking a method to give a voice to the downtrodden in a way that echoes the desires of New Deal program members seeking to be the representatives of those hit hardest by the Depression (*Big Money* 350). The narrator explains that, by rebuilding "the ruined words worn slimy in the mouths of lawyers districtattorneys collegepresidents judges," the American people can recover and rebuild the world of words torn down by capital. For all its critique of the elitist brain power of its time, the trilogy presents the author as a new figure of how that does not presume to take over the oppressed but to assemble their voices in a collective unity and to reclaim the words stolen by those in power. This sentiment is echoed once more in Camera Eye (51), wherein the unnamed author notes that "we have only words against/Power Superpower" (420). In keeping with the ethos of the author as word slinger, Dos Passos again highlights the importance of mental labor for revolutionary ends but does so in a way that decentralizes the individual author and places an emphasis on the fruits of their labors. Words are what will raise class consciousness by forming critique—as in the case of the boy orator—and by giving a true representation of American life, as is the case in the Camera Eye sections. Dos Passos, like Gramsci and Benjamin, saw authors as producers, imbricated within the vast system of production despite any attempts to view themselves otherwise. However, seeing one's self within that system did not signal defeat. Rather, the trilogy articulates the way the author can be both of and against an economic system of oppression.

To view the author as a producer, a mental laborer, or a word slinger is itself the first step in rectifying the divide between the intelligentsia and the working classes. In working against the petty snobberies of his class, Dos Passos's work exposes the ways mental labor can be co-opted as well as its potential to stir emotions and organize revolutionary impulses. The trilogy therefore offers a differing opinion of the New Deal brain trust that does not nostalgically gloss over the theoretical complications that come with assuming a complete union between working-class movements and the intelligentsia. What we are left with is an intellectual who neither bends to capital nor assumes the role of a representative. Rather, the author uses their labor, in the work's creation and through its representations, to chronicle the speech of the people, making the trilogy a process as much as a product of the intellectual activity it theorizes.

WORKS CITED

Benjamin, Walter. *The Work of Art in the Age of its Technological Reproducibility and Other Writings*. Translated by Edmund Jephcott, Rodney Livingstone, and Howard Eiland. Edited by Michael Jennings, Brigid Doherty and Thomas Levin, The Belknap-Harvard UP, 2008.

Casey, Galligani Janet. "Historicizing the Female in *U. S. A.*: Re-Visions of Dos Passos's Trilogy." *Twentieth Century Literature*, vol. 41, no. 3, 1995, pp. 249–64.

Dell, Floyd. *Intellectual Vagabondage: An Apology for the Intelligentsia*. George H. Doran Company, 1926.

Denning, Michael. *The Cultural Front: The Laboring of American Culture in the Twentieth Century*. Verso, 2010.

Diggins, John. "Dos Passos and Veblen's Villains." *The Antioch Review*, vol. 23, no. 4, 1963, pp. 485–500.

Dos Passos, John. *1919*. Houghton Mifflin Company, 1932.

———. *The 42nd Parallel*. Houghton Mifflin Company, 1930.

———. *The Big Money*. Houghton Mifflin Company, 1933.

———. "Every Vote a Blow!" *New Masses*, vol. 8, no. 4, Nov. 1932, p. 4.

———. *Travel Books and Other Writings 1916–1941*. The Library of America, 2003.

———. "The Writer as Technician." *Modernism: An Anthology of Sources and Documents*, edited by Jane Goldman, Olga Taxidou, and Vassiliki Kolocontroni, U of Chicago P, 1998, pp. 545–48.

Fishback, Price, et al. "Did New Deal Grant Programs Stimulate Local Economies? A Study of Federal Grants and Retail Sales during the Great Depression." *The Journal of Economic History*, vol. 65, no. 1, 2005, pp. 36–71.

Fitzpatrick, Ellen. "Rethinking the Intellectual Origins of American Labor History." *The American Historical Review*, vol. 96, no. 2, 1991, pp. 422–28.

Gramsci, Antonio. *Selections From the Prison Notebooks of Antonio Gramsci*, edited and translated by Quintin Hoare and Geoffrey Smith. International Publishers, 2014.

Hofstadter, Richard. *Anti-Intellectualism in American Life*. Vintage Books, 1963.

Jacoby, Russell. *The Last Intellectuals: American Culture in the Age of Academe*. Basic Books, 2000.

Kabal, Jerome. "Revolutionary Contradictions: Antonio Gramsci and the Problem of Intellectuals." *Politics and Society, vol.* 6, 1976, pp. 123–72.

Kallich, Martin. "John Dos Passos Fellow-Traveler: A Dossier with Commentary." *Twentieth Century Literature*, vol. 1, no. 4, 1956, pp. 173–90.

League of Professional Groups for Foster and Ford. *Culture and the crisis: an open letter to the writers, artists, teachers, physicians, engineers, scientists and other professional workers of America*. Workers Library Publishers, 1932.

Lecklider, Aaron. *Inventing the Egghead: The Battle over Brainpower in American Culture*. University of Pennsylvania Press, 2013.

Levin, Harry. "Revisiting Dos Passos' 'U. S. A.'." *The Massachusetts Review*, vol. 20, no. 3, 1979, pp. 401–15.

Mutnick, Deborah. "Toward a Twenty-First-Century Federal Writers' Project." *College English*, vol. 77, no. 2, 2014, pp. 124–45.

Neufeld, Maurice F. "The Historical Relationship of Liberals and Intellectuals to Organized Labor in the United States." *The Annals of the American Academy of Political and Social Science*, vol. 350, 1963, pp. 115–28.

Novak, George. "American Intellectuals and the Crisis." *New International*, vol. 3, no. 1, 1936, pp. 23–27.

Pizer, Donald. "John Dos Passos' 'Rosinante to the Road Again' and the Modernist Expatriate Imagination." *Journal of Modern Literature*, vol. 21, no. 1, 1997, pp. 137–50.

Rutkowski, Sara. *Literary Legacies of the Federal Writers' Project: Voices of the Depression in the American Postwar Era*. Palgrave Macmillan, 2017.

Sassoon, Showstack Anne. *Gramsci's Politics*. Croom Helm, 1980.

Stearns, Harold E. *America and the Young Intellectual*. Greenwood Press, 1973.

Szalay, Michael. *New Deal Modernism: American Literature and the Invention of the Welfare State*. Duke UP, 2000.

Whyte, George R. *The Dreyfus Affair: A Chronological History*. Palgrave Macmillan, 2005.

PART 4

CHRONICLING THE AMERICA-EUROPE DIVIDE

10

TRANSATLANTIC TENSIONS

Changing Views of Europe and the United States in Dos Passos's Interwar Writings

Fredrik Tydal

The relationship between Europe and the United States occupies a central if not always fully acknowledged role in the works of John Dos Passos. In fact, his first published novel, *One Man's Initiation: 1917*, begins aboard an American ocean liner bound for Europe. This setting serves as an appropriate opening for his novelistic career, not only because Dos Passos himself spent a good deal of his life crossing the Atlantic, but also since his work in many ways seems to both navigate and negotiate that transatlantic space.

This essay explores the complex relationship between Europe and the United States that emerges from Dos Passos's interwar writings, both fiction and nonfiction. It argues that the author's shifting attitudes toward Europe and the United States not only offers a window into the tensions of the interwar period, but also provides a new context for his own changing politics. My discussion will be framed around a central contradiction—namely, that while Dos Passos as a young man sees Europe as a role model for the United States, he comes to eventually reverse his position, advocating a cutting of ties between the Old and the New World.

In what follows, then, I will be charting a trajectory in Dos Passos's thinking about Europe and the United States, and in order to do so, a starting point is required. A useful one, I believe, is to be found in the author's formative correspondence with his friend Rumsey Marvin. For in a letter from December 1916, the young Dos Passos's despair over the Great War prompted a revealing reflection on what he saw as the relationship between Europe and the United States: "[T]here is something frightfully paralysing to me in the war—Everything I do, everything I write seems so cheap and futile—If Europe is to senselessly destroy itself—Its [*sic*] as if a crevasse had opened and all the fair things, all the mellow things, all the things that were to teach us in America how to live, were slipping in—a sort of tidal wave and blood and fire . . ." (*Fourteenth Chronicle* 60). The passage is significant not only in terms of content, but also in tone. From these lines, it is clear that Dos Passos saw Europe as a kind of role model or even parent to the United States. Certainly, considering their historical relationship, the latter idea would seem to come naturally; the Old World, Dos Passos suggests, still has something to teach its younger kin. But implicit in these lines is also a certain hereditary fear: Now that Europe is destroying itself, will the United States follow? What if the tidal wave should reach all the way across the Atlantic?

What also stands out about the passage is the emotional tone, suggesting great concern. Naturally, the war troubled many American writers and intellectuals, but given Dos Passos's background, his attachment to Europe was especially strong. To him, Europe was not only the continent of his Portuguese ancestry, but in a psychologically significant way also the place of his childhood. From age one to his enrollment at Harvard at age sixteen, Dos Passos spent the greater part of his life in Europe: living his early years in Wiesbaden, Paris, and Brussels; attending boarding school in England as a boy; and traveling in Italy and Greece in his early teens (Ludington 14–47). It was Europe, in other words, that had not only schooled him, but also, in a sense, raised him—in lieu of a sickly mother and an often absent father.

As the passage from the letter indicates, the war clearly represented a crisis of faith for Dos Passos, casting doubt on the validity of Europe as a role model. As we know, his response to the war and the inner turmoil it provoked in him was to enlist in the ambulance corps, so as to help stop both the literal and figurative blood flow. Although his time of service forever disillusioned him with war, it did restore his faith in Europe—in a way that appears as paradoxical. This is expressed in the two novels produced by his experiences: *One Man's Initiation* (1920) and *Three Soldiers* (1921).

As I have pointed out, *One Man's Initiation* begins with the protagonist Martin Howe setting out for Europe. Although the character is crossing the Atlantic to serve as an ambulance driver on the Western Front, the novel is not only a story of war, but also draws on the motif of the Old World journey—a familiar thematic preoccupation in American literature, extending back to Nathaniel Hawthorne's *The Marble Faun* and Henry James's many transatlantic fictions. In fact, if we look closely at the beginning of the novel, Martin appears to have more in common with an Old World traveler than with someone sailing off to war. As the ship "plows through the long swell, eastward," he senses new beginnings: "a leaf seems to have been turned and a new white page spread before him, clean and unwritten on" (9). As they reach the shores of France, Martin is described as "breath[ing] deep of the new indefinable smell [coming] off the land" (15). The novel, in other words, begins with what is almost a discovery of Europe—which the quasi-epic tone reinforces.

Throughout the novel, the war continues to be pushed into the background, as Martin experiences moments of what I would describe as a conflation of the aesthetic and the historical sublime, which effectively serves to block out the reality of the war. From time to time, Martin is overwhelmed by the sense of beauty and history of the Old World surroundings. At one point, the awe inspired by a tall old abbey gives him the impression that "there might have been no war at all," and he finds himself transported back to the perceived tranquility of medieval times (41–42). On another occasion, he wakes up outside after a night of revelry in Paris and is spellbound by the sight of Notre Dame in the misty morning. As he gazes at the beauty of the cathedral, the reality of the war threatens to intrude through flashes in his mind, but in his newly awakened state, these may as well be residual images from his dreams, which would in that case make the war a nightmare (57–58). Taken together, then, the war appears as something of an aberration to Martin—a bad dream, incongruous with the culture and sophistication of Europe.

Toward the end of the novel, in what may be seen as its climax, this idea is reinforced, as Martin takes part in a political discussion, dominated by a group of young Frenchmen. Here, Martin first offers a criticism of his fellow countrymen: Americans, he comments, "are like children. They believe everything they are told, you see; they have had no experience in international affairs, like you Europeans" (106). The parent-child relationship between Europe and the United States suggested by Dos Passos in his correspondence with Rumsey Marvin is here clearly expressed. One of the Frenchmen then delivers an eloquent critique of contemporary Western civilization, drawing on Greek philosophy, Hindu thought, and socialist ideas. It projects a form of optimism that is almost unique for Dos Passos; there is none of the irony of his later writings, which often undercuts commitment and ambition. As the young men sit down for a final drink, there is a brief moment when the significance of the scene appears to sink in for our protagonist: "Martin took in at a glance the eager sunburned faces, the eyes burning with hope, with determination, and a sudden joy flared through him. 'Oh, there is hope,' he said, drinking down his glass" (115). The point is clear: underneath the chaos of war, despite centuries of conflict and oppression, there is still cultural and political hope in Europe—in marked contrast, by implication, to the United States.

In the subsequent and better-known *Three Soldiers*, this idea finds further expression. While *Three Soldiers* ostensibly differs from *One Man's Initiation* in that its compass is expanded to include the perspective of more than one person, the focus of the novel eventually comes to land on John Andrews, the soldier who most resembles Martin Howe and the author's own experience. After having grown disillusioned with war, Andrews deserts and finds a refuge in Paris—specifically in its cultural life. Making the acquaintance of the vivacious Genevieve, Andrews begins to heal from his wartime psychological scars as the two spend their days listening to music and discussing literature. At one point, he compares himself to "a man who has come up out of a dark cellar" and is "almost too dazzled by the gorgeousness of everything" (295). The formulation not only evokes Plato's allegory of the cave, but also accords with the emancipatory logic implicit in the progression of chapter titles up to that point: from "Making the Mould," "The Metal Cools," "Machines," and "Rust" to finally "The World Outside." The nature of that outside world is twofold: in one sense, it is the world of civilian life, freed from the mechanization of modern warfare. Yet, in another sense, it is the world of European culture, suggested by the element of aesthetic sensation ("dazzled by the gorgeousness of everything"), and made specific by the choice of literary and musical references throughout the Paris part of the novel (most prominently Debussy, but also Flaubert, Bach, and Balzac).

Through his encounter with European culture, Andrews gains new energy and takes up playing the piano again, eventually starting to compose his own material. But this idyllic existence does not last for long, as the novel ends with his arrest for desertion. In the closing scene, Dos Passos depicts how the cultural oasis Andrews had discovered in Europe is rudely trampled on by American military power. Rich in symbolic value, the final paragraph shows his music sheets being disheveled by the wind as he is taken away by soldiers and, by implication, brought back into the fold of army regimentation. Thus, in both of Dos Passos's first two novels, Europe, in contrast to the United States, offers a kind of cultural and political hope, which the protagonists are able to discern beneath the chaos of war. But in *Three Soldiers*, as shown, the United States could be seen as stifling that hope through the twin specters of coercion and conformity.

After two novels predominantly set in Europe, *Manhattan Transfer* (1925) by contrast takes place entirely in the United States. Despite this focused setting, however, Europe still has an important thematic presence in the novel, mainly through how Dos Passos satirizes the European immigrant experience via the characters of Emile and Congo Jake. Both of them from France, the pair is introduced to the reader as their boat makes its way through the swells of the Gulf Stream. This transatlantic, in-between setting serves as an apt background for their conversation, which centers on the differences between Europe and the United States. "Europe's rotten and stinking," Emile comments. "In America a fellow can get ahead. Birth dont matter, education dont matter. It's all getting ahead" (30). Emile, in other words, imagines the United States as freed from the constraints of European class societies, where the individual can reach the top through hard work and ambition. Congo, however, is more interested in the short term and satisfying his immediate desires, as his main priorities are finding women and enjoying himself. As the two friends step ashore, their respective attitudes produce different results. Emile retains his idealism, believing that he can work himself to the top by effort and determination alone, and is thus content beginning at the bottom. Congo, by contrast, is more instinctual, feeling the pulse of the city and eventually striking gold during Prohibition by supplying the pent-up demand for alcohol. Toward the end of the novel, Congo becomes a wealthy bootlegger, while Emile ends up working as his chef—ironically suggesting, of course, that hard work does not pay as well as crime does. But even though Congo ends up wealthy, it is implied to only be fleeting, as the end of the novel sees him under attack from rival bootleggers, and we are made to understand that his fortunes could just as easily reverse. Whereas Dos Passos's first two novels feature Americans journeying to Europe and there paradoxically finding hope in the midst of war, *Manhattan Transfer* shows us two Europeans going to the United States but finding only an unforgiving, dog-eat-dog climate. The only hope there is in modern American society, the novel implies, is in leaving—as the central character Jimmy Herf does at the end.

Interestingly, Jimmy Herf's rejection of modern American city life could be said to be prompted by his encounter with Europe, which figures as an external setting in his part of the story. Between the second and third sections of the novel, Jimmy and his wife-to-be, Ellen, travel to Europe to work for the Red Cross—the details of which are absent from the text, presumably so as to keep the geographical setting constant and maintain the urban atmosphere. Thus, as the third section opens, we only see Jimmy and Ellen returning, and it is implied that their Old World journey has had a profound effect on at least one of them. For as the ship pulls into New York City, Jimmy comments to Ellen: "I kinder wish we were just going on board . . . I hate getting home" (252, ellipsis in original). Despite having been in Europe during a time of war, Jimmy, like Martin Howe and John Andrews before him, paradoxically idealizes the experience, viewing it as a happier time in his life and specifically in his relationship with Ellen. After their return, he fails to reintegrate into

American urban life as he sinks "into dreamier and dreamier reverie," waxing nostalgic about the look in Ellen's eyes while sitting on a hilltop somewhere in France, and remembering pastoral scenes of grazing cows on grassy slopes and fetching milk from a shepherd's hut (290). For the remainder of his story, Jimmy's disillusionment with modern American society, which had previously only been vague and unarticulated, will grow stronger and more purposeful, culminating in his retreat from the city at the end of the novel. Seen this way, it is the encounter with Europe that allows Jimmy to put words to his feelings about the direction of modern American society and finally act on his impulses.

At this point, it is necessary to return to Dos Passos himself in order to explain the shift in attitude toward Europe that begins to take place following *Manhattan Transfer*. To be precise, it is a development set in motion by his involvement in the Sacco-Vanzetti case: the *cause célèbre* of his generation, in which two Italian American radicals were tried for a double homicide during a time of heightened anti-immigrant sentiment. It is generally agreed, of course, that Dos Passos's interest in the case was a watershed moment in his development as a politically conscious writer. However, I want to argue that it also contained the seeds of his shift in attitude to Europe. As so many immigrants before them, Sacco and Vanzetti had moved to the United States in search of a better life. Dos Passos visited both men in prison, and from his writings on the case, he clearly felt strong compassion for them. Yet only two years previously, he had waxed ironical about the European immigrant experience through Emile and Congo Jake in *Manhattan Transfer*. Thus, I propose that his involvement in the Sacco-Vanzetti case forced him to reconsider the assumptions underlying his depiction of the two French immigrants—and, by extension, the view of Europe and the United States that informed it. For, quite contrary to the stock phrases about freedom and opportunity that he has Emile rattling off, Dos Passos's writings on the Sacco-Vanzetti case are filled with highly charged rhetoric and imagery about transatlantic emigration. Essentially, Dos Passos argues that there was a frightening symbolic significance in the image of two European immigrants facing execution in the State of Massachusetts, whose soil had once served as refuge from political oppression and religious persecution. Consider, for example, how he imagines the perspective of Vanzetti:

> Between the houses he could see the gleaming stretch of Plymouth Bay, the sandy islands beyond, the white dories at anchor. About three hundred years before, men from the west of England had first

> sailed into the grey shimmering bay that smelt of woods and wild grape, looking for something; liberty. . . . freedom to worship God in their own manner. . . . space to breathe. ("The Pit and the Pendulum" 85, ellipses in original)

This connection between past and present, suggesting a kinship between the Pilgrims and subsequent generations of immigrants, would shape much of Dos Passos's thinking around the case. In their resistance to oppressive institutions, in their crossing the Atlantic in search of a less stratified society, and in their escape from a continent ravaged by war and persecution, Sacco and Vanzetti, in Dos Passos's mind, embodied the hopes and dreams of all those who had come before them. To be sure, this is a far cry from his depiction of Emile and Congo Jake—from irony to sincerity.

Dos Passos's writings on the Sacco-Vanzetti case, I argue, forced him to acknowledge an essential difference between Europe and the United States, namely the latter's lack of a feudal past. European immigrants, Dos Passos writes, were driven by the dream of a place "where man could reach his full height free from the old snarling obsessions of god and master" (*Facing the Chair* 57). To explain what motivated Sacco and Vanzetti to leave their native country, then, Dos Passos had to contrast the present-day reverberations of Europe's history of oppression and serfdom with the comparative freedom and opportunity of the United States.

This reevaluation of the relationship between the United States and Europe prompted by the Sacco-Vanzetti case must also be placed in a broader context—namely, that of totalitarian developments in Europe. After having completed *Manhattan Transfer* in the summer of 1925, Dos Passos went to Europe, and as part of that journey visited Italy, making a port of call in the city of Savona, of which he had fond memories from an earlier visit. When disembarking, however, he did not recognize the vibrant city he had previously known. He related his immediate impressions in a letter to John Howard Lawson, who had accompanied him on the earlier visit. "Savona is a dead town," he wrote, "do you remember how swell it seemed in 1917—?" A former leftist stronghold, the city had now taken a markedly different turn: "[E]verybody has been killed by the fascisti or chased away," Dos Passos matter-of-factly states, describing the city as "[t]he most fantastically sinister place I've ever been in" (*Fourteenth Chronicle* 363). Three years later, demonstrating the lasting impression it left on him, he published an account of his visit to Savona in the stylized piece "A City That Died by Heartfailure." Written in the form of a detective story, the text seeks to diagnose the eerie atmosphere of a city that had previously bustled with life and energy. Soon, it becomes more and more evident to both narrator and reader that fascism is responsible for having turned the city into a place of paranoia and decay, where "people walked as if they were being followed, talked as if they felt they were being overheard" (107). At the end of story, all ambiguity is removed as a group of local blackshirts appear, at once confirming and taking pride in the political repression installed: "the purification of the city has been complete," they boast (108).

While Europe was beginning to fall under the sway of anti-democratic forces, Dos Passos was composing the *U.S.A.* trilogy. In its middle volume, *1919*, published in 1932, he revisits the same wartime Europe he had previously depicted in *One Man's Initiation* and *Three Soldiers*. Since *Manhattan Transfer* had taken place entirely in the United States, *1919* is also the first time since these novels that Dos Passos returns to an Old World setting in his fiction. The difference, I would argue, is noticeable. While Martin Howe experienced moments of the sublime in wartime Europe, the impressions of Dos Passos's Old World travelers in *1919* suggest the trite and the trivial. Consider, for example, Richard Ellsworth Savage's first impressions of France, ascribed to his own consciousness through the use of free indirect discourse: "Bordeaux, the red Garonne, the pastelcolored streets of old tall mansardroofed houses, the sunlight and shadow so delicately blue and yellow, the names of the stations all out of Shakespeare, the yellowbacked novels on the bookstands, the bottles of wine in the buvettes . . ." Far from Martin Howe's sincere appreciation of the beauty and sense of history of Europe, this description seems straight out of a travel brochure—the type of language Savage's future employer J. Ward Moorehouse would use. In the following sentence, we are then told how the "faintly bluegreen fields were spattered scarlet with poppies like the first lines of a poem . . ." (*U.S.A.* 442). It is overwrought to the point that it becomes bland. Here, then, the irony is clearly directed at the American undertaking the Old World journey, as the reader is made to ponder the absurdity of tourist-like impressions in the midst of war. In comparison with *Manhattan Transfer*, *1919* presents a clear reversal: in the earlier novel, it was Emile's enthusiasm about the United States that was being made fun of, while in the later one, it is Savage's impressions of Europe that are the object of irony.

The tendency is not unique to Savage's narrative, but extends to that of other characters in *1919*. For example, it is particularly prevalent in Eveline Hutchins's narrative sections. Like Savage, she is delighted to be in Europe; but at the level of narration, Dos Passos distorts that delight into something else. The following passage, describing her everyday life as a relief worker in Paris, is worth reproducing at length:

> Eveline never tired of looking out the window, through the delicate tracing of the wroughtiron balcony, at the Seine where toy steamboats bucked the current, towing shinyvarnished barges that had lace curtains and geraniums in the windows of their deckhouses painted green and red, and at the island opposite where the rocketing curves of the flying buttresses shoved the apse of Nôtre Dâme dizzily upwards out of the trees of a little park. They had tea at a small Buhl table in the window almost every evening when they got home from the office on the Rue de Rivoli, after spending the day pasting pictures of ruined French farms and orphaned children and starving warbabies into scrapbooks to be sent home for use in Red Cross drives. (*U.S.A.* 543)

Naturally, this is as much an implied criticism of the character as it is a reflection of the author's attitude toward Europe. In Eveline's mind, the culture and beauty of Paris take center stage, while the reality of the war exists like something of an afterthought. Dos Passos effects this impression at the level of sentence construction: their having tea at the Buhl table is the main clause, to which the war is then made subordinate—both syntactically and perceptually. The overall effect is one of estrangement, of turning the city into something akin to a laughing mirror, in the sense that its features are not only exaggerated, but also made ugly through being put side by side the horrors of war. Comparing these passages and the pattern of which they are part to the descriptions of Europe in Dos Passos's earlier work, readers may find that the Old World has lost its splendor—or more precisely, its hope and potential.

If the emergence of fascism in Italy represented the threat of a new disillusionment with Europe for Dos Passos—another crisis of faith—the events of March 1933 in Germany intensified it. For as disturbing as Mussolini's regime was to Dos Passos, the development in Italy was initially an isolated case; with the rise of Hitler, however, it appeared as part of a larger pattern. In his response to Hitler's coming to power, published in April of that year, Dos Passos attempted to understand the development by pointing to "the grotesque sediment of feudalism that still underlies the German mind." Throughout the article, Dos Passos builds on this idea of regression: that what was happening across Europe was consistent with a longer history of autocracy and oppression. "Americans who don't want to live in a society of slaves can no longer look to Europe for moral countenance," he writes. "That continent, between the false mustache of the Jew-baiter Hitler and Mussolini's castor oil squint, has sunk back to the cultural level of the Thirty Years War."

Evoking the idea of hereditary fear, Dos Passos hopes that the events in Germany will "give a salutary awakening jolt to all Americans," as he goes on to cite several examples of social injustice perpetrated in the United States—including the executions of Sacco and Vanzetti—that to him appear ominous in light of the developments in Europe ("Thank You, Mr. Hitler!" 156).

By the mid-1930s, it seemed inevitable to Dos Passos that Europe was again nearing large-scale conflict. In 1935, he predicted a "coming period of wars and dictatorships" (*Fourteenth Chronicle* 461), and in a letter to F. Scott Fitzgerald the following year, he even formulated himself in terms remarkably similar to those used twenty years before in his correspondence with Rumsey Marvin: "[T]he course of world events seems so frightful that I feel absolutely paralyzed," he despaired (*Fourteenth Chronicle* 488). On the one hand, Dos Passos's fear was prompted by the developments in Italy and Germany, but on the other hand, it was also the result of more recent events. For as Dos Passos was writing the letter to Fitzgerald in September 1936, General Francisco Franco and his Nationalist forces were advancing toward Madrid in the civil war that had broken out only a few months earlier. The viral spread of reaction around Europe deeply troubled Dos Passos: "A fascist Spain will mean a fascist France," he wrote to Malcolm Cowley later the same year (qtd. in Ludington 359). And given the notion of hereditary fear, it should be clear that Dos Passos was afraid the United States might be next.

Things would seem to be moving toward a boiling point for Dos Passos and, in the following year, his disillusionment with Europe became final through his experiences during the Spanish Civil War. Detailed in several recent publications as well as in Sonia Tercero Ramirez's film documentary *Robles: Duelo al sol* (2015), the disappearance of José Robles during the war affected Dos Passos on a deeply personal level, effectively amounting to the traumatic as it became increasingly clear from inquiry and investigation that his friend had been executed. As he assigned blame to the Soviet influence on the Republican side, the affair came to be the decisive factor in Dos Passos's move away from left-wing politics, and marked the start of his well-known journey to the other side of the political spectrum.

When Dos Passos returned from Spain, he published the revealingly titled article "Farewell to Europe," acknowledging his bond to Europe only in order to sever it. In the article, he relates his impressions of his experiences in Europe that spring, warning of impending social and political strife, and recommending that the United States go its own way. "The Atlantic is broad enough to protect us against air raids," he writes, "but it can't protect us against the infectious formulas for slavery that are preparing in Europe on every side," referring here to both fascism and communism. He then goes on to account for the situations in Great Britain, France, and Spain, but finding hope nowhere, due to fascist aggression on the one hand, and Stalinist influence in domestic left-wing politics on the other. "Mother England," Dos Passos writes, using a telling moniker, "is going to be very little help to the democratic idea in the near future," citing the looming possibility of a war with the fascist powers and the inability of a left split along Stalinist-Trotskyist lines to organize themselves (183). In France, he sees on the horizon "a civil war deadlier than the civil war in Spain," with the left compromised as the result of being "hogtied by the internal and international politics of the Kremlin," and the right pushed toward "a pro-German policy that is headed straight for high treason" (184). Lastly, in his beloved Spain, he is afraid that the cost of Soviet aid and influence will prove too high in the event of Republican victory, while the opposite outcome—that is, the success of the rebels—"would mean the final blotting out of hope for Europe" (185).

As Dos Passos moves toward his conclusion, we see the reappearance of the familiar figure of the Old World traveler, in what is a thinly masked generalization of his own recent experience: "An American in 1937 comes back from Europe with a feeling of happiness, the relief of coming up out into the sunlight from a stifling cellar, that some of his grandfathers must have felt coming home from Metternich's Europe after the Napoleonic wars, the feeling all the immigrants have had when they first saw the long low coast and the broad bays of the new world" (185). The choice of metaphor here is striking. In *Three Soldiers*, Dos Passos describes John Andrews's discovery of European culture in terms of coming up from a dark cellar. Now, however, he uses the same metaphor for the opposite purpose: to describe the oppressive climate in Europe in contrast to the freedom of the United States, suggesting a complete reversal. In the closing passage that follows, Dos Passos can be seen working out his post-Robles politics, occupying something of an intermediate position: still using elements of left-wing rhetoric, but also drawing on the American founding mythology more earnestly than before.

> Sure, we've got our class war, we've got our giant bureaucratic machines for antihuman power, but I can't help feeling that we are still moving on a slightly divergent track from the European world. Not all the fascist-hearted newspaper owners in the country, nor the Chambers of Commerce, nor the armies of hired gun-thugs of the great industries can change the fact that we have the Roundhead Revolution in our heritage and the Bill of Rights and the fact that

> the democracy in the past has been able, under Jefferson, Jackson, and Lincoln, and perhaps a fourth time (it's too soon to know yet) under Franklin Roosevelt, to curb powerful ruling groups. America has got to be in a better position to work out the problem: individual liberty vs. bureaucratic industrial organization than any other part of the world. If we don't it means the end of everything we have ever wanted since the first hard winters at Plymouth. (185–86)

Leslie Fiedler once wrote, "The end of the American artist's pilgrimage to Europe is the discovery of America" (124). In light of the development I have charted, this is certainly true of Dos Passos. In the beginning of his writing career, he sets out for Europe with his protagonist Martin Howe, and twenty years later, he comes to indeed "discover America." But for Dos Passos, this is also a political discovery, as his farewell to Europe anticipates—if not coincides with—his farewell to the political left.

In a sense, we may say that Dos Passos's political discovery of the United States is inscribed in the title of the larger work he had just finished. While that ambitious trilogy of his had nominally been completed with the appearance of *The Big Money* in 1936, he did not have to formally put a name to the work as a whole until its publication as a collected volume—which was not always meant to be titled "U.S.A." Dos Passos's notebooks from the period of composition offer several scribbled potential titles, such as "The First 30 Years," "New Century," and "New Era"—but notably no "U.S.A." (Papers of John Dos Passos, Box 48). Dos Passos actually only settled on "U.S.A." as a title at a relatively late stage: in the summer of 1937, following his return from Spain, and coinciding with the appearance of "Farewell to Europe" (*Fourteenth Chronicle* 497). If we think about this chronology, a striking symmetry appears, which, simplistic as it may seem, nonetheless captures something fundamental about the author's changing positions and also provides a denouement of sorts to the trajectory I have charted: "Farewell to Europe, Hello U.S.A." For the rest of his life, Dos Passos would indeed greet the United States with much enthusiasm, and I believe that his disillusionment with Europe must be taken into account when seeking to understand his turn to homegrown conservatism.

WORKS CITED

Dos Passos, John. "A City That Died by Heartfailure." 1928. *The Major Nonfictional Prose*, edited by Donald Pizer, Wayne State UP, 1988, pp. 106–9.

———. *Facing the Chair: Story of the Americanization of Two Foreignborn Workmen.* 1927. Da Capo, 1970.

———. "Farewell to Europe." 1937. *The Major Nonfictional Prose*, edited by Donald Pizer, Wayne State UP, 1988, pp. 183–86.

———. *The Fourteenth Chronicle: Letters and Diaries of John Dos Passos*, edited by Townsend Ludington, Gambit, 1973.

———. *Manhattan Transfer*. 1925. Penguin, 2000.

———. *One Man's Initiation: 1917*. 1920. Aegypan, 2007.

———. Papers of John Dos Passos, Accession #5950, Special Collections, University of Virginia Library, Charlottesville, VA.

———. "The Pit and the Pendulum." 1926. *The Major Nonfictional Prose*, edited by Donald Pizer, Wayne State UP, 1988, pp. 85–91.

———. "Thank You, Mr. Hitler!" 1933. *The Major Nonfictional Prose*, edited by Donald Pizer, Wayne State UP, 1988, pp. 156–57.

———. *Three Soldiers*. 1921. Penguin: 1999.

———. *U.S.A.* 1938. Library of America, 1996.

Fiedler, Leslie A. *An End to Innocence: Essays on Culture and Politics*. Beacon, 1955.

Ludington, Townsend. *John Dos Passos: A Twentieth-Century Odyssey*. 1980. Carroll & Graf, 1998.

11

"ROOTS STRIKING INTO THE INFINITE PAST"

John Dos Passos's Quest for the Modernist Cosmopolitan Subject in *Rosinante to the Road Again*

Eulalia Piñero Gil

In *The Modernist Papers* (2007), Fredric Jameson refers to John Dos Passos's modernist approach toward the fictional space as a "discontinuous literary cross-cutting" (167). The American cultural critic and theorist alludes to the author's transversal and dialectical relationship between creativity and the totality of history. In fact, Dos Passos showed a utopian commitment to ideological radicalism in his early literary aesthetics, and in his historical and political views of America and Europe during his youth. In this regard, Jun Lee draws attention to the fact that "as a modernist he tried to connect his aesthetic creativity to the totality of history in a dialectical way, since the perspective of totality is the core of his political radicalism as well as his art" (18). In his quest for the totality of history, young Dos Passos needed to internationalize his experience and creativity to connect them to the historical context, much like other modernists, who expressed in their artistic creations a deep sense of loss and despair for their society. This was the case of many expatriate writers, namely T. S. Eliot, Gertrude Stein, Scott Fitzgerald, and Ezra Pound. They sought to internationalize their literature, and they lived in European urban centers such as London and Paris to show their disillusion and despair with the materialist ideas of human progress and the invisible role and place of the artist in contemporary life. In my view, distance became a metaphor of their alienation and the urge to convey a de-centered perspective was a crucial aspect of their modernist poetics. Therefore, crossing cultural and ideological frontiers was at the core of their artistic experience.

Dos Passos's journey to Spain in 1916 inspired the travel book *Rosinante to the Road Again* (1922), which is a series of narrative chapters–essays–on his experiences in the villages and cities, and an insightful literary analysis of Spanish poets such as Jorge Manrique, Joan Maragall, Juan Ramón Jiménez, and Antonio Machado. In *Rosinante,* Dos Passos puts Madrid and other Spanish cities on the map of the global scope of modernism in his quest for the modernist cosmopolitan subject, and initiated, at the same time, a very fruitful transatlantic dialogue between American and Spanish literatures. For this purpose, he wrote an innovative modernist epic in which his fictional heroes, Telemachus and Lyaeus, are searching for the transcendental and abstract totality of life. Concretely, their quest focuses on the authentic "Spanish gesture" in a historical period of modernization and deep social transformation. Dos Passos's holistic approach, which can be found in many of the colorful sections of the travel book, shows his experimentation and intense interaction with prose, poetry, and painterly descriptive techniques. Such experimentation illustrates the author's relevant involvement with modernist poetics in his ground-breaking and "discontinuous literary cross-cutting."

In this sense, Ezra Pound's famous avant-garde exhortation "Make it new" is clearly reflected in the rhetorical techniques employed in *Rosinante.* As an experimental travel book that departs from the classical linear descriptions of this kind of texts, it fictionalizes the protagonists and uses discontinuous and fragmentary narrative structures. Thus, Dos Passos's fictional alter ego, Telemachus, becomes a "wanderer in search of a father" (Pizer 144) and an epic hero who undergoes an initiation journey of transformation and spiritual awakening in the Spanish society. For this reason, the author structures his interpretation of contemporary Spain on the parallel mythic pairs of Telemachus and Lyaeus,[1] and of Don Quixote and Sancho Panza: "Telemachus and Quixote constitute the life of the intellect and spirit, Lyaeus and Panza that of the body and the senses" (Pizer 142). In this way, *Don Quixote,* Spain's most famous epic narrative, offered the American writer the opportunity to re-evaluate the complex meanings of the wandering hero from La Mancha and his squire, and through these two figures to evaluate the progress and benefits of modernity.[2]

Most of the critical analyses on *Rosinante* have explored it from different perspectives and theoretical stances: the great impact of Spain in Dos Passos's work (Zardoya, Montes, Marín Madrazo, Ludington), the influences and traces of Cervantes's *Don Quixote* in this early work (Marín Ruíz, Villar Lecumberri), the representation of the modernist expatriate imagination (Pizer), and the importance of the text as a testing ground for later aesthetic experiments (Juncker). However, this interdisciplinary essay represents a shift in focus on Dos Passos's *Rosinante* by analyzing it from a Jamesonian perspective, exploring the implicit dialectical interaction between creativity and the totality of history, the role of the modernist utopian illusion and the quest for return to an Edenic past, the cosmopolitan expatriate individual in the Spanish historical context of the first decades of the twentieth century and, finally, the implications of the literary form in relation to a concrete textual tradition or movement.

In Jameson's *The Political Unconscious: Narrative as a Socially Symbolic Act* (1981), dialectical criticism is the main methodological framework that the critic develops within his complex and influential theories. This critical approach is based on the idea that literary works are always part of a larger structure or a concrete historical situation. Then, in a duality based on the external and the internal conformation of a text, a dialectical criticism will seek "to unmask the inner form of a genre or body of texts and will work from the surface of a work inward to the level where literary form is deeply related to the concrete" (Selden 114). As for the role of the literary text and the artistic artifact in modern societies, Jameson demonstrates that it is inextricably bound up with a larger whole, and part of a historical situation. Therefore, from a Jamesonian perspective, narratives always respond to history and are ideologically conditioned and utopian, and in most cases project an ideal future. In general, as for the role of the work of art in society, Jameson suggests:

> It is clear that the work of art cannot itself be asked to change the world or to transform itself into political praxis; on the other hand, it would be desirable to develop a keener sense of the complexity and ambiguity of that process loosely termed reflection or expression. To think dialectically about such a process means to invent a thought which goes "beyond good and evil" not by abolishing these qualifications or judgments but by understanding their interrelationship. (*Political Unconscious* 223)

In this way, I explore how the experimental fragmentary form of *Rosinante* is also deeply engaged with a specific historical situation and how Dos Passos poses his aesthetic, political, and literary ideas from a comparative perspective in a fruitful translinguistic and transcultural literary dialogue between the United States and Spain. Likewise, the Spanish idealized vision depicted in *Rosinante* becomes a symbol of Dos Passos's quest for the return to the mythic Arcadia and a "counter image to a world destroyed by its devotion to the false gods of modernity" (Pizer 141) previously depicted in *Three Soldiers* (1921); but it also provides compensation for the loss of his homeland, a quest for transformation, and the eradication of the money-making culture that he clearly rejected. In this light, Jameson emphasized the role of purification that most modernist fiction had in an attempt to separate literature from the dissatisfaction and disillusionment of the existing capitalist order, so that it could embody "the great Utopian idea of a purification of language, a recreation of its deeper communal or collective function, a purging of everything instrumental or commercial in it" (*Modernist Papers* 8). Similarly, it is my contention that *Rosinante* represents the Jamesonian quest for purification, and it might be explored as the symbol of Dos Passos's utopian illusion about an ideal future—in contrast to the despair and disillusion that he represents in all of his major novels. As a result, the Spain depicted in *Rosinante* symbolized for the writer the original fullness and "the true gods of the past still potent" (Pizer 141). Nevertheless, as the writer evolved in his literary career, a deep change was depicted in his fiction, a clear image "of the disintegration of America, symbolized by his concept, the two nations in a dialectical tension with his utopian vision of one community where people live together in harmony and are allowed to have their own opportunities of self-realization" (Lee 197).

CHRONICLING SPAIN

Dos Passos discovered Spain in 1916 when he still was a young man full of illusions and expectations about the Old World. His journey to southern Europe also included his painful experience in France as a volunteer ambulance driver during the First World War. The writer's antiwar views and emotional crisis emerged rapidly in the form of writing, and he fictionalized his disappointment in *Three Soldiers* and in many of the poems of *A Pushcart at the Curb* (1922), where his lyrical voice emerges openly with a desperate tone to save the world from the deceptions of the great warlords.[3] Moreover, during that period of his life, the American writer suffered a personal crisis that appeared in part from his Freudian response to his father's values, and the deep sense of displacement he felt from the vital uncertainties of his childhood and early adolescence. As a result, his disappointment with the contradictions of the American economic system, the sense of social uprooting, and the war experience unchained his need to search for an alternative vital experience. In this manner, his discovery of Spain became a sort of positive personal catharsis in a crucial period. Even though his first stay was less than four months, "He had learned a great deal, not only about Spain but also about himself," as Ludington has noted ("I Am So Fascinated" 316). Similarly, the Spanish experience played a central role in Dos Passos's development of his cosmopolitanism as a writer, and "it was the most important factor among many in shaping Dos Passos's ideas and forming the way he saw the world" (Ludington, "I Am So Fascinated" 313). Hence, for the writer, the Iberian Peninsula was, in spite of the social conflicts and injustices he observed, an Arcadian or idyllic society compared to the industrialized European and American countries.[4]

Rosinante consists of seventeen essays and narrative segments Dos Passos wrote in a fragmentary form with the recurrent leitmotif of the journey as a quest of discovery. For Pizer, the text "is a significant expression of what can be called the Modernistic expatriate imagination" (137). The travel book opens in Madrid, which was one of Dos Passos's favorite cities, with a vivid reference to one of Plaza Santa Ana's cafés: "He sat on a yellow plush bench in the café El Oro del Rhin, Plaza Santa Ana, Madrid, swabbing up with a bit of bread the last smudges of brown sauce off a plate of which the edges were piled with the dismembered skeleton of a pigeon" (1). Each of the seventeen sections of this fragmented travel book is a detailed impressionistic word painting of Spanish society, culture, ideology, art, history, and literature. In my view, Dos Passos's fragmented style is related to the complexity of Spanish culture and society as well as to his desire to represent the valuable information he gathered during his intense journeys. One of his most distinctive rhetorical strategies was the direct interaction with ordinary people he met on the road, and in the villages and cities. In fact, the book has five sections titled "Talk by the Road," wherein the author uses an interactive dialogical structure with a polyphonic interplay of various characters' voices, which contributes to a fruitful exchange of ideas. Those conversations were essential materials that showed his interest in how Spaniards lived in a particular historical moment as political subjects and how they expressed themselves about it. As a result, even though he had a very idealized image of Spanish social reality, he was also interested in investigating the Spaniards' response to the political situation and the social unrest as part of a larger structure of a historical situation.

In analyzing Spain's social and political tensions during the first decades of the twentieth century, Dos Passos explores the complex layers of Spanish history and the social influence of the different civilizations. He concludes that Spain's palimpsestic history was an alternative to the capitalist dissolution of history. In one of the many conversations he has in *Rosinante* about the multicultural heritage of Spanish culture, one of his friends observes: "Spain, he said, is the most civilized country in Europe. The growth of our civilization has never been interrupted by outside influence. The Phoenicians, the Romans—Spain's influence on Rome was, I imagine, fully as great as Rome's on Spain; I think of the five Spanish emperors; —the Goths, The Moors; all incidents, absorbed by the changeless Iberian spirit" (31). *Rosinante* is Dos Passos's first publication of European reportage that clearly had ideological implications about his cosmopolitan identity as an American modernist writer and intellectual. But paradoxically this personal analysis had to be achieved abroad during those years in which he was on the road and immersed in a deep cultural exploration in the lands of Castile, La Mancha, Madrid, Andalusia, Toledo, and the Mediterranean coast. The exotic Spain was for the writer the perfect place for this transformation, a kind of peaceful refuge in which he could reflect on his own country from a distance with the necessary detachment to be really critical about his complex American identity. Similarly, it was the social milieu where he found the raw materials from which he crafted his experimental fiction. In this sketchy narrative, he is seeking understanding of himself through self-exile. Moreover, it is an intriguing self-exploration through which he discovers what he considers a positive value system in Spanish culture and life that contrasts with "the materialism and moral narrowness of American life" (Pizer 149). In fact, Spain was "a kind of island apart from the Europe he had previously known" (Ludington, *John Dos Passos* 97), and he enjoyed the relaxed lifestyle, the quality food, the musical sounds of the cities and villages, the importance of culture and tradition and the slow pace of life.

Historian Daniel Aaron has observed that Spanish social and cultural idiosyncrasies had a greater impact in Dos Passos's imagination: "Dos Passos's ancestral roots in Portugal were next door to Spain, whose greatest literary works, such as *Don Quijote*, had a tremendous effect on him, as did the nation itself, with its proud history; its varied, striking landscape; and its national traits of an almost anarchistic individualism and a notable, if not always successful, defiance of oppressive authority" (qtd. in Ludington, "I am so fascinated" 314). I certainly agree with Aaron's view, for in *Rosinante* Dos Passos not only tested his beliefs about the kind of individualism he was looking for in America, but it was also a radical way of approaching life and politics, which was far beyond the limits of capitalist society. The epic journey he initiated in Spain became a sort of quest for the Promised Land in which he discovered a colorful society full of positive aspects in a colorless world. However, the writer also shows that his travel book is deeply engaged with a concrete historical reality such as the social unrest derived from the high prices and the descent of wages of those years. That period of economic instability was a major source of social discontent, and the Labor Unions, the Confederación Nacional del Trabajo (CNT) and the Unión General de los Trabajadores (UGT), demanded wage increases in the twenty-four-hour General Strike of December 1916. In addition, World War I helped to produce a social crisis "almost as great in Spain as in some of the belligerent countries" (Payne 611). The most important social tensions within Spanish life were, according to Payne, "the clash of religious and political ideologies, the atmosphere of publicized violence during the war years, and finally the revolutionary upheavals of eastern and central Europe between 1917 and 1919" (611).

A similar point may be made about Dos Passos's interest in the Spanish historical background, "roots striking into the infinite past," and the connection he established between the palimpsestic history and the positive effects the layers of different civilizations had in that society. In other words, the writer believed that Spain's long history had an extraordinary impact on its paradigmatic social cohesion:

> Everywhere roots striking into the infinite past. . . . In Almorox the foundations of life remained unchanged up to the present. The strong anarchistic reliance on the individual man, the walking, consciously or not, of the way beaten by generations of men who had tilled and loved and lain in the cherishing sun with no feeling of a reality outside of themselves. . . . Here lies the strength and the weakness of Spain. This intense individualism, born of a history whose fundamentals lie in isolated village communities —*pueblos*, as the Spaniards call them—over the changeless face of which, like grass over a field, events spring and mature and die, is the basic fact of Spanish life. (23–25)

At the same time, Dos Passos's political insight was admirable. His remarkable analysis of how centralism was one of the key political debates of Spanish society in the 1920s—as it is today—is prescient: "Spain as a modern centralized nation is an illusion, a very unfortunate one; for the present atrophy, the desolating restlessness of a century of revolution, may very well be due in large measure to the artificial imposition of centralized government on a land essentially centrifugal" (25). In this relevant remark, Dos Passos is alluding to the political impact that Catalan and Basque nationalist movements had in one of the most centralized European countries during a period of political instability and uncertainty. Both regions sought to win autonomy from and within the established system, and the centralized government on its side tried to maintain the unquestioned control of the country's political decisions. It is important to note that Catalonia and the Basque country led the way in the industrial and commercial development due in part to Spain's neutrality during the First World War. This crucial economic fact also influenced their nationalist aspirations. Besides, their cultural and linguistic idiosyncrasies were significant aspects that contributed to the attempts to legislate local government autonomy.

In the same way, Dos Passos foregrounds the conflict between Andalusian peasants and landowners, showing a distinctive capacity to analyze in depth the injustice, poverty, and economic slavery those workers suffered in Cordova. The writer became familiar with the political turmoil of the city, the strikes of farm-laborers, and the fact that the region had been under martial law for months: "we talked about the past and future of Cordova" (53); "many of the peasants had never dared vote, and those that had had been completely under the thumb of the *caciques*, the bosses that control Spanish local politics" (56). It goes without saying that revolutionary syndicalism found in those adverse social conditions an important response from the landless peasants. As a result, labor union leaders organized demonstrations and called for two main strikes. The first came in 1903–1904, when a major strike wave was the response to widespread food shortage. The second was the so-called "Bolshevik triennial period" of 1918–1920, involving mass strikes in 1918–1919. The second wave was encouraged by wartime prosperity and the clear influence of the Russian Revolution (Payne 602). Indeed, the Russian Revolution inspired workers and peasants in Spain and other European countries such as France, Hungary, Germany and Italy. Once again, Dos Passos's insightful historical view on that period was really significant as he observed that "Russia has been the beacon flare" (qtd. in Townson 68) for many European countries.

Another example of Dos Passos's "insider knowledge" of Spanish life and history may be found in section three. Here, the American writer analyses the Spanish political crisis of the early twentieth century with impressive discernment: "At present day, when all is ripe for a new attempt to throw off the atrophy, a sort of despairing inaction causes the Spaniards to remain under a government of unbelievably corrupt and inefficient politicians" (28). Dos Passos was aware of the social and political tensions of the first decades of the twentieth century and how Spain was "irreconcilably polarized" between those who were in favor of modernizing processes and those who resisted it. Among the former group were workers, middle classes in towns and cities, liberal intellectuals, and among the latter group, were those counterrevolutionaries who firmly believed that the most significant features of the Spanish nation were "Catholicism, monarchy, armed forces, and the empire" (Townson 70). Dos Passos unmistakably decried the inaction of those politicians who were more concerned about centralizing power, and who found in repression the only response to the social unrest. He, instead, favored politicians who looked toward modernization and social and political reforms. However, those demands were heavily contested by the most conservative classes of society. In this light, Dos Passos related the underlying social and economic reasons for the pervading Spanish political instability to the fact that three different political regimes were established in a period of twenty-two years. But, in spite of the political and social crisis, he was able to portray in his historical chronicle the positive aspects of "the Spanish gesture" and "the strength and the weakness" (23, 24) of Spain: "the easy acceptance of life, the unashamed joy in food and color," and "the strong anarchistic reliance on the individual man" (32, 24). At the same time, he emphasizes the rich diversity of a complex nation: "In trying to hammer some sort of unified impression out of the scattered pictures of Spain in my mind, one of the first things I realize is that there are many Spains" (25).

DON QUIXOTE AS ALTER EGO

With regard to Dos Passos's decision to articulate his Spanish experience with Cervantes's *Don Quixote* in mind, it seems that the novel was for the writer the perfect representation of the literary archetype of the dreamer and the motif of the epic journey that crosses cultural frontiers. In fact, he was fascinated with the novel and had read it more than nine times, the last time in Spanish. Besides, he also intended to study it in depth because he believed that, among many other things, it represented the palimpsestic Spanish history, and that significant aspect could help him establish the connections between both cultures. In this sense, it is important to draw attention to the fact that Dos Passos belongs to a remarkable tradition of American writers who have established an inter-textual dialogue between their fiction and *Don Quixote of La Mancha*, spanning from the American Renaissance to postmodern literature: Washington Irving, William Dean Howells, Mark Twain, Herman Melville, Eudora Welty, William Faulkner, John Steinbeck, Jack Kerouac and Paul Auster, among others.[5]

Likewise, Dos Passos's alter-ego shows his attraction to Don Quixote because the wanderer hero embarks on an idealist journey of self-discovery and embodies an indestructible chimera that is grounded in a quest for a new utopian dream of human regeneration: "Gentleman, it is a little ridiculous to say so, but we have set out once more with lance and helmet of knight-errantry to free the enslaved, to right the wrongs of the oppressed" (37). It is well-known that Dos Passos showed a striking nostalgia for a golden age during his youth that supposedly was based on a primordial social harmony in which people could survive without the constraints of the materialist society. In other words, he struggled between the old and the new and the loss of innocence in his early literature in what could be described as a quixotic attitude. In this sense, he also identified the fictional character's idealism with what he defines as one of the most extraordinary virtues of the Spanish people: "The Spaniard, like his own don Quixote, mounted the warhorse of his idealism and set out to free the oppressed, alone" (45). As a result, his journey into the heart of the Spanish landscape, culture, and its peoples was embedded in a utopian illusion that foregrounded the interaction between creativity, history, and the role of purification of literature. With this ideological background, the impact of Dos Passos's Spanish experience was so deep that he had to share his discovery with Dudley Poore, one of his many American college friends, when he was about to return to Madrid: "I am mad about Spain—the wonderful mellowness of life, the dignity, the layered ages" (qtd. in Ludington, *John Dos Passos* 110).

From a rhetorical perspective, *Rosinante*, like his poetry collection *A Push-cart at the Curb*, shows an impressive emphasis on visual imagery. According to John Dos Passos Coggin, the writer "always had the eye of a painter and the ear of a poet" (8). In particular, the author was aware of the importance of verbally representing the perceptual information in the absence of visual input. In other words, it seems as if Dos Passos really had a deep need to paint the Spanish images he was describing visually throughout the different sections of *Rosinante*. In fact, he also left a visual testimony of his sensorial perception of the Spanish landscapes in the form of a series of colorful watercolors and canvases as he was also an accomplished painter who created over four hundred artworks during his lifetime. In addition, Dos Passos absorbed from the avant-garde painters of his time elements of Impressionism, Expressionism, and Cubism. The extreme modernity of his early watercolors from the countryside of Spain shows how he opted to combine elements from different styles and textures. There are many relevant examples of his sensorial way of depicting the landscapes, as when he visited the Mediterranean island of Majorca:

> We sat looking at the sea that was violet where the sails of the homecoming fishing boats were the wan yellow of primroses. Behind us the hills were sharp pyrites blue. From a window in the adobe hut at one side of us came a smell of sizzling olive oil and tomatoes and peppers and the muffled sound of eggs being beaten. We were footsore, hungry, and we talked about women and love. (91)

In *Rosinante*, Telemachus, the wandering character, becomes an observer who merges with the landscape and its people. In this process, he learns through the sensorial perception to encompass the enormous variety of sensory expe-

John Dos Passos, "Palma de Majorca," Watercolor, paper, 7 ⅛ x 9 ¼. Lucy Dos Passos Coggin Collection.

riences he found in Spain. Thus, the nomadic character is always accompanied by Lyaeus, who is a faithful counterpoint, a *ficelle*, that inevitably reminds the reader of the special relationship Don Quixote and Sancho Panza develop through their long and adventurous journey. The mythical couple represents for Dos Passos the duality of the Spanish character:

> Telemachus—Don Quixote.
>
> These characters symbolize the intellectual life, a never-ending quest for adventure, and the need to embark on learning adventures.
>
> "Don Quijote, the individualist who believed in the power of man's soul over all things, whose desire included the whole world in himself." (24)
>
> Lyaeus—Sancho Panza, the *ficelle*, a character who is a confidante and provides the reader with significant information about the main protagonist.
>
> These characters represent the body, the senses, and a hedonistic approach to life.

> "Sancho, the individualist to whom all the world was food for his belly." (24)

Dos Passos was also intrigued by the word *"lo flamenco"* which was, in some way, related to the Spanish folkloric world and the sensorial experience. In a long conversation with his friend Don Diego, the narrator insists on the meaning and cultural implications of the expression: "In Spain, we live from the belly and loins, or else from the head and heart: between Don Quixote the mystic and Sancho Panza the sensualist there is no middle ground. The lowest Panza is *lo flamenco*" (17). The response emphasizes the idea of an affective and artistic culture with strong social bonds that relies on the communal experience of music and dancing.

One of the most striking aspects of the mythical couple's journey is that it becomes a personal fictional narrative of Dos Passos's complex relationship with the powerful and successful image of his father, John Randolph Dos Passos. In *Rosinante*, the American writer explores his childhood and adolescence as an immigrant, as a fatherless child who dreams about finding the roots of his origins: "Telemachus had wandered so far in search of his father he had quite forgotten what he was looking for" (1). His successful father embodied the values of the American dream: material progress, social regeneration, and social mobility. However, Dos Passos soon detected the historical tensions of the American Dream and its deep historical contradictions. Therefore, in Spain and from a distance, he was able to see the disturbing proximity of dream and nightmare and the effects of the loss of innocence in American society. As an expatriate in Spain, he discovered "what he was prepared to find in an older and mainly unindustrialized culture, just as a few years afterwards many American artists would find in Paris the freedom they believed lacking in America," as Pizer observes (139). Moreover, in Spain, he found his real self: "I am very happy . . . walking about here in these empty zigzag streets I have suddenly felt familiar with it all, as if it were a part of me, as if I had soaked up some essence out of it" (130).

Similarly, he became the Adamic hero par excellance, separated from his culture in search of a reality more substantial than that embraced by the materialistic society he had rejected. And as mentioned before, Don Quixote, The Knight of the Sorrowful Countenance, "blunderingly trying to remould the world, pitifully sure of the power of his own ideal" (33), was one of Dos Passos's favorite characters (Schwartz 188), and he incorporates this powerful mythical character in the travel book to create a modernist epic narrative based on his Edenic dreams and powerful experiences in Spain. Thus, the writer "made a significant contribution to the modernist revival of the epic as well as a desire for organic totality" (Lee 17) with the inclusion of one of the most influential novels in the Western canon. In this light, Dos Passos also followed the Poundian concept that "considered the aesthetic to include a social purpose" (Matterson 173), something that is clearly reflected in the rhetorical techniques employed in *Rosinante*, as it is an experimental travel narrative that departs from the classical linear descriptions of this kind of texts and introduces the fictionalization of the protagonists. Therefore, Dos Passos's fictional alter ego Telemachus, the son of Odysseus and Penelope, an observer, merges with the landscape and establishes a dialectical criticism between the Edenic Spain and the excesses of American society from a distance. Likewise, the old Spanish culture offered the American writer the opportunity to explore in depth the myth of Don Quixote and Sancho Panza in order to re-evaluate the meanings of the wandering hero from La Mancha and his squire, an aspect that was distinctive of high modernist poetics (Piñero Gil, "La utopía" 175–91). Therefore, *The Odyssey* and *Don Quixote* serve as a literary map for Dos Passos. His reading of these classical epic narratives is that "of the map of a whole complete and equally closed region of the globe, as though somehow the very episodes themselves merged back into space, and the reading of them came to be indistinguishable from map-reading" (Jameson, *The Modernist Papers* 167).

Dos Passos found in the Spanish society of the 1910s and 1920s "the full life of spirit in which the natural, the honest, and the good still existed" in the civilized world (Pizer 149). He also discovered in his idealized image of Spain "a space that resisted capitalism, homogeneity, centralized nationality, and the devastation of modern war, all of which he saw as ingrained in American culture" (Rogers 77). For that reason, the fictional narrator's quest focused on what he described as the "Spanish gesture" embodied by two mythical individuals: the flamenco dancer Pastora Imperio and the baker of Almorox in Toledo. That village of La Mancha becomes a metaphor, a sort of Arcadia, and a vehicle for the expression of his essential beliefs: "men lived in harmony with nature, fulfilled in body and soul" (Pizer 140), and the fact that generations of individuals had had the opportunity to develop their own idiosyncrasies based on the anarchistic spirit that traditionally characterized Spaniards: "Spain is the classic home of the anarchist" (45).

In section two of *Rosinante*, Telemachus has a long dialogue with a donkey boy about the significance of productive work in Spain: "Not on your life, in America they don't do anything except work and rest so to get ready to work again. That's no life for a man. People don't enjoy themselves there"

(11). Throughout the conversation, Dos Passos cleverly contrasts two radically different lifestyles and how the individual's vision and experience is really significant for his own study. Once more, the writer gives voice to a peasant who has a very clear vision of life even though he is young and innocent; his testimony is very helpful, as he is able to articulate the importance of his independence and the real value of time in a hedonistic life:

> On this coast, señor inglés, we don't work much, we are dirty and uninstructed, but by God we live. Why the poor people of the towns, do you know what they do in summer? They hire a fig-tree and go and live under it with their dogs and their cats and their babies, and they eat figs as they ripen and drink the cold water from the mountains, and man-alive they are happy. They fear no one and they are dependent on no one; when they are old they tell stories and bring up their children. You have travelled much; I have travelled little, Madrid, never further, but I swear to you that nowhere in the world are the women lovelier or is the land richer or the cookery more perfect than in this vega of Almuñécar. . . . If only the wine weren't quite so heavy. (16)

The young writer was filled with admiration for this distinctive aspect of the Iberian personality but he was also faithful to the individual in a Thoreauvian way. In other words, he believed deeply in the transcendentalist writer's ideas on self-sufficiency, integrity, and a life in harmony with nature and the community.

TRANSCULTURAL DIALOGUE

In 1916, Dos Passos had spent most of the time in Madrid, which became his center of operations. It was the city that most inspired his need for deepening in the "Spanish gesture" and in its lively streets and people. It was "his adopted city," and, as he confessed many times, the capital was a complete sensorial experience: "Honestly. I've never been in such a musical city as Madrid, everything jingles and rings. . . . I am quite settled in Madrid now, I feel as if I'd lived here all my life" (Ludington, *John Dos Passos* 100–01). His cultural immersion underwent an unusual and intense adaptation to the customs and habits of the people of Madrid. In a letter to his good friend Rumsey Marvin, the writer expressed his enthusiasm about the traditions and the city scenery. In this sense, Bautista Cordero points out that "Dos Passos felt fascinated by *chocolate*, the

Sierra de Guadarrama, *botijos*, donkeys and mules, multicoloured shawls and the hours *madrileños* keep" (57). Nevertheless, he was also aware of the inevitable transformations of modern life and of how the Anglo-American influence was changing the city: "At present in Madrid even café life is receding before the exigencies of business and the hardly excusable mania for imitating English and American manners. Spain is undergoing great changes in its relation to the rest of Europe, to Latin America, in its own internal structure" (102).

Dos Passos's main literary aspiration was to establish a trans-literary dialogue with the most relevant Spanish writers. For this purpose, he got in contact with Antonio Machado, Juan Ramón Jiménez, and other authors whose works he wanted to translate into English. In fact, he attempted to imitate and made a poetic homage to the Castilian poet Machado in "Winter in Castile," which is the longest and more Spanish section of *A Pushcart at the Curb* (Piñero Gil, "Introducción" 36–37). It goes without saying that Dos Passos can be considered a Hispanist, as he not only read Cervantes but became familiar with Baroja, Benavente, Maragall, Manrique and Unamuno, among other Spanish writers: "He saw Spanish literature as a diverse assemblage of styles and ideas rooted in preindustrial artisanship rather than factory-driven commodification" (Rogers 78). In this sense, his readings of the most significant authors of the '98 generation gave him a direct vision of the political and historical crises the Spanish writers were depicting in their work as a result of the War of 1898 that ended Spain's colonial empire in the Americas. And he "essentially agrees with the nationalist line within Spain that '98 is an exceptional generation," as Rogers observes (78).

Therefore, in *Rosinante*, Dos Passos not only makes "a complex fusion of travelogue, literary criticism, translation, autobiography, fiction, propaganda, and socio historical commentary" (Rogers 79); he also attempts to establish a trans-literary and transatlantic dialogue between American and Spanish literatures in his quest for the internationalization of the literary experience. Similarly, he encourages the American public to read Spanish literature in a very persuasive way:

> If the American public is bound to take up Spain it might as well take up the worth-while things instead of the works of popular vulgarization. They have enough of those in their bookcases as it is. And in Spain there are novelists like Baroja, essayists like Unamuno and Azorín, poets like Valle Inclán and Antonio Machado, . . . but I suppose they will shine with the reflected glory of the author of the *Four Horsemen of the Apocalypse*. (66–67)

In section XVI, Dos Passos also pays a tribute to Miguel de Unamuno, one of the leading intellectuals of the period who had been condemned to fifteen years' imprisonment for *lèse majesté* (117) in 1920, for an offence committed against the dignity of the reigning sovereign Alfonso XIII. With this reference, the narrator makes a statement about the right for freedom of opinion and expression that should prevail in any modern society like Spain. In the same way, Dos Passos shows his ideological proximity to the Spanish writer when he stresses Unamuno's resistance to the materialistic "modernization and Europeanization of Spanish life and thought" (121). The philosopher believed that Spanish society had to endorse the democratic political principles in order to be like other European societies. Furthermore, Dos Passos praises the philosopher's views on the chasm between faith and reason and the transcendental significance of each individual in essays such as "Del sentimiento trágico de la vida" (1913), "The Tragic Feeling of Life." Certainly, this is one of Unamuno's most influential essays and Dos Passos stresses its significance when he quotes a long paragraph on Don Quixote's idealism and the hero's importance in Spanish society: "What is, then, the new mission of Don Quixote in this world? To cry, to cry in the wilderness. For the wilderness hears although men do not hear, and one day will turn into a sonorous wood, and that solitary voice that spreads in the desert like seed will sprout into a gigantic cedar" (123). In Dos Passos's *Rosinante,* there is a synthesis between the spirit of American radicalism and the aesthetic techniques of modernism like the implicit dialectical interaction between subject and object, the representation of the cosmopolitan expatriate individual as a fundamental part of a historical situation, the modernist self-referentiality poetics, and, finally, the literary form deeply related to a concrete textual tradition or movement. As a result, the Spanish reality depicted in *Rosinante* becomes a symbol of Dos Passos's quest for the return to the mythic Arcadia, but it also compensates for the loss of his homeland.

In his transnational quest for the Spanish gesture and for a utopian territory, Dos Passos was searching for a way to define his own unstable hybrid modernist identity and establish a dialectical interaction between his artistic subjectivity and his idealization of a new country. Thus, his spiritual journey in Spain was not similar to that of the American nineteenth-century conventional travelers or tourists; rather, his way of travelling and visiting Spain was based on his curiosity and preference for knowing the language, the literature, the food, the politics, and, above all, the idiosyncrasy and the peculiarities of Spanish culture. In this way, *Rosinante* embodies Dos Passos's cosmopolitan modernist quest to internationalize literature, often making powerful connections between his literature and a broad range of literary myths, finding a more meaningful modern culture. Similarly, it becomes a sort of paradigmatic modernist epic in the way in which the American writer experiments with the literary motif of the journey as a form of self-exploration and as a creative way of establishing an original transatlantic literary dialogue. His temporary expatriate condition in Spain, and the reality of being a young American with Portuguese roots, determined, in some way, his need for a more Edenic and epic culture far from the limitations of the excesses of American urban industrialization and cultural materialism. Therefore, we might conclude that Spain became the country that inspired his rebellious spirit and innovative writing in an early period in which he clearly devoted himself to radical politics and experimental modernism to construct a cosmopolitan subjectivity.

Rosinante to the Road Again may be studied from the political and literary perspectives as an example of Dos Passos's early experimentation that embodies the spirit of American radicalism and the aesthetic techniques of modernism. Therefore, it may be explored as the symbol of the writer's idealized vision of literature in a concrete textual tradition and as the paradigm of his early expectations about a more harmonic future for America which was unavoidably connected to the exploration of other countries and cultures. For this purpose, he makes inter-textual allusions to the classical epic narratives, *The Odyssey* and *Don Quixote*, from a modernist perspective. Related to this, it is important to highlight that "epic narratives focus on a crisis in the history of a race or culture" (Peck and Coyle 31), and they are always concerned with crossing cultural frontiers. In the same way, he also pointed out the crisis in which American civilization was immersed and how it had to be explored by crossing literary frontiers, incorporating the deeds of epic warriors and heroes from other cultural contexts. This is how other modernist writers—T. S. Eliot, Gertrude Stein, and Ezra Pound, chief among them—approached the epic conventions in their literature. In other words, their modernist creativity was based on the crossing of cultural and ideological frontiers. Then, for Dos Passos, the epic journey becomes a cross-cultural experience to learn a lesson, change, and later return home after he had achieved self-knowledge, transformation, and the exploration of new cultures and ways of life. In fact, he was restless for travel all his life and believed in travelling as a personal experience of discovery and learning. But his deep sense of social uprooting and displacement had also a significant role in his urgent need for having the perspective of another land.[6] Moreover, he appreciated solitude, independence, and the personal enrichment he found in the exploration of diverse cultures and in the opportunity of looking at his own with a certain critical distance and without prejudices or attachments, aiming to act as an objective chronicler of the times he witnessed. As a result, his journeys in many different countries all over the world became for the writer transcendental processes of personal metamorphosis which provided a great opportunity for exploring his adventurous spirit and never-ending curiosity. As Donald Pizer has cleverly noted, "he sought in his depiction of a foreign culture to explore in striking new forms the meaning of his own" (137).

NOTES

1. Lyaeus is an epithet of Dionysus/Bacchus, who were Greek and Roman mythological variations of the same god. Lyaeus is traditionally considered the lord of exuberance, fertility and drunkenness. Besides, he freed people from care and anxiety.
2. The title of the book itself is a paradigm of the writer's quixotic vision of his epic journey in Spain. To begin with, Rosinante is Don Quixote's old nag, his faithful companion and *doppelgänger*. In fact, the old hidalgo considers it of foremost importance to find a proper name for his steed before his first adventure: "Four days were spent in thinking what name to give him, because (as he said to himself) it was not right that a horse belonging to a knight so famous, and one with such merits of his own, should be without some distinctive name, and he strove to adapt it so as to indicate what he had been before belonging to a knight-errant, and what he then was" (Chapter I). According to Howard Mancing, "Rocinante becomes one of the most important and most comic figures of the novel" (618). Dos Passos is likely to have chosen the name of Rosinante for his travel book as a literary homage to one of the most significant Western epic novels, and more specifically to the protagonist horse who symbolizes the union between the heroic knight and his steed, his master's virtues and the idea of coming back to the road to defend the helpless and destroy the wicked. Telemachus discovers a horse on his way to Toledo and immediately shows his affection and recognition of the heroic animal protagonist:

   > Telemachus got up on his numbed feet and stretched his legs. "Ouf," he said, "I'm tired." Then he walked over to the grey horse that stood with hanging head and drooping knees hitched to one of the acacias.
   >
   > "I wonder what his name is." He stroked the horse's scrawny face. "Is it Rosinante?"
   >
   > The horse twitched his ears, straightened his back and legs and pulled back black lips to show yellow teeth.
   >
   > "Of course it's Rosinante!"

The horse's sides heaved. He threw back his head and whinnied shrilly, exultantly. (38)

3. In the novel, the reader has the opportunity of facing the emotional effects of the European conflict that were devastating for the majority of modernist writers. Thus, these authors concluded that it was the epitome of the human atrocities, the hideous ugliness and the confirmation that history was coming to an end; as a consequence, modern life was confusing, terrible, and futile. His anti-war novel shows a deep sense of loss, despair, disaffection, and a direct questioning of materialism and the evils of industrialism in American society from its very roots.
4. Likewise, during his visits to Portugal, he was also able to appreciate his own ancestry and was eager to compare and contrast its culture and traditions, which he described as "having a certain mildness, a lack of the racial and ideological fanaticism that has brought our civilization to the verge of destruction . . . the more I study it the prouder I am of my Portuguese inheritance" (Ludington, "A Sort of Family Feeling" 133).
5. These authors reveal their debt to Miguel de Cervantes's novel in the genesis of their fiction or in their metafictional essays in the following works: Washington Irving's "The Legend of Sleepy Hollow" and *The Tales of the Alhambra*; Mark Twain's *A Connecticut Yankee*, *The Adventures of Huckleberry Finn* and *The Adventures of Tom Sawyer*; William Dean Howells's "The Spanish Student" and *Criticism and Fiction*; Herman Melville's *Moby-Dick*; Eudora Welty's *The Golden Apples* and *Losing Battles*; William Faulkner's *Light in August*, *Go Down, Moses* and *The Sound and the Fury*; John Steinbeck's *The Wizard of Maine*, *Travels with Charley*, and the prologue to *East of Eden*; Jack Kerouac's *On the Road* and Paul Auster's *City of Glass*.
6. There might be other significant biographical reasons for this need to travel. Dos Passos grew up in European exile as his father was married back in the United States to Mary Dyckman Hays, who was not his mother. As his biographer Townsend Ludington observes, "His first lonely years seemed like a hotel childhood . . . [in which] he felt like a double foreigner . . . [like a] man without a country" ("A Sort of Family Feeling" 121).

WORKS CITED

Bautista Cordero, Rosa María. *A Descriptive Analysis of the Spanish Translations of Manhattan Transfer and Their Role in the Spanish Construction of John Dos Passos*. Universidad Autónoma de Madrid, 2016.

Cervantes, Miguel de. *The Ingenious Hidalgo Don Quixote of La Mancha*. Translated by John Ormsby, T.Y. Corwell and Co., 1981.

Coggin, Dos Passos John. Prefacio. *Invierno en Castilla y otros poemas de John Dos Passos*. Editorial Renacimiento, 2018, pp. 7–9.

Dos Passos, John. (1922). *The Fourteenth Chronicle: Letters and Diaries of John Dos Passos,* edited by Townsend Ludington, Gambit Publishers, 1973.

———. *A Pushcart at the Curb. Travel Books and Other Writings*. Library of America, 2003.

———. *Rosinante to the Road Again*. Onesuch Press, 2011.

Jameson, Fredric. *The Modernist Papers*. Verso, 2007.

———. *The Political Unconscious: Narrative as a Socially Symbolic Act*. Cornell UP, 1981.

Juncker, Clara. "John Dos Passos in Spain." *Miscelánea*, vol. 42, 2010, pp. 91–103.

Lee, Jun Young. *History and Utopian Disillusion. The Dialectical Politics in the Novels of John Dos Passos.* Peter Lang, 2008.

Ludington, Townsend, "'I Am So Fascinated by Spain': John Dos Passos, January 1917." *Nor Shall Diamond Die: American Studies in Honour of Javier Coy*, edited by Carme Manuel and Paul Derrick, Universidad de Valencia, 2003, pp. 303–19.

———. *John Dos Passos. A Twentieth-Century Odyssey*. Carroll & Graf Publishers, 1998.

———. "'A Sort of Family Feeling': The Two Dos Passoses, Portugal and Brazil." *Ilha do Desterro*, vol.15, no. 16, 1986, pp. 116–35.

Mancing, Howard. *The Cervantes Encyclopedia*. Greenwood Press, 2004.

Marín Madrazo, Pilar. *La gran guerra en la obra de Hemingway y Dos Passos*. Almar, 1980.

Marín Ruíz, Ricardo. "Tras los pasos de Rocinante: imitación y re-elaboración del personaje cervantino en John Dos Passos, Graham Greene y John Steinbeck." *Don Quijote en su periplo universal: aspectos de la recepción internacional de la novela cervantina*, edited by Hans Christian Hagedorn, U. de Castilla-La Mancha, 2011, pp. 337–62.

Matterson, Stephen. "Ezra Pound." *American Literature: The Essential Glossary*. Arnold, 2003, pp. 171–73.

Montes, Catalina. *La visión de España en la obra de John Dos Passos*. Almar, 1980.

Payne, Stanley. *Spain and Portugal*. U. of Wiscosin P, 1973.

Peck, John, and Martin Coyle. *Literary Terms and Criticism*. MacMillan, 1984.

Piñero Gil, Eulalia. "Introducción." *Invierno en Castilla y otros poemas de John Dos Passos*. Editorial Renacimiento, 2018, pp. 10–71.

———. "La utopía modernista y don Quijote de la Mancha en *Rosinante to the Road Again* de John Dos Passos." *Cervantes y la posteridad. 400 años de legado cervantino*, edited by Alfredo Moro Martín, Vervuert, 2019, pp. 175–91.

Pizer, Donald. "John Dos Passos's *Rosinante to the Road Again* and the Modernist Expatriate Imagination." *Journal of Modern Literature*, vol. 21, no. 1, Summer 1997, pp. 137–50.

Rogers, Gayle. *Incomparable Empires. Modernism and the Translation of Spanish and American Literature*. Columbia UP, 2016.

Schwartz, Delmore. "John Dos Passos and the Whole Truth." *Dos Passos: The Critical Heritage*, edited by Barry Maine, Routledge, 1988, pp. 175–85.

Selden, Ray, Peter Widdowson, and Peter Brooker. *A Reader's Guide to Contemporary Literary Theory*. Prentice Hall, 1997.

Townson, Nigel. "The Contested Quest for Modernization: 1914–1936." *The History of Modern Spain: Chronologies, Themes, Individuals*, edited by Adrian Shubert and José Álvarez Junco, Bloomsbury, 2107, pp. 64–71.

Villar Lecumberri, Alicia. "Sobre *Rocinante vuelve al camino* de John Dos Passos." *Recreaciones quijotescas y cervantinas en la narrativa*, edited by Carlos Mata Induráin, Eunsa, 2013, pp. 365–78.

Wrenn, John H. *John Dos Passos*. Twayne Publishers, 1961.

Zardoya, Concha. "Madrid en la poesía de John Dos Passos." *Verdad, belleza y expresión: letras anglo-americanas*. EDHASA, 1967, pp. 113–22.

Contributors

Rosa María Bautista-Cordero is an assistant professor of English-Spanish Translation at the Universidad Autónoma de Madrid (Spain) and a member of the John Dos Passos Society since 2014. She is the author of an annotated Spanish edition of *Manhattan Transfer* (Cátedra, 2018), and has written various articles on translation, censorship, and the Spanish reception of John Dos Passos. Among the authors she has translated are John Dos Passos, Allen Ginsberg, Graham Greene, Tom Wolfe, Hugh Thomas, Bruce Chatwin, Philip Roth, V. S. Naipaul, and Peter Balakian. She has taught at Universidad Alfonso X el Sabio, the ILMyT of Universidad Complutense, and New York University (Madrid Campus).

William Brevda is emeritus professor of English at Central Michigan University. He is the author of two books: *Harry Kemp: The Last Bohemian* (Bucknell University Press, 1986) and *Signs of the Signs: The Literary Lights of Incandescence and Neon* (Bucknell University Press, 2011). His most recent articles have appeared in *Joyce Studies Annual* and *Texas Studies in Literature and Language*.

Victoria M. Bryan co-founded the John Dos Passos Society in 2012 and is currently the dean of the Honors College and Academic Enhancement at Cleveland State Community College (Tennessee). She earned her PhD in English from the University of Mississippi in 2014. She is the author of *Prestige Television and Prison in the Age of Mass Incarceration* (Routledge, 2019).

Alberto Lena holds a PhD in American Studies from Exeter University. He is currently working as a civil servant at the Castilla y León Department of Education in Castilla y Leon, Spain. He is the author of essays on Francis Ford Coppola, John Dos Passos, Benjamin Franklin, F. Scott Fitzgerald, and Ernest Hemingway. He has also written a book on Alfred Hitchcock, Thornton Wilder, and *Shadow of a Doubt*. At present he is researching a book project on the representation of the "Other" in Classical Hollywood Cinema.

Keiko Misugi is professor of American literature at Kobe College, Japan. Her recent publications include "John Dos Passos's Corporeal Experimentations through 1920s Theater" (2019), "Jimmy Herf's Yearning for Corporeality in *Manhattan Transfer*" (2018), and "Deromanticizing War: John Dos Passos's Critique of Theodore Roosevelt in *1919*" (2015). Her Japanese-language essays have appeared in *Where Wandering Souls Have Drifted: Saul Bellow's Later Works* (Sairyusha, 2017), *Journal of Mark Twain Studies*, and *Faulkner Journal of Japan.*

David Murad is professor and current co-chair in the Department of English at Lakeland Community College in Kirtland, Ohio. Holding a doctorate from Kent State University, he has published articles in *The Hemingway Review* and *Interdisciplinary Literary Studies*. From 2016–2018 he served as president of the John Dos Passos Society.

Addison T. Palacios is an assistant professor of English at Mt. San Jacinto College in southern California. His research focuses on representations of the intellectual in twentieth-century America alongside the modern university. His work has been supported by the Mellon Foundation, the Modernist Studies Association, and the Nettie Lee Benson archives at the University of Texas at Austin.

Eulalia Piñero Gil is associate professor in American literature and gender studies at the Universidad Autónoma of Madrid. Recently, she has edited *Live Deep and Suck All the Marrow of Life: H. D. Thoreau's Literary Legacy* (Vernon Press, 2020). In 2018, she published the first translation and critical edition of John Dos Passos's *A Pushcart at the Curb*, *Invierno en Castilla y otros Poemas* (Renacimiento, 2018). Currently, she is the president of the Spanish Association for American Studies (SAAS).

Lauro Iglesias Quadrado is an assistant professor of English at the Federal University of Bahia (UFBA) in Salvador, Brazil, where he conducts research on literature and sound media. His doctoral dissertation, granted in 2018 from the Federal University of Rio Grande do Sul (UFRGS) and titled *The Poetics of Noise,* is a study of John Dos Passos's *Manhattan Transfer* and the acoustic tensions of early twentieth-century modernism. He is a literary editor of *Revista Philia*, an academic journal that receives submissions in many languages in the areas of philosophy, literature, and art.

Aaron Shaheen is the George C. Connor Professor of American Literature at the University of Tennessee at Chattanooga and the co-founder of the

John Dos Passos Society. He is the author of two monographs: *Androgynous Democracy: Modern American Literature and the Dual-Sexed Body Politic* (University of Tennessee Press, 2010) and *Great War Prostheses in American Literature and Culture* (Oxford University Press, 2020). His most recent articles have appeared in *PMLA*, *Modernism/modernity*, and *Modern Fiction Studies.*

Jessica E. Teague is an assistant professor of English at the University of Nevada, Las Vegas. She is the author of *Sound Recording Technology and American Literature, from the Phonograph to the Remix* (Cambridge University Press, 2021). Her work has also appeared in journals such as *American Quarterly* and *Sound Studies.*

Fredrik Tydal holds a lectureship in English at the Stockholm School of Economics. His most recent articles have appeared in *Steinbeck Review*, *The Journal of D.H. Lawrence Studies*, and *Transnational Literature*. He is the current president of the John Dos Passos Society.

Index

www.ingramcontent.com/pod-product-compliance
Lightning Source LLC
Chambersburg PA
CBHW030623310726
48979CB00003B/846
* 9 7 8 1 6 2 1 9 0 7 1 3 8 *